CLASSROOM MANAGEMENT:
Building Relationships of Mutual Respect

Edited by Dave F. Brown, Ed. D.
West Chester University

cognella™
San Diego, CA

Bassim Hamadeh, Publisher
Michael Simpson, Vice President of Acquisitions
Christopher Foster, Vice President of Marketing
Jessica Knott, Managing Editor
Stephen Milano, Creative Director
Kevin Fahey, Cognella Marketing Program Manager
Melissa Barcomb, Acquisitions Editor
Luiz Ferreira, Licensing Associate

First published in the United States of America in 2012 by University Readers, Inc.

Trademark Notice: Product or corporate names may be trademarks or registered trademarks, and are used only for identification and explanation without intent to infringe.

15 14 13 12 11 1 2 3 4 5

Printed in the United States of America

ISBN: 978-1-60927-028-5

www.cognella.com 800.200.3908

Contents

Section One

Developing Mutually Respectful Relationships With Children

Introduction

Developing Mutually Respectful Relationships with Children

By Dave F. Brown

Developing and implementing an effective plan for classroom management is critical to every teacher's success. The primary reason that teachers leave the profession is failure to gain students' cooperation needed for the type of classroom order required for meaningful student learning. Each article in this initial section provides teaching candidates with perspectives on how to create the classroom community needed to ensure cooperation among students. These initial management practices create the base for healthy relationships between students and teachers.

Teachers initiate the development of these relationships on the first day as they help students feel psychologically comfortable. Comfort for students means that they initiate friendships with fellow students and that they understand that their teacher cares about them. This first section includes articles on

- the importance of building relationships with students;
- what to do on the first day of school;
- strategies for developing class rules with students; and

- qualities of effective teaching.

I chose the articles for this book based on each author's ability to stimulate conversation among teaching candidates. Some of the articles provide step-by-step procedures for resolving issues and effective strategies for solving problems. Several other articles present challenges rather than solutions. With instructor guidance, students using this book can engage in the processes of critical and creative thinking and problem solving that are inherent in the daily lives of teachers.

I offer a set of questions that accompany each article as a possible guide for class discussions, but I intend these questions only as possible prompts rather than the sole method to engage students in conversation. Effective management is not a linear path—there are not simple solutions to every incident that arises in the daily lives of teachers. Because of the nature of children, no cookie-cutter plans can exist—children are young, immature, constantly growing individuals who are more different than they are alike. Predicting the behavior of children is often precarious, and because of their nature, much of effective management is trial and error. Yet a set of research-based processes does exist that every successful teacher uses to maintain a classroom of optimal learning. Those basic processes of effective teaching are described by James H. Stronge in an excerpt from his book, *Qualities of Effective Teachers*, titled "Section II: Teacher Responsibilities and Behaviors," contained in the first section.

If following Stronge's research-based list (article #6) were enough to be an effective teacher, anyone could become one. Every experienced educator knows that effective classroom management is so much more. Effective management is as much demonstrations of appropriate social behaviors by teachers as it is following the research on proper procedures and guidelines. Hopefully by reading these articles, teaching candidates will begin to "see" themselves implementing these strategies and enjoying their students in the process of learning as a result.

Relationships Matter

By Deborah Stipek

In this era of accountability and No Child Left Behind (NCLB), test scores are all that matter. Or are they? Could our preoccupation with test scores be producing classroom conditions that actually undermine student learning? When tests become high-stakes, teachers naturally focus their attention on the knowledge and skills the tests measure—leaving less time to engage students in conversation about personal issues or make them feel valued and supported. Feeling pressured to produce higher test scores, teachers become more controlling and less patient, particularly with students who lag behind.

Ironically, these effects of NCLB get in the way of achieving the very goals the law aims to promote. Learning requires effort, and one of the best predictors of students' effort and engagement in school is the relationships they have with their teachers (Osterman, 2000). To promote high academic standards, teachers need to create supportive social contexts and develop positive relationships with students.

For 30 years, I have been conducting research on students' motivation to learn. I have interviewed hundreds of students from preschool through high school to identify the classroom practices that engender effort in schoolwork. My observations confirm a broad body of research that has demonstrated that students function more effectively when they feel respected and valued and function poorly when they feel disrespected or marginalized (National Research Council, 2004; Ryan & Deci, 2000). When students have a secure relationship with their teachers, they are more comfortable taking risks that enhance learning—tackling challenging tasks, persisting when they run into difficulty, or asking questions when they are confused. Urban students claim that when a teacher shows genuine concern for them, they feel that they owe the teacher something in return. They don't want to disappoint a teacher who cares about them (Davidson, 1999). Fortunately, research has revealed a great deal about the kinds of teacher behavior and the school structures that promote students' feelings of belonging.

How Students Know Teachers Care

Young children share their feelings and information about themselves with teachers who are affectionate and nurturing. These close relationships with teachers lead to higher levels of student engagement and achievement (Pianta, 1999). Specific behaviors that promote positive relationships with young children include listening to their concerns, responding to transgressions gently and with explanations rather than sharply and with punishment, and showing positive emotions (smiling, being playful). When young children are asked how they know their teachers care about them, they refer to teachers being attentive ("She says hi to me when I come in the room"); addressing their nonacademic needs ("She saves a snack for me if I miss snack time"); and being fair ("She makes sure I get a turn"). The personal relationships that these behaviors engender are particularly valuable for children who come to school with poor social skills (Pianta, Stuhlman, & Hamre, 2002).

Adolescents report that they work harder for teachers who treat them as individuals and express interest in their personal lives outside school. Caring teachers, they report, are also honest, fair, and trusting (Davidson & Phelan, 1999). These teachers grant students some autonomy and opportunities for decision making—for example, by giving them choices in assignments, engaging them in developing classroom rules, and encouraging them to express their opinions in classroom discussions.

The social dimension of classrooms may be particularly important for at-risk youth. When researchers ask youths who have dropped out of high school why they left school, the young people frequently say it was because no one cared. Those who stay in school cite meaningful relationships with adults who show an interest in them as individuals (National Research Council, 2004). In a 1997 Public Agenda phone survey, 64 percent of students claimed that they would learn more if their teachers "personally cared about their students as people"; unfortunately, only 30 percent claimed that most of their teachers did care. According to a recent large survey of high school students, African American students were particularly responsive to teachers who showed that they cared about the students' learning (Ferguson, 2002). When asked why they worked hard when they did, 47 percent checked "My teachers encourage me to work hard"; only 15 percent checked "My teacher demanded it."

Nurturing Through High Expectations

Being a caring and supportive teacher does not mean coddling; rather, it means holding students accountable while providing the support they need to succeed. One adolescent in a low-income, high-crime community in California told me that he liked his high school because the teachers "sit on your face." He explained that when the teachers weren't sure that students really understood something, they stuck with them, got them help, or gave them some materials to help them figure it out. If students hadn't done their homework, teachers made them stay in at lunch or after school to finish it. If they didn't do their homework for several days in a row, teachers called their parents. Conversations with students in both urban and suburban schools have convinced me that as long as teachers are providing the support students need, the students interpret teachers' efforts to hold them accountable as evidence that they care.

Consistent with my own observations, research on adolescents finds that students in this age group define caring teachers as those who communicate directly and regularly with them about their academic progress and make sure they understand what has been taught (Wentzel,

2002). When researchers asked urban high school students what advice they would give a new teacher, one student replied,

> If there's confusion on my face, I want you to see it. If there's disagreement, I want you to say, "You disagree? Why?"

Another student complained about a particularly uncaring teacher:

> He's just writing things on the board. … He doesn't look at the class like, "Do you understand?" He's just teaching it to us. He sees that a couple of students understand it and he moves on. He doesn't make a space for us to ask. (Cushman, 2002, p. 8)

The press for learning that many adolescents view as evidence of a caring teacher differs from the pressure for learning created by NCLB. Teachers press students to learn by encouraging them, paying attention to their work and giving constructive feedback, refusing to accept halfhearted efforts, providing assistance when students need it, and refusing to give up on students. Holding students accountable without this support and encouragement is likely to discourage and alienate them rather than motivate them.

Supporting Positive Student–Teacher Relationships

What goes around comes around. The social context for adults affects the social context for students. Teachers who feel respected, trusted, and cared about as individuals are in a much better position to offer the same support to their students. School administrators can emphasize that relationships matter by devoting professional development time to the social context of classrooms. It's equally important, however, that administrators provide time and opportunities for teachers to develop common goals and to build close, collegial relationships with one another.

It is crucial to structure schools to allow for sustained contact between students and teachers. Small schools and class sizes help. Schools can also organize classes and teaching schedules to reduce the number of students a teacher sees each day. Middle and high schools, for example, have experimented with teams of teachers who work with 60–100 students.

Multiyear grouping is one scheduling option that enables teachers to develop sustained relationships with students. For example, a school may establish K–1, 2–3, and 4–5 classes so that students are with the same teacher or set of teachers for two years. Another option is looping, in which one teacher or a set of teachers moves up with a group of students for two or more years.

In secondary schools, block scheduling, involving classes at least 90 minutes long, gives teachers more opportunity to interact with students for sustained periods of time; classes are less rushed and thus more likely to encourage informal as well as academic interactions. Policies that facilitate one-on-one access to teachers, such as having teachers in their classrooms 30 minutes before or after school—or allocating some other specific time during the day when they are available for help or conversation—also help build strong student–teacher relationships.

Advisory groups are another common strategy that schools use to ensure that every student has a close personal relationship with at least one adult. Each adult in the school—including teachers and sometimes nonprofessional staff—serves as advisor for a small group of students (usually about 20) for the entire time the students are at the school. When I talk to students from low-income communities in high schools that have such a program, they invariably refer to their advisor as playing a crucial role in their persistence and commitment to finishing high school. Many refer to their advisor as a parent figure: "She's like a mom; she really knows me and keeps an eye on me." "He really wants me to go to college, and I don't want to disappoint him."

Schools should take particular care to promote good relationships with the students who are most at risk academically. Unfortunately, teachers often favor and develop more personal, supportive relationships with high-achieving students than with low-achieving students. Tracking magnifies this effect (Osterman, 2000). Eliminating tracking can go a long way toward reducing differential teacher treatment of students and giving more students an opportunity to feel supported and valued by their teachers. Even within individual classes, however, students who struggle academically typically have the worst relationships with their teacher. Teachers need to make special efforts to show a personal interest in and interact positively with the students whom they find most difficult to teach—by going out of their way to compliment positive behaviors, showing an interest in the students' lives outside school, listening to the students' perspectives on the problems they are having, and collaborating with them on developing strategies to address these problems.

Relationships Support Achievement

The spotlight on performance created by NCLB and other accountability policies must not distract us from attending to factors that substantially affect how well students perform. The most difficult-to-reach students will often go all out for a teacher who demonstrates caring for them as individuals and commitment to their success. School policies that support positive relationships between teachers and students can contribute significantly, not only to students' social-emotional health and

well-being, but also to their academic performance. That's why paying attention to students' nonacademic needs is a key ingredient in schools' efforts to meet today's high academic expectations.

References

Cushman, K. (2002). *Fires in the bathroom: Advice from kids on the front lines of high school.* Available: www.whatkidscando.org/firesinthebathroom.pdf

Davidson, A. (1999). Negotiating social differences: Youths' assessments of educators' strategies. *Urban Education, 34,* 338–369.

Davidson, A., & Phelan, P. (1999). Students' multiple worlds. In *Advances in motivation and achievement: Role of context, Vol. 2* (pp. 233–283). Stamford, CT: JAI Press.

Ferguson, R. (2002). *Who doesn't meet the eye.* Naperville, IL: North Central Regional Educational Laboratory.

National Research Council Committee on Increasing High School Students' Engagement and Motivation to Learn. (2004). *Engaging schools: Fostering high school motivation to learn.* Washington, DC: National Academies Press.

Osterman, K. (2000). Students' need for belonging in the school community. *Review of Educational Research, 70(3),* 323–367.

Pianta, R. (1999). *Enhancing relationships between children and teachers.* Washington, DC: American Psychological Association.

Pianta, R., Stuhlman, M., & Hamre, B. (2002). How schools can do better: Fostering stronger connections between teachers and students. *New Directions for Youth Development, 93,* 91–107.

Ryan, R., & Deci, E. (2000). Self-determination theory and the facilitation of intrinsic motivation, social development, and well being. *American Psychologist, 55,* 68–78.

Wentzel, K. (2002). Are effective teachers like good parents? *Child Development, 73,* 287–301.

Discussion Questions

1. What is the role of emotion in the learning process? Do teachers need to concern themselves with students' emotional states of mind each day?

2. How did you know that former teachers cared about you?

3. How would you describe "care" for students; that is, what does caring for a student look like?

4. What are several ways that students describe caring teachers?

5. What are some strategies that schools can adopt for helping students and teachers to develop strong relationships?

6. What is the role of assertiveness in a caring relationship with students?

7. What are several strategies for developing healthy caring relationships with students who are not socially adept, or have a history of unco-operative behavior?

8. What are some daily strategies for discovering more about your students' lives outside of school?

Preparing for the School Year

By Paul R. Burden

If you surveyed experienced teachers about the role of management at the beginning of the school year, you would undoubtedly hear comments about management and instructional preparations before school starts and about ways to plan for the first days of the school year. Studies on classroom management have verified that the first few days of the school year set the tone for the entire year (Emmer et al., 2000; Evertson et al., 2000).

To prepare, you can make management preparations, make instructional preparations, establish a plan for misbehavior, and also prepare for the first day of school. When the school year finally begins, there are certain actions that are appropriate during the first day and over the following few days. A number of these issues are addressed in this section. There are a number of resources that provide more details than can be discussed in this chapter. Resources are available for the elementary grades (Bosch & Kersey, 2000; Canter & Associates, 1998; Jonson, 2001; Moran et al., 2000; Roberts, 2001; Williamson, 1998), secondary grades (Arnold, 2001; Wyatt & White,

2001), and K–12 grades (Schell & Burden, 2000; Wong & Wong, 1998).

Making Management Preparations

It is important to consider carefully a variety of management issues such as your school environment, room and seating arrangements, materials, rules and procedures, communication with parents, and other issues. Based on a study of experienced teachers (Schell & Burden, 2000), you could direct your attention to the following classroom management issues.

1. The school environment. The first step is to become thoroughly familiar with the total environment before school starts: the room, school, facilities, personnel, services, resources, policies and procedures, other teachers, children, and the community. You will then have more information upon which to base decisions, will probably feel more confident about your job, and will not need to devote time in the first few weeks to gather this information.

2. Gather support materials. After examining the curriculum guide and the textbooks, you might have ideas about activities for a certain unit or lesson. Supplementary materials may be needed when the time comes to teach that lesson. This is the time to gather any additional support materials such as games and devices, pictures, cassette tapes, ideas for activities, charts, maps, and graphs. The school may have discretionary funds for the purchase of these types of resources. They may be obtained from school supply catalogs, a local teacher store, or even at garage sales.

3. Organize materials. It is useful to set up a filing system for storing district and school communications and other important documents. Papers kept in a filing cabinet include the district's policy handbook; correspondence from the principal, superintendent, or other supervisors; correspondence from professional organizations; lesson plans; and items on curricular content.

Some teachers use file folders. A separate file folder may be created for each course unit to hold pertinent notes and resource materials. Textbooks, resource books, manipulative materials, and other types of instructional supplies and materials also need to be organized and stored.

4. Classroom procedures. You can follow various procedures to accomplish specific tasks. Procedures may be identified regarding handing in completed work, sharpening a pencil, using the restroom, or putting away supplies. Before school starts, identify actions or activities requiring procedures that would contribute to a smoothly running classroom, and then decide what those procedures should be.

5. Classroom helpers. Teachers call upon students at all grade levels as helpers to perform various classroom tasks. Make a list of tasks that need to be done and then decide which ones students could perform. Give attention to how task assignment will be rotated to give every student an opportunity to help. Roles are often held for one

or two weeks before the assignments are rotated. Depending on the grade level and circumstances, some tasks may include students as line leader, light switcher, pencil sharpener, paper collector, plant waterer, chalkboard eraser, window and blind opener, and supply manager.

6. Class lists and rosters. It is useful to plan a means to record whether students have returned their book orders, picture money, field trip permission forms, and so on. You can prepare a generic class roster listing the students' names in alphabetical order in the left column, with blank columns on the right to check off the action. It is helpful to input the list on a computer disk so that an updated sheet can be easily generated when the roster changes.

7. School/home communication. Open communication with parents is vital. Before school starts, many teachers prepare an introductory letter to parents to welcome them and to inform them about the teacher, the curriculum, grading practices and standards, the homework policy, rules and procedures, and so on (discussed more fully in Chapter 4). This letter can be sent home with the students on the first day of school. Teachers can also make plans for other types of parental communication such as phone calls, progress reports, or a Back-to-School Night.

To establish good relationships with students, you might send a postcard or a letter to them before school starts. The greeting could include a personal and positive welcome, a list of some activities you plan for the school year, and perhaps a request that the student bring something special to school.

8. Birthdays and other celebrations. Depending on your grade level, you may want to recognize student birthdays. Most schools have very specific policies for celebrating major holidays, such as Halloween, Christmas, Hanukkah, Martin Luther King, Jr. Day, and Easter. Inquire about these policies so you'll understand what is expected.

9. Distributing textbooks. Sometime in the first few days of school, you will need to distribute textbooks. You need to obtain the textbooks and prepare an inventory from on which to record each book number, with a space in which to write the student's name.

You need to think about when and how the textbooks will be distributed. Since the first day of school often necessitates many announcements and activities, you might want to wait until the second or third day before distributing textbooks, or distribute them just before they are needed for the first time. Attention might be given to the specific means of distribution. One way is to have students line up one row at a time and go to the table where the books are stacked. When giving the book to the student, you can record the student's name on the inventory form.

10. Room identification. On the first day of school, students need to locate your classroom. Especially for students new to the building, it is important to have the room clearly labeled. A poster on the outside doorway should include the room number, the teacher's name, the grade level and/or subject (Room 221, Mr. Wagner, world History).

This information should be written on the chalkboard so students see that they are in the correct classroom. Some type of welcoming statement should also be placed on the chalkboard, such as, "Welcome, I'm glad you're here."

11. Room arrangement. Room arrangement is an issue that can be decided before school starts. Take into account the fixed features in the room, instructional materials and supplies, traffic areas, work areas, boundaries for activity areas, visibility to see all students, and the purposes of various seating arrangements. Determine the arrangement in the classroom for your desk, the students' desks, tables, book shelves, filling cabinets, and other furniture. The room arrangement you select should be consistent with your instructional goals and activities. Teacher-led instructional approaches such as presentations and demonstrations will require one type of room arrangement, whereas small-group work would require a different type of arrangement.

12. Seat selections and arrangements. One teacher may prefer to select each student's seat, while another lets the students select their seats. This decision should be made before school starts. In either case, be sure that there are enough seats for the number of students you expect. You might take the age level and maturity of the students into account as you select the manner of assigning seats.

Inspect the seats to be sure they are not damaged and that they are of sizes to accommodate your students. You might change the seating arrangements during the school year to accommodate work groups, to move students who need close supervision to more accessible seats, or simply to provide a change.

13. Room decoration. It is important to make your classroom an attractive, comfortable place. Consider having some plants in the classroom, or even an aquarium. Displays of pictures, posters, charts, and maps also help cover the walls with informative and appealing materials. Attractive bulletin boards add color. You might prepare one bulletin board listing classroom information and use another one to display seasonal items. After school starts, you could have students prepare bulletin boards.

Making Instructional Preparations

Prior to the start of the school year, carefully consider a variety of instructional issues such as long-range plans, supplementary materials, student assessment, a folder for substitute teachers, a syllabus, and so on. Based on a study of experienced teachers (Schell & Burden, 2000), you could direct your attention to the following instructional issues.

1. Long-range plans. It is helpful to peruse the curriculum guides and other related materials so you can appreciate what should be covered by the end of the school year. Some tentative decisions need to be made on the amount of time to be spent on each particular unit. Some curriculum guides include recommendations for the number of weeks to spend on each unit.

You may want to solicit advice from other teachers, particularly from those who teach your same subject or grade level. To the extent possible, make these rough schedules conform to the school calendar by taking into account grading periods and holidays. Be careful not to overschedule yourself. Leave some time for review near the end of each unit or chapter, for reteaching as the situation warrants, and for unexpected occurrences such as school closings due to inclement weather.

2. Supplementary materials. For each major curricular topic in your rough long-range plans, start an ongoing list of related supplementary materials or activities. It may include field trip locations, resource people, media, games, assignments, bulletin boards, and additional books. Inquire about library or media center resources, such as films or videotapes, and order and reserve them. You might prepare other supplementary materials to use during the first few weeks of school.

3. Skeleton plans. A skeleton plan is a brief overview of intended accomplishments. It often includes a weekly list of expected accomplishments. Skeleton plans include more details than the long-range, yearly plans, but not the detail needed for daily lesson plans. Skeleton plans for the first three or four weeks serve as a guide for preparing the more detailed lesson plans.

4. Weekly time schedules. You should establish your weekly schedule before school starts and include a copy in a handy place such as in your lesson plan book. The weekly schedule is often displayed in a chart, with the weekdays listed at the top and the hours listed on the left-hand column. The class schedule for middle and secondary teachers probably will be determined by the principal or others in the school building, and

it will show what grade level and subject is taught during each class period.

5. Daily lesson plans. After you have completed the skeleton plans for the first three or four weeks, it is time to prepare the daily lesson plans for the first week of school. Lesson plan formats vary; one that is often used includes boxes for the days of the week and the subjects taught. In these boxes, notes may be included about objectives, a list of topics to be covered or activities to be conducted, materials, and means of assessment. Beginning and probationary teachers are often required to show the principal or assistant principal their weekly lesson plans for the coming week.

Many teachers prefer to begin the school year with an interesting review of the content the students had in the subject area in the previous year. This is a time to consolidate learnings and review while giving you opportunities to reinforce subject matter and identify the students' level of understanding.

6. Syllabus. You need to give students information about each course at the start of the year. You could plan and prepare this information as well as any related materials before school starts.

The course syllabus includes the course title, the title of the textbook and any other primary resource materials, a brief course description, a list of course objectives, a content outline, course requirements (e.g., tests, homework, projects), how grades will be calculated (e.g., the points for each requirement and the point total needed for certain grades), a description of the homework policy, the attendance and tardiness policy, and a listing of classroom rules and procedures. Some teachers also include a description of the instructional methods and activities that students are to engage in.

7. Policy sheets. The syllabus might include all related classroom policies and procedures,

though some teachers do not include these items. Depending on the grade level and circumstances, some teachers do not provide a course syllabus.

As a result, a teacher might prepare a separate policy sheet for the students. The sheet may state the classroom rules and procedures, the policy for attendance and tardiness, and the like. If a course syllabus is not used, this policy sheet might also state the grading policy.

8. Tentative student assessment. It is useful to make an initial assessment of the students' understanding and skills at the start of the school year so you can better recognize the abilities and differences within the class. These assessments could be conducted sometime during the first week of school, but you should think about how to plan for the assessment and then make any necessary arrangements before school starts. Assessment procedures might include worksheets, oral activities, observation checklists, pretests, or review lessons. After conducting these early assessments, you could then record the results on a class roster that was drawn up earlier.

9. Homework. Give careful consideration to how you will evaluate students and determine report card grades. One element of student evaluation often involves homework, and preparation for developing a homework policy can be done before school starts.

Prepare a homework policy in the form of a letter that is sent to parents at the start of the school year (see Chapter 4). The homework policy should explain why homework is assigned, explain the types of homework you will assign, inform parents of the amount and frequency of homework, provide guidelines for when and how students are to complete homework, let parents know you will positively reinforce students who complete homework, explain what you will do when students do not complete homework, and clarify what is expected of the parent (Sarka & Shank, 1990).

10. Backup materials. It is useful to have some backup materials available when instruction takes less time than anticipated, when a change of plans is necessary, or when students finish their activities early. These backup materials may be related to the particular topics being covered at the time. Many teachers have a collection of puzzles, educational games, discussion questions, brain teasers, creative writing, word searches, and riddles. You can gather these materials before school starts.

11. Opening class routine. Students often perform better when they know that a particular routine will be regularly followed at the start of class. You can decide on the particular actions to be taken. You may need to take attendance, make announcements, and attend to other tasks at the start of the class period. The purpose of having a routine is to provide an orderly transition as students enter the room and get ready for instruction. Some teachers have students review vocabulary words or other problems related to the curriculum while other tasks are performed.

12. Folder for substitute teachers. A substitute teacher will take your place when you are absent. It is important to prepare materials for substitute teachers to help support what they do, maximize the learning, and minimize any off-task behavior. Many teachers keep a folder for substitute

teachers that includes important information. It can be kept on your desk with the plan book.

The type of material in a folder for substitute teachers varies, but the following information would be useful to include: a copy of the daily schedule, times of recess and lunch, a list of the classroom rules, a list of classroom procedures (e.g., morning opening, taking attendance, lunch count, lunch, dismissal, fire drills), a list of reliable students in each class period, hall pass procedures (to go to the rest room, library, or office), information on where to find certain items (e.g., lesson plans, audiovisual equipment, supplies), others to contact for information or help (e.g., a nearby teacher with room number), and a list and description of students with special needs. Much of this information can be collected before school starts, and additional information can be added as needed.

Establishing a Plan to Deal with Misbehavior

With an understanding of classroom management and discipline, you will need to develop a plan for dealing with misbehavior in the classroom. A seven-step plan is presented here that begins with the establishment of a system of rules and procedures. You need to provide a supportive environment during instruction and also provide situational assistance when students get off-task. If the student does not get back on-task, you need to move through advancing levels of consequences. If none of these actions work, you may need to involve other personnel.

You should deal with misbehavior in a way that is effective while also avoiding unnecessary disruptions. Researchers and educators have proposed movement from low to high intervention when developing a plan to address misbehavior (e.g., Charles, 2002; Levin & Nolan, 2000; Wolfgang, 2002). Once the rules and procedures and a supportive classroom environment are in

Creating a Learning Community

Seeking Student Feedback

Developing an inviting classroom is facilitated by listening to the views of your students and making appropriate adjustments in rules, procedures, instructional strategies, activities, and other aspects of the classroom. Feedback that students provide can help in making adjustments to better meet the students' needs and to create a positive learning community.

This feedback could be obtained during classroom meetings, informal discussions, questionnaires, or other approaches. Open-ended questions often stimulate discussion of these issues. Sample questions are listed here. What further questions could you add to the list?

My favorite activity in class is …
I like this class because …
I would like this class better if …
I don't like it when other students …
I think I could learn better if …
I get discouraged when …
In this class, I wish we spent more time …

place, the teacher moves from low to high interventions as described below.

1. *Establish your system of rules and procedures.* Establish an appropriate of rules and procedures as a foundation for dealing with discipline (discussed more fully in Chapter 5). It is vital that you select a system of rules and procedures appropriate to the situation. This system should incorporate reward or reinforcement for desirable behavior and the consequences of misbehavior.

No single approach is best for all teachers and all teachers and all teaching situations. For instance, rules and procedures for a tenth-grade English class would not be appropriate for a third-grade class. Furthermore, the system needs to be consistent with established school and district policies and with your own educational philosophy, personality, and preferences.

2. *Provide a supportive environment during class sessions.* Once the system of rules and procedures has been established at the start of the school year, you need to maintain a supportive environment. Actions taken in the normal course of instruction are for the purpose of guiding and reinforcing students for positive behavior (discussed more fully in Chapter 6). You would follow them even in the absence of misbehavior.

Providing a supportive environment is accomplished primarily through cueing and reinforcing appropriate behaviors; and getting and holding attention. Cueing and reinforcing involves stressing positive, desirable behaviors; recognizing and reinforcing desired behaviors; and praising effectively. Getting and holding attention necessitates focusing attention at the start of lessons; keeping lessons moving at a good pace; monitoring attention during lessons; stimulating attention periodically; maintaining accountability; and terminating lessons that have gone on too long. Treat students with dignity and respect, and offer challenging, interesting, and exciting classes.

3. *Provide situational assistance during class sessions.* Students may get off-task during a lesson. This off-task behavior may be in the form of misbehavior or may simply be a lapse in attention. Either way, you need to promptly provide situational assistance. Situational assistance denotes actions you take to get the student back on-task with the least amount of intervention and disruption possible; it does not involve delivering aversive nonpunitive or punitive consequences. You should be alert to lack of involvement in learning activities, prolonged inattention or work avoidance, and obvious violations of classroom rules and procedures. These behaviors can be dealt with directly and without overreaction.

Situational assistance can be provided by removing distracting objects, reinforcing appropriate behaviors, boosting student interest, providing cues, helping students over hurdles, redirecting the behavior, altering the lesson, and other approaches (discussed more fully in Chapter 11).

Some inappropriate behaviors are of such short duration and are so insignificant that they can be safely ignored. Your use of situational assistance might be considered a "forgiveness step" for the student by recognizing that the off-task behavior is minor or fleeting and by allowing the student to get back on-task without penalty.

4. *Use mild responses.* If a student continues to be off-task after situational assistance is provided, then you need to use mild responses to correct the student's behavior. These are not intended to be punitive. Mild responses may be nonverbal or verbal (see Chapter 11).

Nonverbal responses include ignoring the behavior, using signal interference, using proximity control, or using touch control. Verbal responses include reinforcing peers, calling on the student during the lesson, using humor, giving a direct appeal or command, reminding the student of the rule, and several other approaches.

5. Use moderate responses. If students do not respond favorably to mild responses and continue to exhibit off-task behavior, you need to deliver moderate responses (see Chapter 11). These punitive responses deal with misbehavior by removing the desired stimulus so as to minimize the inappropriate behavior. Moderate responses include the use of logical consequences and various behavior modification techniques such as time-out and loss of privileges.

6. Use stronger responses. If moderate responses are insufficient, you need to move to a more intrusive type of intervention (see Chapter 11). These stronger responses are intended to be punitive, by adding aversive stimuli such as reprimands and overcorrection. The purpose of aversive stimuli is to decrease unwanted behavior.

7. Involve others when necessary. If all efforts have failed to get the student to behave properly, then you need to involve other persons in the process. This occurs most commonly with chronic or severe behaviors. You may consult or involve counselors, psychologists, principals and assistant principals, teaching colleagues, college personnel, mental health centers, school social workers, school nurses, supervisors and department heads, and parents (see Chapter 12). Their assistance and involvement will vary depending on their expertise.

Planning for the First Day

Starting the school year effectively is vitally important when establishing a system of classroom management. Several principles should guide your decisions about planning the start of the school year and your actions in the first few days (Emmer et al., 2000; Evertson et al., 2000; Good & Brophy, 2000).

1. *Plan to clearly state your rules, procedures, and academic expectations.* When students arrive in your class for the first time, they may have uncertainties. They will want to know your expectations for behavior and for academic work. They will want to know what the rules are for general behavior and also the consequences for adhering to or breaking them (discussed more fully in Chapter 5). Students also will wonder how you will monitor the rules and how consistently you will enforce them.

They want to know what the procedures are for going to the restroom, turning in homework, sharpening their pencils, talking during seatwork, and other specific activities. They will be interested in finding out about course requirements, grading policies, standards for work, and other aspects of the academic program.

Your philosophical perspective about classroom management will likely affect your decisions. As discussed in Chapter 2 on the models of discipline, you need to consider the degree you want to involve students in identifying the rules and procedures. Some teachers like to determine the rules before school starts, while other teachers

Classroom Decisions

Before using mild responses for off-task behavior, teachers often provide situational assistance to get students back on-task. What are the benefits of using situational assistance? How might situational assistance differ among first, seventh, and eleventh grade? How might cultural differences of students affect your decisions about the ways to provide situational assistance?

prefer to involve students in the discussion of the rules to develop a sense of ownership. Still other teachers let the students discuss and determine the rules themselves. You need to decide on your approach to the selection of rules and procedures prior to the start of school.

It is especially important to take the necessary time during the first few days of school to describe your expectations in detail about behavior and work. Emphasize and be explicit about desirable behavior. Combine learning about procedures, rules, and course requirements with your initial content activities to build a good foundation for the year.

2. *Plan uncomplicated lessons to help students be successful.* Content activities and assignments during the first week should be designed to ensure maximum student success. Select relatively uncomplicated lessons at the start of the school year so that few students will likely need individual help. This allows you to focus on monitoring behavior and to respond to students in ways that shape and reinforce appropriate behavior.

It provides you with opportunities to reinforce students for their academic work and to begin to develop positive relationships with students.

3. *Keep a whole-class focus.* Plan activities for the first week that have a whole-class focus, rather than small-group activities. Whole-class activities make it easier to monitor student behavior and performance. In this way, you can focus on reinforcing appropriate behavior and preventing inappropriate behavior.

4. *Be available, visible, and in charge.* You must be in charge of students at all times. Move around and be physically near the students, and maintain a good field of vision to see all students wherever you stand. Move around during seatwork to check on student progress.

5. *Plan strategies to deal with potential problems.* Unexpected events can develop when you meet your students for the first time. These might include (a) interruptions by parents, office staff, custodians, or others; (b) late arrivals on the first day; (c) one or more students being assigned to your class after the first day; and (d)

Teachers in Action

Conducting Yourself on the First Day

Beatrice Gilkes, high school computer science teacher, Washington, DC:
The image that I project on the first day when the students enter is very important, so I take time to plan carefully what I am going to do. It is a day that is usually very hectic and filled with monumental record-keeping chores, statistical reports, and directions. In spite of these distractions, it is important that the students develop a positive image of me as a reasonable, caring, intelligent, and compassionate human being.

I use the following questions as guides as I start planning for the first day and as I try to get to know my students:

- What do I really expect of my students?
- What do my students expect of me?
- What do I need to know about them?
- How can I plan for their interests, talents and deficiencies?
- What will make me special to them?

an insufficient number of textbooks or necessary materials. While you cannot foresee events, you can give thought to how you would deal with the unexpected, should it occur.

Treat each unexpected situation in a calm, professional manner. This will serve as a good model for your students when they confront unexpected or challenging events. Treat students respectfully and deal with some of the needed details later. For example, you can ask a late enrolling student to take a seat and begin work, and then you could handle the particular enrollment procedures later.

6. *Closely monitor student compliance with rules and procedures.* By closely monitoring students, you can provide cues and reinforcement for appropriate behavior. Better classroom managers monitor their students' compliance with rules consistently, intervene to correct inappropriate behavior whenever necessary, and mention rules or describe desirable behavior when giving feedback. Effective managers stress specific corrective feedback rather than criticism or threat of punishment when students fail to comply with rules and procedures.

7. *Quickly stop inappropriate behavior.* Inappropriate or disruptive behavior should be handled quickly and consistently. Minor misbehavior that is not corrected often increases in intensity or is taken up by other students. Quickly respond to inappropriate behavior to maximize on-task behavior. Act in a professional manner to settle the difficulty and preserve the student's dignity in front of the other students.

8. *Organize instruction on the basis of ability levels.* The cumulative record folders will indicate students' prior academic performance in reading, math, and other subjects. Select instructional content and activities to meet the ability levels of your students.

9. *Hold students academically accountable.* Develop procedures that keep students accountable for their academic work. This may include papers to be turned in at the end of class, homework, in-class activities, or other means. Return the completed papers promptly and with feedback. Some teachers give a weekly assignment sheet to each student. This sheet is completed by the student, checked by the parent, and returned to the teacher daily.

10. *Be clear when communicating information.* Effective teachers clearly and explicitly present information, give directions, and state objectives. When discussing complex tasks, break them down into step-by-step procedures.

11. *Maintain students' attention.* Arrange seating so all students can easily face the area where their main attention needs to be held. Get everyone's focused attention before starting a lesson. Monitor students for signs of confusion or inattention, and be sensitive to student concerns.

12. *Organize the flow of lesson activities.* Effective classroom managers waste little time getting the students organized for the lesson. They maximize student attention and task engagement during activities by maintaining momentum and providing signals and cues. They successfully deal with more than one thing at a time (e.g., talking with one student but also keeping an eye on the rest of the class).

Classroom Decisions

Effective teachers are available, visible, and in charge. Suppose that you are ready for your math class on the first day of school. How could you exhibit this take-charge behavior as students come into the room and as you begin opening announcements and activities in a lesson? How might your approach differ for a sixth grade class compared to a twelfth grade class?

Conducting the First Day

The first day of school is often a time of nervousness for teachers and students. Fortunately, you can make decisions about a number of issues as you prepare for the first day. Students, on the other hand, enter school on the first day with a lot of uncertainty. They will have questions on the first day (Wong & Wong, 1998):

- Am I in the right room?
- Where am I supposed to sit?
- What are the rules in this classroom?
- What will I be doing this year?
- How will I be graded?
- Who is the teacher as a person?
- Will the teacher treat me as a human being?

You can do a number of things on the first day to address these student concerns, as discussed below.

1. *Greet the students.* Stand by the classroom door before class begins. When students are about to enter your classroom, greet them with a smile and a handshake. As you do this, tell them your name, your room number, the subject or period, if needed; the grade level and anything else appropriate, such as the student's seating assignment (Wong & Wong, 1998). Your name, room number, section or period, and grade level or subject should be posted outside your door and on the chalkboard.

2. *Tell students about their seat assignment.* There are various ways to handle seat assignments for students. Some teachers prefer to let students select their seats while other teachers prefer to assign seats. Either way, students should be told what to do as they enter the classroom for the first time.

If you determine the seating assignment, there are several possible ways to inform students of their seat assignment as they enter the room. You might have a transparency showing on an overhead projector indicating the seating arrangement. A different transparency would be used for each of your class sections. Also have a copy of the seating chart in hand as the students are greeted at the door.

3. *Correct improper room entry.* Observe students as they enter the room and take their seats. Some students may not go directly to their seats or may behave inappropriately. It is important to ask a student who enters the room inappropriately to return to the door and enter properly.

Be calm, but firm; tell the student why this is being done, give specific directions, check for understanding, and acknowledge the understanding (Wong & Wong, 1998). The communication might be something like this:

> Todd, please come back to the door.
> I am sorry, but that is not the way you enter our classroom every day. You were noisy, you did not go to your seat, and you pushed Ann.
> When you enter this classroom, you walk in quietly, go directly to your seat, and get to work immediately on the assignment that is posted.
> Are there any questions?
> Thank you, Todd. Now show me that you can go to your seat properly.

During this interaction, be sure to use the student's name and be polite with a "please" and "thank you."

4. *Handle administrative tasks.* Taking attendance is one of the first administrative tasks to be done at the start of the class period. Have the students raise their hands when called to indicate that they are present and to give you an opportunity to see the face that goes with the name. As you call each name, ask the student whether you pronounced it correctly.

After the first day of school, some teachers prefer not to take attendance at the start of class. Instead, they give an assignment that the students are to begin as soon as they enter the classroom. After the students are underway, the teacher can take attendance by visually scanning the room; the names do not need to be called. This approach, or one similar to it, takes very little time and allows students to move quickly into the academic work.

5. *Make introductions.* Students appreciate knowing something about the teacher. At the start of the class period, tell the students your name and some personal information, such as the number of years you have been teaching, professional development activities, family, personal interests and activities, hobbies, and other background information. This helps the students know you as a person and may be informative and comforting to them. This is also the time to let the students know that you are enthusiastic about working with them and that you will be reasonable and fair with them.

Some teachers like to use this opening time to have the students briefly introduce themselves. Some get-acquainted activities for students could be included on the first day to help promote good feelings.

6. *Discuss classroom rules and procedures.* All classrooms need rules and procedures if they are to run smoothly and efficiently. Rules should be taught on the first day of class to establish the general code of conduct (discussed more fully in Chapter 5). Post the rules in a conspicuous place in the classroom. If a letter has been prepared for parents that describes the rules and procedures, this should be given to the students so they can take it home.

Some classroom procedures may be taught on the first day of school, but many teachers prefer to teach procedures (e.g., distributing materials, getting ready to leave the classroom, handing in papers) over the next several school days instead (Leinhardt, Weidman, & Hammond, 1987). In this way, all the procedures are not taught at the same time, and the students might be less overwhelmed by them and will more likely remember them when they are covered in several brief sessions. Procedures can be taught when the need for them first occurs. For example, when it is time to collect papers at the end of an activity, you could teach students the appropriate procedure.

7. Present course requirements. Before school started, you would have prepared the course requirements and syllabus. On the first day, students want to know what content will be covered and what is expected of them concerning grading. Take time to discuss the course content and some of the activities planned for the year. If you have prepared a syllabus, hand it out. Discuss the grading requirements concerning tests, homework, projects, and the like and indicate what levels are needed for the various letter grades.

8. Conduct an initial activity. Depending on the amount of time available on the first day, many teachers plan an initial activity related to the curriculum. It should provide a review of some material that students had in the previous year, or may be a preview of content to be covered. Either way, the activity should be designed so that the students can complete it without much

---

Classroom Decisions

An initial activity will focus on some aspect of the curriculum. How might you provide variations of that activity based on the varied ability levels of the students? How might you relate the content to various cultural backgrounds of your students? How might you modify the activity due to the varied learning styles of the students?

assistance and with much success. This leaves you free to monitor the students during the activity, to provide assistance when necessary, and to take corrective action on off-task behavior.

9. End the class period. A routine to end the class period is needed, and this must be taught to students. Procedures need to be established and time saved for actions such as returning books and supplies, disposing of scrap paper and cleaning up the classroom, and putting away books and other materials in preparation for leaving the classroom.

Organizing Your Classroom and Materials

Decisions about room arrangement must be made before students arrive on the first day of school. Before arranging the classroom, consider: (a) the movement patterns of students throughout the classroom; (b) the need for students to obtain a variety of materials, texts, reference books, equipment, and supplies; and (c) the need for students to see the instructional presentations and display materials. Good room arrangement can help teachers cope with the complex demands of teaching by minimizing interruptions, delays, and dead times. Based on studies of effective classroom managers, there are five keys to good room arrangement (Emmer et al., 2000; Evertson et al., 2000).

1. *Use a room arrangement consistent with your instructional goals and activities.* You will need to think about the main types of instructional activities that will be used in your classes and then organize the seating, materials, and equipment compatibly. Teacher-led presentations, demonstrations, or recitations will require students to be seated so they can see the instructional area. In contrast, small-group work will require very different room arrangements.

2. *Keep high traffic areas free of congestion.* High traffic areas include the space around doorways, the pencil sharpener and trash can, group work areas, certain book shelves and supply areas, the teacher's desk, and student desks. High traffic areas should be kept away from each other, have plenty of space, and be easily accessible. For example, try not to seat a student next to the pencil sharpener because of the heavy traffic and the possibility of inappropriate behavior.

3. *Be sure students are easily seen by the teacher.* It is important that teachers easily see students to identify when a student needs assistance or to prevent task avoidance or disruption. Clear lines of sight must be maintained between student work areas and areas of the room that the teacher will frequent.

4. *Keep frequently used teaching materials and student supplies readily accessible.* By having easy access and efficient storage of these materials, activities are more likely to begin and end promptly, and time spent on getting ready and cleaning up will be minimized. Establishing regulated storage areas can help reduce the occurrence of students leaving materials in their desks or taking them out of the room.

5. *Be certain students can easily see instructional presentations and displays.* The seating arrangement should allow all students to see the chalkboard or the multimedia screen without moving their chairs, turning their desks around, or craning their necks. Place the primary instructional area in a prominent location to help students pay attention and to facilitate note taking.

Floor Space

A classroom typically contains many items such as student desks, the teacher's desk, bookcases, tables, and activity centers that take up floor space. When determining how to arrange the classroom, you need to consider the functions of the space and the various factors mentioned earlier in an effort to facilitate learning and to minimize interruptions and delays. Visiting other teachers' classrooms can provide ideas for effective ways to arrange the floor space in your own classroom.

A good starting point in planning the floor plan is to decide where you will conduct whole-group instruction. Examine the room and identify where you will stand or work when you address the entire class to conduct lessons or give directions. This area should have a chalkboard, an overhead projector screen, a table on which to place the overhead projector, a small table to hold items needed during instruction, and an electrical outlet. Consider the following items:

- Student desks. Even if other arrangements are to be used later in the year, you might start the year with student desks in rows facing the major instructional area, since it is easier to manage students with this pattern. Be sure all students can see the major instructional area without having their backs to the area and without having to get out of their seats.

It is important to keep student desks away from high traffic areas. Avoid placing their desks near the door, pencil sharpener, trash can, and supply areas. Leave ample aisles between the desks to enable easy movement of students and yourself when monitoring seatwork.

- The teacher's desk. Your desk should be situated so that you can see the students, but it is not essential that the desk be at the front of the room. Placement of your desk at the rear of the room, in fact, may help when monitoring students during independent work. Students facing away from you cannot discern when you are looking at them unless they turn around. This tends to encourage students to stay at their assigned

tasks. Instead of sitting at their desk during independent work, many teachers prefer to move around the room to monitor and assist students.

If you plan to work with individual students at your desk, you need to consider traffic patterns to and from the desk. Student desks should not be so close to yours that the seated students will be distracted by other students approaching your desk or working with you there.

- Bookcases and filing cabinets. These should be placed so students' visibility of chalkboards or relevant displays is not obstructed. They also should not prevent your monitoring. If a bookcase contains frequently used items such as resource books, dictionaries, or supplies, then it should be conveniently located and monitored. If it contains seldom-used items, an out-of-the-way place is best. If there is only one bookcase, it is helpful to use it for frequently used items.
- Activity centers or work areas. An activity center is an area where one or more students come to work on a special activity. It may be in the form of a learning center or a computer work area. One or more tables commonly serve as the work surfaces. When you select the placement of tables for this area, be sure that you can see all students in the work area, keep traffic lanes clear, and avoid congested areas. A center often will have special equipment such as tape recorders with headphones, a computer, a filmstrip projector, or other materials and supplies. Enough table and work space must be provided for students to work efficiently. It is useful to place the work area at the side or the back of the room and to the backs of other students. Figure 3.1 shows a number of possible seating arrangements.

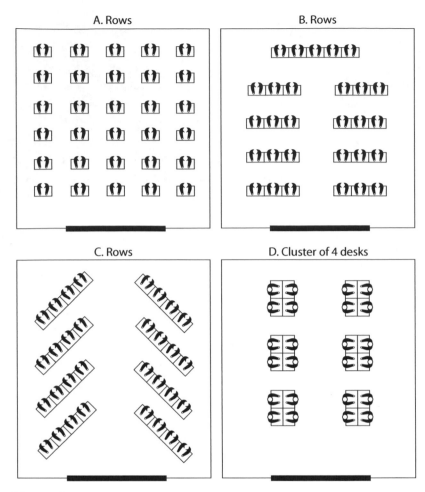

A. Rows   B. Rows

C. Rows   D. Cluster of 4 desks

Figure 3.1 Possible seating arrangements

Storage Space

Teachers and students use a wide variety of instructional materials. All of these materials are not used every day and must be stored when not in use. Therefore, storage space must be provided for textbooks and resource books, frequently used instructional materials, teacher's supplies and instructional materials, equipment, and infrequently used materials.

1. Textbooks and resource books. Some textbooks are not retained by students and thus must be stored in the classroom for easy access. Resource books obtained from the school library,

public library, or other sources may be available for student use. All of these books should be stored in a bookcase that enables easy access.

2. Instructional materials. Instructional materials that students need will vary with the subject area that you teach. These may include rulers, scissors, special paper, pencils, staplers, tape, glue, and other supplies. As with textbooks and resource books, a storage location should be selected to enable easy access to the materials. Clearly labeled containers for each of the supply items are often very helpful in maintaining an orderly supply area. These materials may be stored on shelves of a bookcase or cabinet, or on a counter.

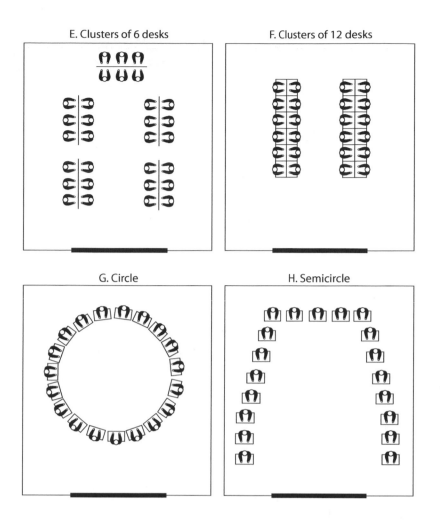

E. Clusters of 6 desks

F. Clusters of 12 desks

G. Circle

H. Semicircle

3. Teacher supplies. Supplies that only you would use should be kept in your desk or in storage areas used only by you. These supplies include items such as hall passes, attendance and lunch count forms, ditto masters, computer disks, computer programs, lesson plan book, tablets, file folders, and chalk. These items should be placed in secure places so students don't have access to them.

4. Equipment. Items like an overhead projector, tape recorders, computers, or other instructional media may not be used every day. Therefore, these items must be stored when not in use.

5. Infrequently used items. Some instructional materials are used only once a year. These include seasonal decorations (e.g., Halloween, Thanksgiving), bulletin board displays, or special project materials. Certain instructional materials may be used for only one unit, as in the case of a model of the human eye for a science class. Some teachers prefer to keep seasonal decorations or other infrequently used materials at their homes.

Bulletin Boards and Wall Space

Constructive use of bulletin boards and wall space can contribute to a positive classroom environment. This can be achieved by displaying relevant instructional material, assignments, rules, schedules, student work, and other items of interest. Many teachers involve students in the selection of content and the preparation of bulletin boards and the use of wall space. One approach is to select a different group of students to plan and prepare a bulletin board each month.

Some teachers prefer to dedicate each bulletin board to a certain purpose. For example, one bulletin board could be used to post classroom rules, a daily or weekly schedule, classroom helpers, lunch menus, a school map, emergency information, or any other procedural information. Another bulletin board could be used to display student work. A third type of bulletin board could be simply for decoration, with seasonal, motivational, or artistic items. Other bulletin boards can be used to post information and news articles about school or community events. In addition, bulletin boards can also be used to post content- related news articles, posters, or information.

Discussion Questions

1. What aspects of your first day as a teacher on the first day of school make you somewhat nervous or anxious?

2. What do you want to know about the first day of school?

3. What should students learn on the first day of school about your expectations?

4. How can you teach students what they need to know about your policies, procedures/routines, and philosophy on the first day?

5. Which policies and procedures must students learn on the first day?

6. What are the advantages and disadvantages of teachers assigning seats on the first day?

7. Describe several games to use to learn students' names.

8. What is the importance of providing children with choices on the first day of school?

9. What are the advantages and disadvantages of assigning homework on the first day?

10. How can teachers preview on the first day what students will be learning throughout the year?

11. Make a list of the tasks you should complete before the first day the students arrive.

12. Which seating arrangements match your philosophy of teaching and learning?

Using Classroom Rules
to Construct Behavior

By David F. Bicard

I've come to a frightening conclusion that I am the decisive element in the classroom. It's my approach that creates the climate. It's my daily mood that makes the weather. As a teacher, I possess a tremendous power to make a child's life miserable or joyous. I can be a tool of torture or an instrument of inspiration. I can humiliate or humor, hurt or heal. In all situations, it is my response that decides whether a crisis will be escalated or de-escalated and a child humanized or dehumanized. (Haim Ginott, The Teacher, January 2000)

In many middle school classrooms, teachers attempt to influence the behavior of students through the use of rules. However, rules alone exert little effect on student behavior. Teachers may sometimes be unaware of the effects their actions have on the behavior of their students. Two classic studies may help to illustrate the effects of teacher-made rules and teacher behavior on the activity of their students. Madsen, Becker, and Thomas (1968) found that when a teacher provided rules alone to her students, the students' appropriate and inappropriate behavior remained at relatively the same level as when she provided no rules. Major decreases in inappropriate conduct and increases in appropriate conduct occurred when the teacher showed approval for appropriate behavior in combination with ignoring some inappropriate behavior. Similarly, Thomas, Becker, and Armstrong (1968) found that teachers could produce or eliminate appropriate and inappropriate behavior by varying approval and disapproval statements. When the teachers delivered positive statements to their students regarding their classroom behavior, the students maintained appropriate conduct; and when the teachers withdrew positive statements and delivered frequent disapproval statements, inappropriate behavior increased.

While rules by themselves may not be effective, they do provide structure, communicate teacher expectations, provide a foundation for learning, and help maintain a well-run and organized classroom. Positive rules, along with consistent action by the teacher, set the stage for praising student achievement that benefits the teacher as much as the students. Good classrooms where students are highly involved do not just happen. They exist because effective teachers have constructed the types of classroom conditions and student interactions necessary for a positive learning environment (Emmer, Evertson, Clements, & Worsham, 1994). In Middle School Journal, Mills (1997) described how one effective teacher named Suzan constructed her classroom to ensure successful learning. Suzan "modeled a way of teaching, learning, and behaving that she shared, both explicitly and implicitly, with her students. … [Her approach] held expectations for student responsibility, for a caring atmosphere, and for student success" (p. 32). Throughout this article we will return to Suzan's classroom to demonstrate how effective teachers can use words and actions to construct positive rules for their students.

Rules are one of the most cost effective forms of classroom management available to teachers (Catania, 1998). However, not all teachers recognize the benefit of teaching rules. In *Setting Limits in the Classroom,* Mackenzie (1996) noted 10 common misconceptions held by teachers about the use of rules, among them, "teaching rules is the parents' job," "students should know what I expect," "I can't afford to take precious time away from instruction," and "explaining my rules to students should be enough." The reality is that in the classroom, teaching rules is one of the teacher's jobs, with parents' help. In addition, students need time to learn the rules and expectations of their teachers. Rules need to be taught with words as well as actions; the time invested up front will pay huge dividends in the end.

Ginott (2000) suggested that teachers are the decisive element in the classroom. In that role, they should take the responsibility for constructing and implementing positive rules as a management system to build academic success. This article describes the characteristics of positive rules,

offers suggestions for developing and implementing the rules, and provides guidelines for what to do when students break the rules.

Characteristics of Positive Rules

The first part of this section will describe the differences between some common rules that exist in many middle school classrooms. The second part discusses an often overlooked, yet extremely important, component of effective rules. These small differences in the way teachers construct rules may have a big influence on the way students behave in the classroom.

Positive rules specify appropriate student behavior in observable terms

Rules come in three basic varieties: positive rules that communicate how to behave, negative rules that communicate how not to behave, and vague rules that communicate neither how nor how not to behave (Figure 1). A common rule about completing assigned work can be worded positively ("Answer each problem until you are done"), negatively ('Don't stop unless you are done"), or vaguely ("Stay on task"). Small differences in wording make a substantial difference in the way students will respond and how teachers will focus their attention. The positive version of the rule lets the student know how to behave so that teachers can provide approval when students follow the rule. Conversely, in the negative and vague examples, nothing has been said on how to respond: the student is left with only how not to respond. More important, in the negative and vague examples, teachers are more likely to recognize students only when they do not follow the rule. When rules state what the student can do in specific and observable terms, both teachers and students can easily recognize whether a rule is

Examples of Positive, Negative, and Vague Rules		
Positive	**Negative**	**Vague**
Raise your hand when you want to talk.	Don't interrupt others.	Respect others.
Keep your eyes on the teacher.	Don't look around the room.	Listen to the teacher.
Bring a pencil to class every day.	Don't come to class without a pencil.	Come to class prepared.
Before you leave make sure your desk is clean.	You are not ready to leave until your desk is clean.	Keep the classroom neat.
Be in you seat when the bell rings.	Don't be out of your seat when the bell rings.	Be on time for class.

being followed. Teachers are more likely to notice appropriate behavior and celebrate student success. Positive rules tell students what to do instead of what not to do and are thus more instructive (Paine, Radicchi. Roseliini. Deutchman, & Darch, 1983).

When rules state only what the student cannot do or are vague, teacher attention will likely be on punishment for inappropriate behavior (Zirpoli & Melloy, 1993). When teacher attention is focused on punishment, the classroom becomes coercive, authoritarian, and punitive. It becomes a teacher's job to investigate violations, determine guilt, and mete out sentences. Less time is left for teaching. Frequent disapproval may also deter student learning in other ways. Greer (1981) found that the use of disapproval statements by teachers resulted in the students avoiding what was taught during free time. For example, if when teaching reading a teacher delivers frequent disapproval statements to his or her students, the students will be less likely to read books when they have leisure time. As Sufcer-Azaroff and Mayer (1986) noted. "One more critical disadvantage to resorting to punishment too frequently is that the practice inadvertently may teach others to use it as well" (p. 146).

A key component of effective rules is that the rules specify observable student behavior. In this respect observable means something a teacher can count, for example raising a hand. When a teacher can count behaviors, students become accountable for those behaviors. Vague rules such as "respect others" or "stay on task" may be as difficult for students to follow as they are for teachers to enforce because behaviors are extremely difficult to count. A teacher who can observe specific instances of appropriate student conduct is prepared to celebrate students' successes.

When attention is focused on appropriate behavior through the use of positive rules, teachers promote a sense of personal efficacy in students that communicates the trust, competence, responsibility, affiliation, and awareness so important in middle level curriculum (Stevenson, 1998). In short teachers should be in the business of constructing behaviors not eliminating them (W. L Heward, personal communication, February 12,1998).

Suzan "told her students what she expected and wanted. … She reminded the students of proper lab behavior before each lab activity. … She gave examples of acceptable comments that focused on their learning and encouraged students" (Mills,

1997, pp. 33–34). Yet simply stating positive rules is only the first step of effective classroom management.

Positive rules specify observable consequences

Another important, though often overlooked, component of effective rules is a statement of consequences. Consequences are the quid pro quo of rules, letting students know what they get in return. Classroom studies conducted by Braam and Malott (1990) and Mistr and Glenn (1992) have shown that rules specifying only response requirements did not reliably guide student behavior; conversely when rules specified observable behavior and consequences, they were effective in maintaining appropriate behavior. Consequences are important because they teach

responsibility and accountability to the teacher as well as the student. Providing clear consequences will help to break the cycle of limit-testing so common with middle school students. In the example, "Raise your hand when you want to talk," the students are left to discover what will happen next; they may raise their hands and then begin to talk, if the teacher provides a consequence, for example, "and I will call on you when it's your turn," the students will not have to guess. This is especially significant when we look at negative rules, such as "Don't talk until called upon." When a consequence is provided, "or your name will be written on the board," the focus of attention will necessarily be on elimination of behavior.

It is also important that students be aware of the consequences for not following the rules. For example, during science experiments Mills' (1997) expert teacher "reminded the students of

Keys to Developing and Implemating Positive Rules in Classrooms
Characteristics of Positive Rules
• Positive rules specify appropriate behaviour in observable terms • Positive rules specify observable consequences
Developing Positive Rules
• Develop a framework before the school year begins • Include students in the decision-making process • Get agreement by students, teachers, and parents
Using Positive Rules Effectively
• Teach the rules • Catch students following the rules • Monitor your behaviour • Include students as monitors
What To Do When Students Break the Rules
• Use the least intrusive procedures first • Praise other students for following the rules • Give verbal redirection • Remain unemotional yet firm when interveing

the cost of activities and suggested the principal, 'won't give me money for labs if you're not mature enough to handle them well'" (p. 34).

Developing Positive Rules

Three strategies help develop effective rules. The first strategy helps teachers to conceptualize a basic framework for identifying situations in which rules should be specified. The next two strategies are specific processes teachers can use to develop successful classroom rules.

Develop a framework before the school year

All rules must follow the policies and procedures of the school; however, these are typically general guidelines that can easily be incorporated into a set of classroom rules. Once teachers, or a team of teachers, have information about school policy and procedures, they can begin to plan rules for their classrooms and team areas. Paine and associates (1983) maintained that the best time to develop rules is before the school year begins. Teachers should decide what kinds of situations to cover and what kinds of rules to write for those situations. For example, a science teacher may have one set of rules during experiments and another during whole-class time. This basic framework will help teachers to guide students toward a formalized version of the rules.

Include students in the decision-making process

Once the guidelines are in place, the next step is involving students in deciding the specific rules.

Student participation in rule setting has been demonstrated to be effective for increased compliance (Dickerson & Creedon, 1981),

lower numbers of violations (Felixbrod & O'Leary, 1974), and academic success (Lovitt & Curtis, 1969). Emmer, Evertson, Clements, and Worsham (1994) noted that involving students in rule setting helps to promote student ownership and responsibility. Incorporating students in the process communicates respect and concern, lets students know they are important elements in the classroom, and serves to promote student acceptance.

There are a number of techniques teachers can use. For example, the first day of class can begin with a discussion of the role of rules in society and their application to the classroom. A teacher could ask the students to describe model behavior, then use this as a basis for discussing what types of rules are appropriate in the classroom. Specifying student behaviors in observable terms provides the foundation for the rules, and identifying teacher behavior provides the foundation for the consequences. The teacher may need to guide the students in providing positive examples, as middle school students tend to focus on violations (Emmer et al., 1994). Suzan had students "brainstorm appropriate comments and role-play supportive situations" (Mills, 1997, p 35). It is important to note that student-made rules are sometimes too stringent, so again, it is a good idea to have a basic framework in mind prior to discussing rules with the students.

Try to keep the rules to a minimum: It is recommended that teachers use no more than three or four rules for each situation. To help students remember the rules and help teachers make praise statements within the wording of the rules, keep the wording as simple as possible. When the rules are established consequences must also be established. A simple method for achieving positive rules and consequences is to ask students to list possible consequences for following classroom rules. These can be favorite classroom activities, free time, or a note to parents. Students should also list consequences for not following the rules—for example, a "three strikes policy," then loss of free time, then a note to parents. An example of a positive rule might be when a student completes assigned work before the end of class, the teacher will give him or her five minutes of free time. Teachers can decide on whole class and individual contingencies based on the list each student completes. This process will allow flexibility in classroom management.

Create a contract for the students, teachers, and parents

Once the rules are in place have each student write the rules on a piece of paper, sign it, take it home for the parents or guardians to sign, and bring it back to school the next day. Jones and Jones (1990) recommended including a statement about classroom philosophy regarding management and instruction: "This lets you present the issues of rules in a positive manner that indicates their relationship to effective instruction and student learning" (p. 285). The contingency contract provides a number of useful advantages: students cannot say they were unaware of the rules; parents know the expectations of the teachers and have agreed, fostering a home-school partnership; and there is a record on file for future reference. (For more information regarding contingency contracts see Cooper, Heron, & Heward, 1987, pp. 466–485.)

Using Rules Effectively

Now that the rules have been specified and the consequences set forth, teachers are ready to begin using the rules to guide student learning. It is worth mentioning again that, without reliable enforcement by teachers, rules have very little effect on student conduct.

Teach the rules

A crucial component of positive classroom management is how teachers implement the rules. The first step in teaching the rules is to post them prominently in the classroom. Suzan, "at the beginning of the year displayed a life-size female adolescent labeled 'scientist,' a smaller poster of rules near a frog saying 'hop to it'" (Mills, 1997, p. 33). An effective strategy is to designate a student from each class to make a poster listing the rules and consequences, or, if teachers decide on one set of rules for all their classes, a competition can be held and prizes awarded for the three best posters. For the first two or three days after the rules are in place, devote five minutes of class time to teaching the rules through examples. Doing this at the beginning of each class is an excellent way to keep the students engaged while taking attendance or gathering materials. Teachers can guide this discussion or designate a student to lead the class. It is important to have all the students state the rules, then have students role-play acceptable and unacceptable behavior. This is a perfect time to begin to catch students following the rules and praise them. Teachers can continue teaching the rules in this fashion each Monday for the first month of the school year and again the first Monday after long breaks. Whenever students need a "booster shot" during the school year, teachers can go back to this activity. Although this procedure may seem somewhat elementary, it is useful to teach rule following just as one would teach any other subject.

Catch students following the rules

Teaching positive rules does not end in the first five minutes of class or in the first week of school; it continues throughout the school year. Suzan "provided numerous opportunities for students to experience success. Her students experienced frequent success and received teacher praise for their efforts" (Mills, 1997, p. 35). Praise should be immediate, consistent, and contingent upon "catching' the students being good." Consistent means a teacher reliably recognizes student behavior as it occurs. Contingent specifies a relationship between praise and the student's behavior. When students are behaving appropriately, follow the "if, then rule"—*if* students have done something appropriate, *then* praise them (Paine et al., 1983). An example from Mills (1997) illustrates this point, "Suzan once shared the compliments that a substitute teacher had made about the students and thanked them for their good behavior. … 'When I saw the work you had done in groups [while I was gone] I knew you had been wonderful'"(p.35).

When praising always identify the rule, the behavior, and the student or students by name, "I like the way Jennifer put things away when the bell rang because that shows she is ready to learn. Nice job Jennifer." Public praise can occur in several situations: while teaching, when near a student, or in the presence of other teachers. This may be especially helpful for some students who are having difficulty in other classrooms. Sometimes public praise might be a problem with middle school students, so teachers may want to praise some students only when nearby or in private. Teachers can write a note on a student's paper or praise the student during individual seat work. Sometimes a call home to parents or even to a student is a good technique. For Suzan, "quiet, supportive exchanges with individual students took place literally during every occasion" (Mills, 1997, p. 34).

Monitor teacher behavior

An effective way to achieve success using positive rules is for teachers to monitor their own behavior. Initially, teachers can count the number of approval and disapproval statements. It is not as difficult as one would think. Generally, middle level teachers are excellent time managers. Begin counting, and when five minutes have passed, note the number of approval and disapproval statements. This then becomes a measure per unit of time. Teachers may be surprised and somewhat shocked at how little praise has been given. A good rule of thumb is to have a 3:1 ratio of approval to disapproval statements (Engiemann & Carnine, 1991).

One technique for helping to pinpoint specific approval statements is a variation of "the timer game" (Lovitt, 1995, p. 322). Identify the behaviors to "catch," for example, students active at work stations making entries in their notebooks. Set a goal such as five praise statements in five minutes. The next and easiest step is for teachers to identify a reward for themselves, maybe a chocolate bar at lunch. Once these are in place, teachers can set a timer for five minutes and begin teaching. During teaching simply make a mark on a spare piece of paper for every praise statement. When the timer goes off, students will probably be very interested in what is going on. This is a good time to let them in on the secret. Take a few minutes to discuss this practice and why it is being used. The students may be willing to assist in counting. It also has the added benefit of notifying students of what behaviors are being monitored and may help to promote appropriate classroom conduct.

Another useful strategy is to place "reminders" in the classroom such as a sign in the back of the room to prompt the teacher. Mills (1997) reported that in Suzan's classroom, "Virtually every week, new student work was displayed. … Before class started, Suzan would call my attention to the students' work, call students over to show me their efforts or explain the concept, and tell me loudly how proud she was of their efforts" (pp. 35–36). Monitoring teacher behavior helps to promote a positive classroom environment. In the classroom it is the teacher who sets the standards.

By modeling appropriate behavior teachers communicate with words and actions that they value a supportive, responsible, and respectful, classroom.

Include students as monitors

Students play an active role in controlling peer behavior (Lovitt, 1995). Middle school teachers are well aware of the effects of peer attention on student behavior. Unfortunately, this has usually been correlated with inappropriate behavior. The results of a study by Carden-Smith and Fowler (1984) suggested that peers can serve to increase and maintain appropriate classroom behavior, provided they are given proper instruction and feedback from a teacher. Here is how Suzan involved students as monitors, "One particular day, the students had given oral reports and presented visuals on different animals; following each report the students asked for questions and comments. All students received praise from classmates about some aspect of their reports or drawings" (Mills, 1997, p. 35). Suzan "reminded her students during lab activities to 'check with your buddy' or 'help your partner'" (Mills, 1997 p. 34). Encouraging students to praise their peers has many benefits. In the above example, a mutually reinforcing relationship is established that will increase the probability of more praise statements to follow. Another example shows how involving students frees the teacher to take on other responsibilities:

> During the first observation, a group of students who finished their assignments early were designated by Suzan as "wizards." Suzan explained the next assignment to the wizards, and they were to provide and explain the worksheet to other students as they completed their work. All students were to seek help from the wizards before they asked questions of Suzan. (Mills. 1997, p. 35)

A useful and highly effective strategy for involving students as peer monitors is a variation of "the good behavior game" (Barrish, Saunders, & Wolf. 1969). This strategy is appropriate for whole groups or individual students. The technique requires teachers to model appropriate behaviors and then designate a student or group of students to identify instances of appropriate behavior by other students. In this game all students can win if they simply engage in appropriate behavior. Each team or individual can choose rewards the students and teacher have selected prior to the game. Successfully including peers as monitors may take some time and creativity on the part of a teacher, but the benefits of a cohesive, nurturing classroom are well worth the investment.

What to Do When Students Break the Rules

There will be times when students behave in unacceptable ways. This is as true for the best students as it is for the worst. The decisions teachers make during these times can escalate or de-escalate an already unfavorable situation. Heward has noted that teachers can maintain and increase deviant behavioral patterns even though they are trying to help their students. This process

> begins with a teacher request that the student ignores and follows a predictable and escalating sequence of teacher pleas and threats that the student counters with excuses, arguments, and eventually a full-blown tantrum. The aggression and tantrumming is so aversive to the teacher that she withdraws the request (thereby reinforcing and

strengthening the student's disruptive behavior) so the student will stop the tormenting (thereby reinforcing the teacher for withdrawing the request). (Heward, 2000)

This increasing escalation of disruptive behavior is called coercive pain control (Rhode, Jensen, & Reavis, 1998) because the student learns to use painful behavior to escape or avoid the teacher's requests. It is best to try to anticipate these times by preparing a plan of action before the situation occurs. The following five proven strategies can be used separately or in combination to assist teachers when students behave unacceptable in the classroom.

Use the least intrusive procedures first

The first technique to use is simply to arrange seating patterns so teachers can reach every part of their classrooms. Second, certain objects may be removed from the classroom if they prove to be distracting. However, keep in mind that having interesting objects in the classroom provides a great teaching opportunity since the student's attention is naturally directed toward the object. Another useful, unobtrusive technique is known as "planned ignoring" (Walker & Shea, 1995). Before attempting to use this technique, first try to determine why the student is engaging in unacceptable behavior. If it is determined he or she is doing this to get attention, then any response (positive or negative) will increase the probability of this behavior re-occurring in the future. With planned ignoring the teacher does not make any contact with the student. This technique works especially well in combination with praising other students, When a teacher uses this technique, at first unacceptable behavior may increase in intensity or duration. This should not be cause for alarm because it is an indication

that the technique is working, it is important to resist the temptation to react. Once the student stops the unacceptable behavior the teacher can catch some appropriate behavior and praise it. If the teacher determines the unacceptable behavior is maintained by other students or is dangerous, then planned ignoring will not work and should not be attempted. At this point a teacher may want to intervene directly.

Praise other students for following the rules

Praising other students for following the rules serves as a reminder to a student that he or she is not behaving appropriately. This reminder encourages the student to adjust his or her own behavior (Sulzer-Azaroff & Mayer, 1986). For example, if James is staring out the window when most of the other students are working diligently on math problems, the teacher may call a student by name and praise him—"I like the way DeMarco is working; one bonus point for DeMarco." More often than not, James will then begin to work on his math. After a few seconds, praise James to encourage him to keep working. This strategy is effective and has the benefit of notifying the student who is acting inappropriately without having to single him out. At the same time, it recognizes a student who is behaving appropriately.

Use proximity control and signal interference

Proximity control and signal interference are two less obtrusive techniques that are frequently used in conjunction with one another (Walker & Shea, 1995). When teachers move around the classroom their presence often serves as a cue to students, who stop behaving unacceptably. When a student is misbehaving, casually move in the direction of the student and attempt to make eye contact. Sometimes simply making eye contact is enough, other times nonverbal cues such as facial expressions, toe taps, or body language may be necessary. These nonverbal signals may alert a student that a behavior is disruptive. Walker and Shea noted, "In addition, proximity can have a positive effect on students experiencing anxiety and frustration. The physical presence of a teacher or parent available to assist has a calming effect on troubled children" (p. 228). Often nonverbal signals help the student to "save face" with his peers and promote a sense of respect on the part of the teacher. This technique is also appropriate for reinforcing acceptable behavior. After making eye contact, the teacher can simply smile or give a thumbs-up sign (Walker & Shea, 1995).

Give verbal redirection

Occasionally students engage in minor disruptions during daily classroom routines such as attendance, returning homework, or when listening to daily messages over the intercom. This is a good time to channel their energy toward acceptable behavior. For example, Lynn passes a note to Juan through Chuck. Ask Lynn to assist in passing out homework. Ask Juan a question about an upcoming activity and tell Chuck to read today's assignment off the blackboard. Verbal redirection can be an extremely effective technique, but caution should be used if the student is engaging in the behavior to get the teacher's attention.

Remain unemotional yet firm when intervening

It is best to remain unemotional yet firm when dealing with rule violations. As classroom leaders, teachers set the tone when things do not go as planned. The most effective strategy teachers can use is to handle minor disruptions before they become worse. Jones and Jones (1990) noted, "An inappropriately angry teacher's response creates tension and increases disobedience and disruptive behavior. When a teacher reacts calmly and quickly to a student's disruptive behavior, other students respond by improving their own behavior" (p. 295). The first step when intervening is to make contact with the student. Never assume the student is aware he or she is breaking a classroom rule; let the student know what is unacceptable: "Carlos, the rule is, raise your hand when you want to speak, and I will call on you as soon as possible." As soon as Carlos raises his hand, the teacher should call on him and praise him for behaving responsibly. Teachers can intervene publicly as a message to the entire class; however, it is best to deliver reprimands in private. When teachers show respect for students, they will be more likely to comply with the teacher's instructions, and the teacher has averted turning a minor disruption into a major catastrophe.

Conclusion

Following this four-part framework for constructing behaviors can result in positive approaches to middle level classroom management. Figure 2 provides an outline of this approach for reference. The goal of setting positive rules and procedures is to maintain a healthy and respectful classroom. As the decisive element, teachers can create a supportive, caring community of learners through the words they choose and the actions they take Mills (1997) captured this approach this way: "Suzan communicated to her students a pervasive caring by helping them feel a sense of belonging; learn acceptable, supportive behaviors; experience frequent success; and assume they have a promising future" (p. 34).

References

Banish, H. H., Saunders. M.. & Wolf, M. M (1969). Good behavior game: Effects of individual contingencies for group consequences on disruptive behavior in a classroom. *Journal of Applied Behavior Analysis, 2,* 119–124.

Braam, C., & Malott, R. M. (1990). "I'll do it when the snow melts": The effects of deadlines and delayed outcomes on rule-governed behavior in preschool children. *The Analysis of Verbal Behavior, 5,* 67–76.

Carden-Smith. L. K. & Fowler. S. A. (1984). Positive peer pressure. The effects of peer monitoring on children's disruptive behavior. *Journal of Applied Behavior Analysis, 17,* 213–227.

Catania. A. C. (1998). *Learning (4th ed.).* Upper Saddle River. NJ: Prentice Hall.

Cooper. J. O., Heron, T. E., & Heward, W. L. (1987). *Applied behavior analysis.* Upper Saddle River, NJ: Prentice Hall/Memill.

Dickerson, E A. & Creedon. C F. (1981). Self-selection of standards by children: The relative effectiveness of pupil-selected and teacher-selected standards of performance. *Journal of Applied Behavior Analysis. 14,* 425–433.

Engiemann, S., & Camine. D. (1991). *Theory of instruction (rev. ed).* Eugene. OR: ADI Press.

Emmer. E T.. Evertson, C. M., Clements, B. S., & Worsham, M. E. (1994). *Classroom management for secondary teachers (3rd ed.).* Needham, MA: Allyn and Bacon.

Felixbrod. J., & O'Leary, K. (1974). Self-detennination of academic standards by children: Toward freedom from external control. *Journal of Educational Psychology, 66,* 845–850.

Ginott, H. (2000). *The teacher.* Retrieved January 6, 2000 from the World Wide Web: http://m-w.geocities.com/Heanland/Piains/3565/aimginott.htm

Greer, R. D. (1981). An operant approach to motivation and affect: Ten years of research in music learning. In *Documentary report of the Ann Arbor symposium: Application of psychology to the teaching and learning of music.* Washington, DC: Music Educators National Conference.

Heward W. L (2000). *Exceptional children: An introduction to special education (6th ed).* Upper Saddle River, NJ: Prentice Hall.

Jones, V. F., & Jones, L S. (1990). *Comprehensive classroom management.* Needham Heights, MA: Allyn and Bacon.

Lovitt T C. (1995). *Tactics for teaching (2nd ed).* Upper Saddle River, NJ: Prentice Hall.

Lovia T. C. & Curis, K (1969). Academic response rate as a function of teacher and self-imposed contingencies. *Journal of applied Behavior Analysis, 2,* 49–53.

Madsen, C. H., Becker, W. C., & Thomas, D. R. (1968). Rules, praise, and ignoring: Elements of elementary classroom control. *Journal of Applied Behavior Analysis, 1,* 139–150.

Mackenzie, R J. (1996). *Setting limits in the classroom.* Rocklin, CA: Prima Publishing.

Mills, R. A. (1997). Expert teaching and successful learning, at the middle level: One teacher's story. *Middle School Journal, 29(1),* 30–38.

Mistr, K. N., & Glenn, S. S. (1992). Evocative and function-altering effects of contingency-specifying stimuli. *The Analysis of Verbal Behavior, 10,* 11–21.

Paine, S. C., Radicchi, J., Rosellini, L C., Deucchman, L. & Darch, C B. (1983). *Structuring your classroom for academic success.* Champaign, IL: Research Press.

Rhode, G. Jensen, W. R, & Reavis, H. K. (1998). *The tough kid book: Practical classroom management strategies.* Longmont, CO: Sopris West.

Stevenson, C (1998). Finding our priorities for middle level curriculum. *Middle School Journal, 29(4),* 53–57.

Suizer-Azaroff, B, & Mayer, G. R (1986). *Achieving educational excellence using behavioral strategies.* New York: CBS College Publishing.

Thomas, D. R, Becker, W. G, & Armstrong, M. (1968). Production and elimination of disruptive classroom behavior by systematically varying teachers' behavior. *Journal of Applied Behavior Analysts, 1,* 35–45.

Walker, J., & Shea, T. M. (1995). Behavior management: A practical approach for educators. Engiewood Cliffe, NJ: Prentice Hall.

Zirpoli,, T. J., & Meiloy, K. J. (1993). Behavior management: Applications for teachers and parents. Don Mills, Ontario: Macmillan Publishing.

Discussion Questions

1. What are some classroom rules that you recall from your experiences as a student?

2. Describe the difference between telling students the rules and teaching students the rules.

3. State five positively worded rules that you are interested in using in your classroom.

4. State five rules that are worded negatively that you have seen or heard of in other classrooms.

5. What are observable rules? State three rules that are observable.

6. What are the advantages and disadvantages of vaguely worded rules?

7. How can teachers encourage students to follow the rules without using consequences during the first weeks of school?

8. Why should teachers include students in the process of establishing rules?

9. How can teachers include students in the process of establishing rules?

10. What is the role of consequences in enforcing the rules?

Teacher Responsibilities
and Behaviors

By James H. Stronge

The teacher responsibilities and teacher behaviors, or qualities, are designed primarily to assist administrators and peer coaches in identifying key components of effectiveness as they visit classrooms and observe teachers in action. In essence, they are intended to facilitate a type of action research focused on behaviors that teachers exhibit in their daily work. For some teachers, the guidance that can emerge from feedback on the classroom qualities may be the impetus to refine a strategy or add something new to their toolkit of skills and techniques.

The positive and negative behaviors exhibited by teachers determine, to a great extent, their effectiveness in the classroom and, ultimately, the impact they have on student achievement. Several specific characteristics of teacher responsibilities and behaviors that contribute directly to effective teaching are listed for each of the following categories:

- The teacher as a person
- Classroom management and organization
- Organizing and orienting for instruction
- Implementing instruction

- Monitoring student progress and potential
- Professionalism

Red flags signaling ineffective teaching are presented at the end of each section. Both positive and negative characteristics are based on a plethora of research-based studies that address the concept of improving the educational system for both students and teachers. These qualities are general for any content area or grade level. Subject-specific qualities presented for the four content areas typically found in all schools include

- English
- History and Social Studies
- Mathematics
- Science

The lists are provided as a vehicle to promote teacher effectiveness.

The Teacher as a Person

The teacher is the representative of the content and the school. How a teacher presents himself makes an impression on administrators, colleagues, parents, and students. Often a student links the preference for a particular subject to a teacher and the way the subject was taught. A teacher who exudes enthusiasm and competence for a content area may transfer those feelings to the students. In addition, how the teacher relates to the pupils has an impact on the students' experience in the class. The teacher's personality is one of the first sets of characteristics to look for in an effective teacher. Many aspects of effective teaching can be cultivated, but it is difficult to effect change in an individual's personality.

Positive Qualities

- Assumes ownership for the classroom and the students' success
- Uses personal experiences as examples in teaching
- Understands feelings of students
- Communicates clearly
- Admits to mistakes and corrects them immediately
- Thinks about and reflects on practice
- Displays a sense of humor
- Dresses appropriately for the position
- Maintains confidential trust and respect
- Is structured, yet flexible and spontaneous
- Is responsive to situations and students needs
- Enjoys teaching and expects students to enjoy learning
- Looks for the win-win solution in conflict situations
- Listens attentively to student questions and comments
- Responds to students with respect, even in difficult situations

- Communicates high expectations consistently
- Conducts one-on-one conversations with students
- Treats students equally and fairly
- Has positive dialogue and interactions with students outside the classroom
- Invests time with single students or small groups of students outside the classroom
- Maintains a professional manner at all times
- Addresses students by name
- Speaks in an appropriate tone and volume
- Works actively with students

Red Flags of Ineffective Teaching

- Believes that teaching is just a job
- Arrives late to school and class on a regular basis
- Has classroom discipline problems
- Is not sensitive to a student's culture or heritage
- Expresses bias (positive or negative) with regard to students
- Works on paperwork during class rather than working with students
- Has parents complaining about what is going on in the classroom
- Uses inappropriate language
- Demeans or ridicules students
- Exhibits defensive behavior for no apparent reason
- Is confrontational with students
- Lacks conflict resolution skills
- Does not accept responsibility for what occurs in the classroom

Classroom Management and Organization

A classroom reveals telltale signs of its user's style. Typically, a well-organized classroom has various instructional organizers, such as rules, posted-on walls. Books and supplies are organized so that often needed ones are easily accessible. The furniture arrangement and classroom displays often reveal how the teacher uses the space. Once the students enter, the details of a classroom at work are evident. The teacher's plan for the environment, both the organization of the classroom and of students, allows the classroom to run itself amid the buzz of student and teacher interaction.

Positive Qualities

- Positions chairs in groups or around tables to promote interaction
- Manages classroom procedures to facilitate smooth transitions, instructional groups, procurement of materials and supplies, and supervision of volunteers and paraprofessionals in the classroom
- Manages student behavior through clear expectations and firm and consistent responses to student actions
- Maintains a physical environment where instructional materials and equipment are in good repair
- Covers walls with student work, student made signs, memos, and calendars of student events
- Has students welcome visitors and observers and explain activities
- Emphasizes students addressing one another in a positive and respectful manner
- Encourages interactions and allows low hum of conversations about activities or tasks
- Maximizes the physical aspect of the environment
- Manages emergency situations as they occur
- Maintains acceptable personal work space
- Establishes routines for the running of the classroom and the handling of routine student needs (e.g., bathroom visits, pencil sharpening, and throwing away trash)
- Provides positive reinforcement and feedback
- Disciplines students with dignity and respect
- Shows evidence of established student routines for responsibilities and student leadership
- Exhibits consistency in management style
- Posts classroom and school rules
- Posts appropriate safety procedures

Red Flags of Ineffective Teaching

- Arranges desks and chairs in rows facing forward (without regrouping)
- Displays inconsistencies in enforcing class, school, and district rules
- Is not prepared with responses to common issues (bathroom visits, pencil sharpening, and disruptions)
- Uses strictly commercial posters to decorate walls
- Lists rules and consequences for negative behaviors (teacher formulated)
- Ranks student progress on charts for all to view
- Emphasizes facts and correct answers
- Assigns one task to be completed by all students
- Does not post or is not clear about expectations of students
- Does not display school or classroom rules

- Allows student disengagement from learning
- Is unavailable outside of class for students
- Complains inappropriately about all the administrative details that must be done before class begins
- Maintains an unsafe environment or equipment
- Students have no specific routines or responsibilities
- Keeps an unclean or disorderly classroom
- Uses many discipline referrals
- Makes up rules and consequences or punishment according to mood; unpredictable
- Does not start class immediately, takes roll and dallies

Organizing and Orienting for Instruction

Some teachers plan at home, and others work after school, crafting unit plans that incorporate various objectives. Regardless where or how teachers plan and organize for instruction, the evidence of effective work is seen in the classroom. An observer in the classroom of an effective teacher can quickly understand the work by viewing the daily lesson objectives and activities posted. Further, the teacher is able to share what the class will be doing to follow-up the lesson of the day. In many schools, teachers are required to submit weekly lesson plans; these plans typically note accommodations for different learning styles or needs, and the variety of instructional approaches that will be used. It is important to note, however, that a lesson plan is not an end-all; it is merely a description of what should be occurring in the classroom. Thus, a good plan doesn't guarantee high-quality instruction, but a poor plan most certainly contributes to ineffective instruction.

Positive Qualities

- Lesson plans are written for every school day
- Students know the daily plan because an agenda of objectives and activities is given
- Student assessment and diagnostic data are available
- Assessment data and pretest results are included in the preparation of lesson plans
- Student work samples are available and considered when writing lesson plans
- Lesson plans are aligned with division curriculum guides
- Teacher-developed assessments are aligned with curriculum guides
- State learning objectives are incorporated into lesson plans
- Lesson plans have clearly stated objectives
- Lesson plans include use of available materials
- Lesson plans include activities and strategies to engage students of various ability levels
- Lesson plans address different learning modalities and styles
- Lesson plans include required accommodations for students with special needs
- State standards are posted in classroom
- Lesson plans include pacing information
- Lesson plans for a substitute or an emergency are located in an easily accessible area of the classroom containing all necessary information

Red Flags of Ineffective Teaching

- No (or very few) lesson plans are available
- Student assessment and diagnostic data are not available
- No connection between assessment data and lesson plans is evident
- No differentiated instruction is provided

- Lesson plans are not aligned with local or district curriculum guides
- State learning objectives are not incorporated into lesson plans
- Activities that are unrelated to the learning objective are selected
- No plans for or anticipation of potential problems
- Lesson plans mainly consist of text or worksheets.
- Students are not engaged in learning
- Lesson plans do not address different learning styles of students
- Lesson plans do not reflect accommodations for students with special needs
- State standards are not posted in the classroom
- Information on pacing is not discernible in lesson plans
- Lesson plans are disjointed
- Lesson plans are short and do not allow for smooth transitions between activities
- Poor or inconsistent student achievement is the prevalent pattern
- Emergency lesson plans are not available
- Materials for substitutes are not available (attendance rolls, class procedures, lesson plans, fire and tornado drill evacuation route maps)

Implementing Instruction

Effective teaching combines the essence of good classroom management, organization, effective planning, and the teacher's personal characteristics. The classroom presentation of the material to the students and the provision of experiences for the students to make authentic connections to the material are vital. The effective teacher facilitates the classroom like a symphony conductor who brings out the best performance from each musician to make a beautiful sound. In the case of the classroom, each student is achieving instructional goals in a positive classroom environment that is supportive, challenging, and nurturing of those goals. The best lesson plan is of little use if the classroom management component is lacking or the teacher lacks rapport with the students. Implementing instruction is like opening night at the theater where all the behind-the-scenes work is hidden and only the magic is seen by the audience. Effective teachers seem to achieve classroom magic effortlessly. The trained observer, on the other hand, is likely to feel great empathy and appreciation for the carefully orchestrated art of teaching.

Positive Qualities

- Uses student questions to guide the lesson
- Uses pre-assessments to guide instruction
- Develops elements of an effective lesson
- Uses established routines to capture more class time (e.g., students have roles to play, such as passing out materials so the teacher need not stop the momentum of the lesson)
- Incorporates higher-order thinking strategies
- Uses a variety of activities and strategies to engage students
- Monitors student engagement in all activities and strategies
- Has high numbers of students actively engaged in the class continuously
- Adjusts the delivery and pacing of the lesson in response to student cues
- Effectively uses the entire classroom (e.g., teacher movement throughout the room)
- Student-centered classroom rather than teacher-centered classroom
- Provides feedback (verbal, nonverbal, and written)
- Designs and bases assignments on objectives

- Assists students in planning for homework assignments

Red Flags of Ineffective Teaching

- Experiences student behavior problems
- Has unengaged students (e.g., bored, off-task, asleep)
- Has poor student performance in class and on assessments
- Gives vague instructions for seatwork, projects, and activities
- Unresponsive to student cues that the delivery of instruction is ineffective
- Lacks variety in instructional methods used
- Has difficulty individualizing instruction
- Uses outdated material or terminology
- Fails to implement needed changes pointed out by peers or supervisors
- Tells students to "know the material"
- Does not apply current strategies or best practices
- Uses poor examples of or improper English
- Transitions slowly between activities or lessons

Monitoring Student Progress and Potential

Effective teachers have a sense of how each student is doing in the classes that they teach. They use a variety of formal and informal measures to monitor and assess their pupils' mastery of a concept or skill. When a student is having difficulty, the teacher targets the knowledge or skill that is troubling the student and provides remediation as necessary to fill in that gap. Communication with all parties vested in the success of the student is important since parents and instructional teams are also interested in monitoring the student's progress. Monitoring of student progress and potential need not be solely the responsibility of the teacher; indeed, an effective teacher facilitates students' understanding of how to assess their own performance, that is, assists them in metacognition. However, ultimate accountability does lie with each teacher, so documenting a student's progress and performance needs to be accomplished. An effective teacher who has observed and worked with a student has a sense of the potential that student possesses, encourages the student to excel, and provides the push to motivate the student to make a sustained effort when needed.

Positive Qualities

- Enables students to track their own performances
- Grades homework
- Gives oral and written feedback
- Documents student progress and achievement
- Makes instructional decisions based on student achievement data analysis
- Circulates in the room to assist students and provide praise
- Gives pretests and graphs results
- Considers multiple assessments to determine whether a student has mastered a skill
- Keeps a log of parent communication
- Uses student intervention plans and maintains records of the plan's implementation.
- Records team conference or teacher conference with students
- Gives assessments on a regular basis
- Makes use of a variety of assessments
- Uses rubrics for student assignments, products, and projects
- Practices differentiated instruction based on assessment analysis

- Exercises testing accommodations for special-needs students.
- Maintains copies of all correspondence (written, e-mail) concerning student progress
- Holds teacher-parent-student conferences and meetings
- Produces class newsletters
- Invites parents and guests to special class events
- Maintains class Web page featuring student work, homework assignments
- Communicates with informal progress reports
- Uses appropriate and clear language in communications
- Participates in Individualized Education Program (IEP) meetings for special-needs students

Red Flags of Ineffective Teaching

- Does not monitor student progress or allow for questions
- Infrequently analyzes or lacks appropriate data
- Infrequently or fails to monitor student progress
- Does not keep a communication log
- Does not record conferences with students or parents and guardians
- Uses extremes in grading—high failure rates or unrealistically high percentage of excellent grades
- Fails to reteach after assessments to correct gaps in student learning
- Offers little or no variety of assessments
- Ignores testing accommodations for special-needs students
- Does not document or holds few parent communications (communication may include conferences, phone calls, e-mail, newsletters, Web sites)
- Uses vague, technical, or inappropriate language in communications
- Does not participate in or attend IEP meetings for students with special needs

Professionalism

Teachers have been portrayed in a variety of ways in the media, ranging from detrimental images to beloved masters of their craft who inspire students to excel. Effective teachers can be seen, heard, and sensed. The effective teacher engages in dialogue with students, colleagues, parents, and administrators and consistently demonstrates respect, accessibility, and expertise. Effective teachers are easily identified through their adept use of questioning and instruction given in the classroom. Finally, an observer who knows from all sources that this person truly makes a difference in the classroom can sense the presence of an effective teacher. The true teacher is a master of teaching.

Positive Qualities

- Practices honest two-way communication between teacher and administrators
- Communicates with families of students
- Maintains accurate records
- Reflects on teaching, personally and with peers
- Attends grade-level meetings; is a team player
- Attends and participates in faculty and other school committee meetings
- Focuses on students
- Performs assigned duties
- Implements school and school district goals and policies

- Acts "globally" around the school for the benefit of the whole school
- Volunteers to assist others
- Seeks community involvement
- Seeks leadership roles on school committees and teams
- Contacts central office personnel for technical support when needed
- Treats colleagues with respect and collegiality
- Works collaboratively with faculty and staff
- Attends professional development opportunities (e.g., conferences, graduate classes, workshops)
- Maintains current teaching certification
- Submits required reports on time and accurately
- Writes constructive, grammatically correct communications
- Writes appropriately for the intended audience
- No testing irregularities found that are within the control of the teacher
- Submits lesson plans and assessment documents on time
- Submits grades on time
- Maintains a calendar of report deadlines
- Keeps an accurate and complete grade book

Red Flags of Ineffective Teaching

- Gives negative feedback routinely at meetings
- Displays unwillingness to contribute to the mission and vision of the school
- Refuses to meet with parents and guardians or colleagues outside of contract hours
- Resents or is threatened by other adults visiting the classroom
- Does the minimum required to maintain certification or emergency certification status

- Submits reports late
- Submits grades late
- Writes inaccurate or unclear reports
- Does not update grade book or it is "inaccurate"

Subject Specific Qualities

Most teachers have been in an unfamiliar situation where they were not certain of what would be considered normal versus questionable. For example, while a chemical fume hood would look out of place in a history classroom, it is a common element in a chemistry classroom. The following subject specific qualities and red flags are shared to equip the reader with some indicators of what may be observed in effective and ineffective teachers' rooms.

English and Language Arts

An effective English teacher has a classroom that is text-rich and integrates the elements of the English language through writing, reading, and oral expression, including listening. The teacher is well read in the subject area and works diligently to convey enthusiasm for the subject. The teacher encourages the reading of great works of literature for class projects and for pleasure, maintains writing portfolios, provides opportunities for discussion, and gives plenty of feedback. In today's changing technological classrooms, software programs may be used to help enhance reading and writing instruction as well as research skills. The effective teacher's classroom integrates all key components of the English curriculum.

To enhance oral language in students, the teacher may

- Provide instruction in listening
- Model good listening behaviors

- Give instruction in speaking skills and verbal and nonverbal messages
- Provide activities for the preparation, practice, and presentation of formal speeches
- Demonstrate and practice the adaptation of oral communication strategies to match the needs of the situation and setting
- Offer opportunities to participate in role-plays, interviews, and impromptu speeches
- Lead discussion groups
- Give instruction in dialect, pronunciation, and articulation
- Use vocal elements in oral presentations: pitch, volume, rate, quality, animation, and pause
- Give instruction on how to use media for research, analysis, and evaluation of media messages

The teacher uses strategies in reading instruction, including

- Read-alouds
- Independent reading
- Dyad reading (paired reading)
- Library visits to promote use of the media center and facilitate book choice
- Classroom libraries
- Providing blocks of time for students to read
- Cause-and-effect frame
- Sequence of events
- Compare and contrast matrix
- Proposition and support outline
- Debriefing
- Discussion web
- Word wall
- Think-pair-share
- Literature circles
- Reader's workshop

Writing instruction may include these types of activities

- POWER writing (prewriting, organizing, writing, editing, rewriting)
- Peer-reviews and constructive criticism
- In-class writing and publishing
- Writer's workshop
- Journals
- Use of technology to facilitate the writing process
- Writing in different forms (technical, persuasive, research, expository, narrative, and poetry)
- Grammar, instruction
- Outlining
- Note-taking (e.g., Cornell notes)

History and Social Studies

The effective teacher empowers students to think about history and the implications of past choices, in order to guide thinking about the future or to find patterns within history. Students are taught a blend of essential facts and skills that enable them to access knowledge and make interpretations of history. The effective history or social studies teacher usually has an area of historical expertise that is evident in discussions and interactions with students on that period in history. Teachers use their own understanding of how history works to teach students to construct their own personal bank of tools to critically examine current news and past events. The effective teacher finds ways to make the events of old become relevant to the students of today.

The teacher uses a variety of preteaching strategies including

- K-W-L charts (Know, Want to Know, Learned)
- Learning logs
- Timelines
- Anticipation guides
- Graphic organizers

The teacher uses a variety of classroom practices, such as

- Simulations
- Debates

- Independent research projects
- Socratic seminar
- Internet and technology based activities
- Historical archives and primary document analysis
- Current events
- Mapping (globes, wall maps, flat maps, computer maps, and sketched maps)

The teacher may use a variety of assessment strategies

- Close read activities
- Multimedia presentations
- Reaction papers
- Historical interpretation
- Rubrics
- Teacher-made tests, both objective and essay

Mathematics

An effective mathematics teacher has the ability to facilitate students' ability to understand, analyze, and solve problems. The teacher presents real-world applications of the math concepts to make the application real for the students. The teacher facilitates students thinking beyond the paper and the pencil to how mathematics is evident and applied to everyday life. The room probably is filled with manipulatives and decorated with math-related posters and 3-D constructions. The chalkboard tray holds oversized tools of the ones students use, such as protractors and compasses. The teacher uses the tools to break down the process and provide meaning for the class. If a student is having difficulty, the teacher is able to diagnose and remediate the gap in prior knowledge or identify where the student has misunderstood the process and gets the child back on track. Students are asked to compute problems, write about solutions, and discuss mathematics. Mathematics is not just numbers and symbols; it is a language for understanding.

The mathematics teacher uses a variety of tools and manipulatives to teach, including

- Various papers (grid, dot, patty, and notebook)
- Calculators (4-function, scientific, and graphing)
- Measurement tools (angle ruler, balance, compass, protractor, ruler, and thermometer)
- Mathematical software programs and spreadsheets
- Commercial manipulatives (algebra tiles, cubes, Cusinaire rods, decimal blocks, fraction circles, Geo boards, Hands-on Algebra, and tangrams)
- Common materials (spinners, coins, dice, and yarn)
- Chalkboards or white boards that have grids
- Overhead calculator and transparent tiles

The effective mathematics teacher uses a variety of approaches to teaching the content, including

- Application problems using real-life data
- 3-D constructions
- Reading and writing story problems
- Using visuals in problems
- Mental mathematics
- Estimation
- Discussing mathematical concepts
- Talking through how to do the problem by students
- Tessellations
- Examining musical patterns in algebra
- Considering angles and proportions in art when studying measurement
- Venn diagrams

Science

Scientific discoveries are constantly adding to and changing the body of science knowledge. Effective teachers engage students in experimentation and discussion of the findings. They are aware of changes and highlight new and older discoveries with students as, together, they investigate and develop an understanding of science.

The science classroom has safety as a focus with the following items displayed or easily available

- Posted safety rules
- Available protective materials (lab aprons and goggles)
- Fire extinguisher or fire blanket in rooms using flammable materials
- Classroom shut-off valves, if present, are labeled
- Chemicals are stored with MSDS sheets (materials safety data sheets)
- Marked disposal bin for broken glass

The science teacher uses a variety of techniques to facilitate the learning of the curriculum objectives

- Cooperative learning groups
- Computer simulations
- Laboratory investigations and experiments
- Lab write-ups
- Hands-on activities
- Demonstrations
- Reading scientific articles and journals

The science classroom contains a variety of equipment, including

- Beakers
- Graduated cylinders
- Flasks
- Rulers, compasses, and protractors
- Balances
- CBL (computer-based laboratory) probes
- Graphing calculators and scientific calculators
- Plant grow light
- Dissection tools

A teacher is not simply effective because of the presence of qualities. Likewise, red flags do not necessarily signal an ineffective teacher, just a behavior that needs improvement. Just as teachers must differentiate for student needs, additional qualities and red flags may be applicable to your unique situation. Teachers are effective because of how various personal and professional factors combine and are executed in a classroom.

You Say Multitasking Like It's a Good Thing

By Charles J. Abate

Multitasking has developed a certain mantra in our culture, repeated and indiscriminately accepted so often that it has become a commonplace—not only in colloquial conversation, but among normally astute academics. According to this widely held axiom, people in general, and our students in particular, can and do function productively and learn efficiently doing several things at once. Scarcely a day goes by, it seems, that we do not hear at least one of our colleagues mention the ubiquitous "m" word. Our hipper, more progressive (and perhaps younger) colleagues brag about their prowess at juggling many tasks simultaneously, while our more seasoned colleagues often bemoan their inability to master this elusive and mind-muddling aptitude. For almost everyone, however, there is the unshakable conviction that our young students excel in a multitasking environment.

In what follows, I try to refute the presumed efficacy of multitasking by drawing on the results of some of the recent neurophysiological experiments. I also examine the concept of multitasking itself, of which the analytical philosopher in me demands a more careful scrutiny than what is usually conducted in more casual conversation. I eventually conclude that multitasking, as we ordinarily understand it, is both impractical and counterproductive to successful conceptual learning and scholastic education.

The term "multitasking" was coined in the computer engineering industry. In that context, it denotes the ability of a microprocessor (the "brain" of a computer) to process several tasks simultaneously. Ironically, even the paradigmatic use of this term is demonstrably false. Microprocessors, as well as their current programmable cousins, cannot literally perform several tasks simultaneously. They are inherently linear in their operation and can perform only one task at a time. This simple fact explains the justification for the dual-core and quad-core microprocessors in current PC applications, where it is deemed advantageous to have multiple microprocessors literally running simultaneously to increase operational speed in computer operations. But even here, the notion of simultaneity breaks down when we note that the several microprocessors in a multi-core system must occasionally interrupt each other for purposes of synchronicity in PC operations.

Master Multitaskers or Just Distracted Students?

Are you mystified when students complain about spending hours on a homework assignment that should have taken about 30 minutes? Remember, your students are likely working under the same assumptions about multitasking as most of the rest of us, thinking they can listen to their iPods, IM their friends, and solve those trig equations at the same time. But reviewing the latest neurological evidence that suggests otherwise might not be the best way to show your students that multitasking is a myth. Let them see for themselves by trying the following exercise in class:

Remove the face cards from a standard deck and select 15–20 random numbered cards. Have your subject mentally add the black cards and subtract the red cards from a running subtotal as quickly as possible, while being timed. (Younger students simply may add all card values.)

Next, call off a list of 15–20 random alphabetic characters while the subject mentally keeps track of the number of vowels recited, while being timed. Then add the times of both exercises.

Finally, repeat the first experiment, but this time interrupt the subject's addition periodically with recited alphabetic characters, while the student attempts to keep track of both results simultaneously. Odds are that the final experiment will take measurably longer than each exercise conducted individually. (It is likely that the final experiment will yield fewer correct answers, besides.)

In a recent study conducted by Paul Dux, Jason Ivanoff, Christopher Asplund, and Rene Marois, using MRI testing, the researchers discovered a neural "bottleneck" in the brain's processing of (nearly) simultaneous tasks. The bottleneck delay increases with the complexity and unfamiliarity of the tasks performed, and with the frequency of interruptions. Their conclusion: The brain itself impedes our ability to carry out higher-level, or conceptual, multitasking.

The results of your in-class experiment just might convince your students that concentrating on the task at hand will result in far fewer "hours of homework" … which will result in more time for the 500 other things they'd rather be doing.

Reference

Dux, Paul, Jason Ivanoff, Christopher Asplund, and Rene Marois, "Isolation of a Central Bottleneck of Information Processing with Time-Resolved fMRI." *Neuron, 52* (December 20, 2006), 1109–20.

For certain kinds of behavior, brains (like microprocessors) are essentially linear devices that are incapable of performing two separate tasks simultaneously. In a more colloquial sense, though, it seems quite obvious that people are capable of at least some level of simultaneous activity. After all, it's only the rare klutz who is called out for not being able to "walk and chew gum at the same time." And certain types of tasks truly can be performed simultaneously. Most of us are quite capable of riding an exercise bike and listening to music at the same time. What is far less obvious is our ability to engage in conceptual learning—the type of learning we expect to foster in the classroom—along with other simultaneous activities, such as watching television or text messaging.

When I use the term "multitasking," I refer to an attempt by individuals to engage in several tasks in rapid linear succession (rather than simultaneously) where at least one of the tasks is a conceptual learning activity. Implicit in this understanding of multitasking is that the performance of multiple activities will entail frequent interruptions to segue from one task to another, as well as the ability to pick up where one previously left off—a model that directly mirrors the type of multitasking carried out by microprocessors.

A cursory survey of recent references to multitasking, especially in the typically non-technical realm of Web blogs and other non-professional postings on the Internet, exposes an interesting dichotomy in general attitudes about the presumed upside of multitasking. Those who extol the virtues (or at least proclaim the necessity) of multitasking behavior seem typically to constitute three non-technical and non-professional communities: career professionals already saddled with overwhelming job-related expectations; young students who seem intent on justifying their "attention deficit" practices; and, interestingly enough, academic administrators and humanities educators.

When one turns from these non-technical discussions to the more research-oriented milieu of the neurophysiologist, one quickly learns that multitasking is not at all the handy panacea for too much to do and too little time to do if that it's often purported to be. In fact, recent experiments provide strong evidence that multitasking is counterproductive, particularly when at least one of the tasks involves higher-level conceptual learning. As one Wall Street Journal columnist quips, multitasking is "the wellspring of office gaffes, as well as the stock answer to how we do more with less when in fact we're usually doing less with more. What now passes for multitasking was once called not paying attention." The most convincing of these recent studies succeeded in exposing three fundamental myths that have arisen about the virtues of multitasking.

Myth One: Multitasking Saves Time

In a study published in the Journal of Experimental Psychology, Joshua Rubinstein, David Meyer, and Jeffrey Poldrack discovered that people who multitask actually prove more inefficient than people who focus on one task at a time. Because our brains are incapable of performing two conceptual tasks literally simultaneously, the process of multitasking entails our alternating rapidly among the various projects. As with a microprocessor, the interruption of one task requires us to remember where we stopped, so that when we return to this task we can resume the activity. The same is true, of course, for the alternate task(s). Now, whereas microprocessors are quite efficient at storing and retrieving these interruption points, brains are decidedly not. They discovered that the time lost while the brain continually reorients itself during the stop-and-go process increases with the complexity and relative unfamiliarity of the tasks, and takes longer when the switching period is extended over a longer time period. In short multitasking proves less efficient than performing the same tasks one at a time.

The explanation for our apparent inefficiency in switching back and forth between projects has to do with the manner in which our brains process conceptual or higher-level information. Using functional magnetic resonance imaging experiments, researchers in a recent study published in *Neuron* were able to identify those areas of the brain that are responsible for the so-called bottleneck that impedes our ability to perform more than one conceptual task at a time. This bottleneck effect helps explain the critical limitations to our ability to carry out higher-level multitasking.

Let us grant that multitasking of higher-level projects may take longer than their completion in a linear fashion. Still, learning is learning, regardless of how long it takes to acquire, right?

So what's the problem with students texting, surfing the Web, listening to music, and so on while attending a lecture, or working on homework?

Myth Two: Multitasked Learning is as Good as Single-Task Learning

Recent neurophysiological experiments expose the fallacy of this presumption about multitasking. In a study funded by the National Science Foundation and published in the *Proceedings of the National Academy of Sciences,* Karin Foerde, Barbara J. Knowlton, and Russell Poldrack discovered that even if learning is possible in a frequently interrupted environment—like that inherent in the process of multitasking—such learning has a different cognitive status than that of uninterrupted learning, and is actually less efficient and useful than uninterrupted learning.

According to the article, brains acquire learning in two fundamentally different manners. Declarative learning (or what I have previously called conceptual or higher-level learning) involves the hippocampus area of the brain and results in the acquisition of information that can be easily recalled and applied to a variety of new and unfamiliar situations. Habitual learning (or what is sometimes referred to as procedural learning) on the other hand, occurs in the brain's striatum, and results in learning that is basically automatic, almost subconscious, but much more limited in its applicability to new situations.

The researchers discovered that the brain uses its hippocampus for single-task learning, but diverts dual-task learning to its striatum. Thus, when a person is distracted, habitual learning actually takes over from declarative learning. In this sense, the two types of learning appear to compete with each other. And because procedural learning is more limited in applicability than declarative learning, it is "inferior" learning, to the extent that

it is less capable of being manipulated, organized, and applied to new and unfamiliar situations than declarative learning. In short, multitasking actually changes the manner in which people learn and retain information.

Given the results of this experiment, one can conclude that learning stored in different areas of the brain may well foretell serious limitations on the overall usefulness and future applicability of the stored information. Is it any wonder that professors increasingly bemoan students' inability to analyze and synthesize information, despite the ever-growing wealth of information available to them?

Myth Three: Multitasking, Forte of The Young

Even those reasonably sane and insightful individuals who are loath to accept the touted advantages of multitasking are prone to grant that "we sure can't multitask like the kids today do." Many of us seem almost resigned to the conclusion that, whatever its potential drawbacks, multitasking is now a way of life and, despite our own personal failings, at least young people can multitask effectively because they've grown up of learning, and adjust our educational practices and expectations accordingly. Fortunately for us dinosaurs, there is now significant evidence that multitasking is not the blessing of youth that it is generally purported to be.

Martin Westwell, deputy director of the Institute for the Future of the Mind, reported on an experiment conducted with two age groups: 18- to 21-year-olds and 35- to 39-year-olds. Both groups were assigned the task of translating images into numbers, using a simple code (an activity requiring declarative learning skills). When both groups were tested without being interrupted, the younger group performed the task about 10 percent faster than the older group. But when both groups were interrupted by a phone call, instant message, or cell phone text message, the older group matched the younger group in both speed and accuracy. Westwell concludes that although older people may process information more slowly than younger people, they seem to have a "faster fluid intelligence" so they are more adept at blocking out interruptions and deciding what to focus on.

We should not draw the conclusion from this research that every age group is equally gifted with the skill of multitasking, only that young people have no advantage or special edge over those who are older when it comes to multitasking, despite their lifelong acquaintance with such efforts, and despite anyone's inclination to believe otherwise.

Like many stories that if repeated often enough become accepted as unquestionably true, multitasking has an aura that people seem to find irresistibly appealing. In her news article, "Multitasking Wastes Time and Money" Megan Santosus writes: "Unfortunately, even in the face of the mounting scientific and anecdotal evidence (not to mention individual blood pressure and stress levels) that multitasking doesn't work, companies cling to it like shipwrecked survivors to flotsam. They believe that asking employees to multitask saves them money and time when chances are good that it will do neither."

The false hopes raised by multitasking are unfortunate enough in the business environment. But they are possibly more pernicious in academia. These false hopes purport to justify all sorts of counterproductive behavior that may seem too universally accepted to rebel against, such as allowing laptop computers and cell phones into the classroom when we know that such devices will interfere with instruction.

What drives the persistent faith in the efficacy of multitasking? Perhaps it is the illusory dream of getting something for nothing; the hope of

accomplishing increasing numbers of activities in the time that was formerly wasted on just one task. Or perhaps we have created a culture, complete with myriad diversions and nifty electronic devices, in which there is simply too little time to do everything we need and want to do. Perhaps we are unable to set priorities for optimal use of our time for fear of missing out on some fascinating activity or other.

Whatever the case, the implicit acceptance of multitasking as a viable and productive strategy cannot, and should not, be encouraged in the academic environment—at least not if we hope to maintain the level of educational efficacy of generations past.

The consequence of tolerating these behaviors is an education that is fundamentally superficial, short-term-memory-based, and limited in its adaptability to new circumstances. We are, unfortunately, already seeing some of the effects of this practice in our classrooms. To further encourage this practice—discredited by significant neurophysiological testing—is to invite academic implosion.

Bibliography

American Psychological Association. "Is Multitasking More Efficient? Shifting Mental Gears Costs Time, Especially When Shifting to Less Familiar Tasks." August 5, 2001.

Dux, Paul, Jason Ivanoff, Christopher L. Asplund, and Rene Marois. "Isolation of a Central Bottleneck of Information Processing with Time-Resolved fMRI." *Neuron, Vol 52* (December 20, 2006): 1109–20.

eSchool News Staff. "Study: Multitasking Hinders Learning" July 26, 2006. www.eschoolnews.com/news/showstoryts.cfrn?Articleid-6453.

Foerde, Karin, Barbara Knowlton, and Russell Poldrack. "Modulation of Competing Memory Systems by Distraction" *Proceedings of the National*

Academy of Sciences, 103, 31 (August 1, 2006), 11778–83.

Lohr, Steve. "Slow Down, Brave Multitasker, and Don't Read This in Traffic." *The New York Times,* March 25, 2007.

Rubinstein, Joshua, David Meyer, and Jeffrey Evans. "Executive Control of Cognitive Processes in Task Switching." *Journal of Experimental Psychology, 27,* 4 (2001): 763–97.

Sandberg, Jared. "Yes, Sell All My Stocks. No, the 3:15 From JFK. And Get Me Mr. Sister." *The Wall Street Journal Online,* September 12, 2006. http://online.wsj.com/public/artide_print/SB115801096324259803.html.

Santosus, Megan. "Multitasking Wastes Time and Money." *CIO,* September 15, 2003.

Wallis, Claudia. "The Multitasking Generation." *Time,* March 19, 2006.

Discussion Questions

1. Describe how and when you multitask with all of the electronic equipment that you use.

2. What electronic devices are the children whom you teach most likely to own and use?

3. Under what conditions do you usually study best?

4. Describe how you establish a routine for studying that permits you to focus well and without disruption.

5. How did you learn to discipline yourself so as to focus well when studying or doing homework?

6. Describe why multitasking is a poor way to save time and accomplish your goals.

7. Describe how the brain handles multitasking, and the connections between that process and a narrow tube being used simultaneously for several different ingredients being poured into it.

8. What is the significance of learning taking place in the hippocampus versus the striatum?

9. Which is more negatively affected by multitasking: declarative or habitual learning?

10. How can laptops and cell phones prevent you from getting your money's worth from your college classes?

Section Two

Communicating Effectively with Parents and Caregivers

Introduction

Communicating Effectively with Parents and Caregivers

By Dave F. Brown

Success in teaching requires implementing many research-based practices and developing healthy relationships with children. Children's academic growth also requires the attention and assistance of parents and caregivers. Teachers' ability to influence children's academic growth is based on securing the support of those who care for youth when they're not at school.

The authors in this second section offer insights on the following:

- adults' perceptions of their parental roles and responsibilities;
- inappropriate parental interventions and their impact on children;
- strategies for initiating the first contact with parents/caregivers;
- tips for conducting successful conferences;
- developing an appropriate homework philosophy and policy;
- effects of reward systems on student motivation and learning; and
- strategies for communicating effectively with children.

Each article in this section is connected by the strand of developing relationships with all stakeholders in each child's education. Teachers with a clearly defined homework policy help to create expectations for children and their parents/caregivers. Rewards are common in elementary schools, but teachers must understand how reward structures often diminish students' motivation. The way in which teachers communicate with children impacts their ability to gain students' cooperation, and the empathetic responses suggested by Englander are preferable to the traditional roadblocks to communication so frequently used by adults. Hopefully after reading these articles, teachers will begin to formulate philosophies and policies that promote optimal academic engagement and success.

Welcome to the Hothouse

By Hara Estroff Marano

"I've just been in the emergency room for two and a half hours," Sarah announced, pushing on as we passed on the street, "and I've *got* to see my daughter." I had seen Sarah, the daughter of a neighbor, grow up, a few years ahead of my two children, and nowadays run into her only when she comes to visit her parents with her own family. Her right foot was freshly cradled in the clunky contraption doctors call a walking boot but is more accurately a limping boot.

"How old is your daughter now?" I asked. "Almost four," she said. "And," she added, her voice suddenly shaky panic, "I've never been separated from her this long before. And she's never been away from me."

There was a time when two and a half hours away from one's four-year-old would not have been seen as a separation. It would have been sought after and thought of as a respite, a reprieve, a welcome break for both mother and child. It would have been seen as a small but necessary step on the march toward independence, toward a child's adaptation to a world composed of people who are not biologically devoted to satisfying her every wish and making her happy. And it would

have been seen as a chance for the parent to reconnect, however briefly, with interests in the world at large. But this is 2008 and the children—or at least many of them—are never safe enough, never happy enough, unless they are directly in the laser sights of Mommy, and sometimes Daddy. The perpetual presence of Mom is supported by a burgeoning belief that only she is competent enough, that no one can provide care for the children or meet their needs as well as she can, that depriving the child of her direct attention in the first few years could, in fact, cause psychological damage for life. For this, a growing number of successful women are giving up significant careers to stay at home with the little ones, demographers report. It seems that to justify such application of their skills and education, they have to elevate child rearing to a challenge worthy of their time.

Parental hyperconcern about safety and well-being turns a two-and-a- half-hour interlude of what once, in calmer days, may have been looked on as a break from the kids into a window of intense worry. Hyper-attendance to children falsely breeds a sense of control and erroneously endows every action of the child with an importance it does not have. It also violates a cardinal rule of development: attentive and responsive care to an infant is absolutely necessary, but there comes a point when it is oppressive, robbing children of the very thing they need for continued growth. In small doses at first, and larger ones later, separation is essential to activate the system the infant will call on for exploring the world and mastering inner and outer life. Buried in overattachment and overinvolvement is an assumption of fragility, the belief that by not having some nuance of need met, the child will be irrevocably harmed. The paradox of parenting is that the pressure to make it perfect can undermine the outcome.

Parents, nevertheless, will not have to relinquish scrutiny of their children to others, even trained professionals, when the kids enter school. Many live in a school district that maintains a Web site just for parents and runs a computer program that allows them to keep an obsessive eye on their kids throughout the school day, from the minute they enter kindergarten to the day they graduate from twelfth grade. Zangle is one such program favored by a number of mid-western school districts. Parents in affluent areas like Bloomfield Hills and Birmingham, Michigan, where up to 70 percent of the highly educated mothers may be stay-at-home moms, are so tickled by the remote control it provides them that they spend hours "zangling" their kids—and comparing the results with other parents passing their days the same way. With a secret password, they log on and check whether their kids have turned in their homework assignments, review the grades they are getting on tests and reports and daily homework assignments, discover whether there have been any "behavioral incidents," and even find out whether their kids chose chocolate milk or Pepsi with their burger and fries in the school cafeteria.

Programs like Zangle are "feeding parental obsessiveness," insists a parent of two young girls in Birmingham, Michigan, who "forced myself to pull back and not do what everyone else does—because I'm not the one who has to prepare for college. The parents spend all day checking in on their kids. They demand to see all their kids' assignments. Sometimes the teachers are forced to say, "It's your son's homework, not yours"

Do We Need a Speech Therapist?

Parental pushiness and protectionism gain momentum as children move from preschool to primary school to high school. Not long ago, parents might have thought their function was, say, to provide good nutrition at home, recognize that direct parental control extends only so far, and, on a sliding scale from begrudgingly to confidently, grant their kids increments of freedom along with allowance money to make choices on their own outside the house, even if the choices were sometimes less than perfect. Zangle and other monitoring programs beginning with kindergarten train parents in intrusiveness and normalize it, even celebrate it, without accommodating so much as a whimper of protest—all the while disrupting the fragile flow of trust that development toward independence has always required and still does.

"I noticed it immediately with my then-one-year-old when we moved to suburban Connecticut from a more alternative community in the Southwest," reports the mother of a four year-old boy and a seventeen-month-old daughter. "How many words were my child saying? Did he know his alphabet? When could he write his name? Do we need a speech therapist? I know parents of a three-year-old who monitor their child so obsessively they send him to an occupational therapist two times a week to work on scissor skills—for no discernible reason." The mother of two confesses that she herself "took my son in to the occupational therapist to be evaluated after his preschool teacher said something about his fine motor skills. Now, mind you, he is highly verbal, he can read, he is a fine artist. But I took him in for an evaluation. I'm not proud of it. It forced me to do some soul-searching, and we never went back."

The push for achievement in all quantifiable realms, especially the academic, begins so early that preschools all around the country are focusing less and less on the development of social skills and self-regulation and more and more on academics. However, children of that age are so unready for curricular focus that preschools report a rising tide of behavioral problems—and wind up expelling six out of every thousand students. Imagine: expelled from preschool! With so much expected of them when they have not yet mastered socialization and self-regulation—two skills that are intricately interconnected and both of which foster academic excellence—more of them are acting out. Expectations for children have gone completely haywire, untethered from any reference to children's developmental needs, referenced only to deep adult anxieties. "The great effect of Head Start was to convince the upper middle class that their children needed a head start and they could do it better," says the historian Steven Mintz, professor at the University of Houston and author of *Huck's Raft: A History of American Childhood.*

Inside the Hothouse

Childhood under the constant gaze of adults is a new and growing phenomenon. The idea that a life—anyone's life—is on some precise schedule amenable to control is a by-product of the syllogisms of success that parents today are frenetically writing for their children.

The giant Citigroup company was rocked by scandal in 2002 when one of its superstar stock analysts, Jack Grubman, bragged in an e-mail that he had upgraded the rating of then-flagging AT&T stock to curry favor with Citigroup's then chairman, Sanford Weill. Grubman's overarching goal was to get Weill, a prominent New York figure, to exert his influence to get Grubman's twin toddlers into one of New York's prestigious preschools. (AT&T's chairman sat on the board of Citigroup and was a client of Citigroup, and Weill sat on the AT&T board.) What made the preschool so essential, apparently, was its track record in sending its graduates to the elite private grammar schools that in turn feed the prestigious prep schools which in turn dump their graduates into the Ivy League. It was the first logical step in the syllogism of academic success that parents construct for their children: if this is the right kindergarten for Harvard and Elijah gets into it, then he will be on track for Harvard. In the hothouse that child raising has become, nothing is left to chance. (Weill made the call, and the Grubman twins were admitted, once Citigroup pledged a million dollars to the school's umbrella organization.)

In the hothouse, parents plan out the lives of their children and propel them into a variety of programmed activities that are intended to have Ivy League appeal; they then ferry the kids around to classes and activities. The critical element in this setup is not that it leaves the kids with little unstructured time but that there is no way of opting out. Someone is always there to see that they get to the next stop in the circuit of activities. Playing hooky daydreaming, or just kicking back is out of the question, and the programming starts early in order to carve the groove as deeply as possible. "My neighbor's boy goes to karate, soccer, swimming, and baseball after going to school four days a week from 8:30 to 2:30," says one mother in suburban Connecticut. "He's five years old. And he has no free time." Neither does his mother.

The Hottest of Hothouses

The ultimate in hothouse parenting is undoubtedly homeschooling, a phenomenon so appealing to today's parents that it is growing at the rate, of 7 to 15 percent a year. To the best that anyone knows, well more than 1.1 million children in the United States are now schooled at home, by their parents, perhaps 2.1 million, with or without additional tutors. Homeschooling is now legal in every state in the United States, but it is not uniformly regulated, and in some states it is not regulated at all; whatever parents choose to do, they can. The adults often provide many rationales for homeschooling, from the inculcation of religious or political values to inferior public school instruction to the avoidance of educational regimentation that does not keep pace with their child's needs. Their children may even excel academically.

That is not its danger. Whatever else it does, homeschooling deprives children of any chance to breathe, of opportunities to discover themselves on their own and to escape from parental vigilance, parental bias, or parental ignorance. It gives parents license to micromanage every detail of their children's lives. It gives children a false sense of their own preciousness; many parents, in fact, choose to homeschool their children because they feel their kids are "special," surveys show. There is a deeper, more subtle issue: the nonstop scrutiny that comes with making the home a school disables in children the mental mechanism that is activated only by separation from parents, the mechanism that will endow children with the eventual ability to navigate securely on their own in the world.

"I'm My Parents' Hobby"

If you're searching for someone to blame, consider Dr. Seuss. "Parents have told their kids from day one that there's no end to what they are capable of doing," says John Portmann, an assistant professor who teaches in the religious studies department at the University of Virginia. "They read them the Dr. Seuss book *Oh, the Places You'll Go!* and create bumper stickers telling the world their child is an honor student. American parents today expect their children to be perfect—the smartest, fastest, most charming people in the universe. And if they can't get a child to prove it on their own, they'll turn to doctors to make their kids into the people that parents want to believe their kids are." What they're really doing, he stresses, is "showing kids how to work the system for their own benefit."

And subjecting them to intense scrutiny. "I wish my parents had some other hobby than me," one young patient told David Anderegg, a child psychologist in Lenox, Massachusetts, and professor of psychology at Bennington College. The author of *Worried All the Time,* Anderegg finds parents are anxious and hyperattentive to their kids, reactive to every blip of their child's day, eager to solve every problem for their child—and believe that's good parenting. "If you have an infant and the baby has gas, burping the baby is being a good parent. But when you have a ten-year-old who has metaphorical gas, you don't have to burp them. You have to let them sit with it, try to figure out what to do about it. They then learn to tolerate moderate amounts of difficulty, and it's not the end of the world."

And "best" now means only one thing. "I have found, both as a [former] student and in working with students, that young adults are pushed by parents and society to be 'the best'" says Alison Maimon, founder of Active Minds, an organization devoted to improving campus mental health.

"But 'the best' means only: get into the best college, excel once there, and get a high-paying job right after graduation."

Invasion of the Mind Snatchers

Talk to a college president and you're almost certainly bound to hear tales of the parents who call at 2:00 a.m. to protest Johnny's C in economics because it's going to damage his life. The thinking is, "If my son doesn't get this course, then he's not going to get the internship he wants, he's not going to get into the grad school he wants, and he's not going to get to become a judge." Too often, say administrators, that's how detailed the parents have gotten in their thinking about collecting "the right combination of stuff," foreclosing the possibility their child might by serendipity discover something that interests him.

Not long ago, Judith Shapiro, president of Barnard College, wrote an article in the New York Times urging parents to back off their desire to manage all aspects of their children's college lives. "One mother," she recounted, "accompanied her daughter to a meeting with her dean to discuss a supposedly independent research project." Then there was the father who called his daughter's career counselor so he could contact her prospective employers to extol her qualifications. And the one who took a year off to supervise the preparation of his daughter's admissions portfolio.

Shortly after the California psychologist Robert Epstein announced to his university students that he expected them to work hard and would hold them to high standards, he heard from a parent—on official judicial stationery—asking how he could dare mistreat the young. Epstein eventually filed a complaint with the California commission on judicial misconduct, and the judge was censured for abusing his office—but not before he created havoc in the psychology department.

Enter grade inflation. When he took over as president of Harvard, Lawrence Summers publicly ridiculed the value of honors after discovering that 94 percent of the college's seniors were graduating with them. Safer to lower the bar than to raise the discomfort level. In 1968, 17.6 percent of students received As in high school, and 23.1 percent got Cs. In 2004, 47.5 percent of students had an A averages, and only 5 percent had a C average. Educators view the current generation as brighter only on paper; in the aggregate, they are less prepared to take on the challenges of college. In 1987, 47 percent of high school students studied six or more hours a week; in 2004, 33.3 percent did; six-plus hours is the time most college professors expect to be devoted to each course.

It is a mark of the devaluation of education at every level that a C serves as the impetus not for the hard work of self-improvement but for parental intercession. The institutional response to parental anxiety about school demands on children, grade inflation is a pure index of emotional overinvestment in their children's success, contends the social historian Peter Stearns of George Mason University. And it rests on a notion of children's frailty—"the assumption that children are easily bruised and need explicit uplift," he says.

Through the syllogisms of success that parents establish, the grades their children receive from preschool through college become markers not merely of the children's academic achievement but of adult success at parenting. That transaction, however, commodifies their children and their children's efforts; even learning, insofar as it is pursued to be translated into a transcript with Ivy potential, is a commodity with exchange value. Learning isn't the joy of finding things out, as the physicist Richard Feynman once described it, or even excelling at finding things out. It is an instrument with no intrinsic value. All it has is commercial utility in wowing the gatekeepers at

Harvard. And so parents are poised to put pressure on schools to enhance their children's grades when they don't score well. These are the same parents who are transforming schooling into a consumer experience.

Parents who pay forty thousand dollars a year, says Arthur Levine, former president of Columbia University's Teachers College and an expert on grading, expect nothing less than As in return. "If the teacher gives you a B, that's not acceptable, because the teacher works for you … If I'm getting Bs, I'm not getting my money's worth." True grades are critical, he argues, because they provide invaluable feedback. They let you know what you are good at and what you are not. You can use that information to direct your efforts in learning. But instead, teachers are more like service employees, and parents call professors and administrators to complain. When he surveyed his faculty on the phenomenon, one college administrator was told of an overwrought mother who called a professor directly to voice her discontent. She introduced herself by saying that she and her husband were both attorneys. The professor understood that was meant to intimidate him.

At a small eastern liberal arts college, a father recently yanked his freshman daughter out of school before the end of the first week because she was unable to get a specific course. "This is her first semester," says a top administrator, incredulous that anyone would not welcome college as a time and place for exploration and exposure to new ideas. "Of course, the reason they sent her to a small college—I guess the rest of the sentence is, so they can have everything that they wanted. They say lots of different things, but that's what they mean. This father had planned out his daughter's college career for four years, and he knew what courses she needed to take every semester for the four years she was going to be here. And if she could not get this course and we could not make that possible for her, she had to go home.

We had to say bye." The administrator sighs and says: "We now have a generation of students who believe that you can make one mistake and ruin everything, as if their entire future rests on every single step. That makes it so hard for them to explore. That doesn't give them permission to fail. It doesn't give them permission to test—because the stakes are so high."

The vice president for student affairs at a well-known East Coast university insists that students whose parents are pathologically overinvolved still make up a minority of the campus population—but they hog administrative resources. They make a disproportionate amount of "noise." They make incessant demands and want frequent reports and constant feedback from the deans. In addition, they're constantly on the cell phone with their kids—"living and breathing for their kids." It's not unheard of for a kid to be facing a standard decision point, such as choice of a major, and to have a parent book a hotel room on or near campus for a month, the easier to oversee the child and the school administration. "I want to tell them to let the kid handle it," the administrator says, "to remind them that the goal of education is to have kids develop their own judgment, their own decision-making ability, their self-confidence."

Officials at one well-known university thought they had heard everything when they received a call from a father complaining that his daughter was stressed out over a roommate problem. It seems the roommate didn't do her laundry often enough, and there was a smell. The daughter felt she couldn't study in the room with a smell, so she picked up her cell phone and dialed her father, over a thousand miles away. The father didn't tell her to talk to the roommate. He didn't coach her on how to do it or what she might say. He didn't even expect his daughter to have the social skills to talk to her roommate. He called the vice president for student affairs.

One or two of these parents "is equal to a thousand others." That, says the East Coast vice president, may make them seem more numerous than they actually are. What's more, as the affluent educated elite, they have the time, the resources, and the knowledge to manipulate the system to their benefit. And because they are the culture shapers and standard-bearers, they set the style for all parents and children.

Let schools at any level try to raise the bar for students and parents protest forcefully. Tiny Duvall, Washington, is a town of fifty-five hundred near Seattle. In 1993, the town's Cedarcrest High School instituted a senior project as a requirement for graduation. Students had to write an eight-page paper, make an oral presentation lasting eight to twelve minutes, and create some kind of related product. Things seemed to be working just fine until recently, when one senior failed his project. His parents got furious—but not at him. They hired a lawyer to protest his grade. So many parents disliked the project and the weight the grade carried that the school was forced to halve the requirement to a paper of four pages. Moreover, it pared down the weight of the grade, too, making it just part of an overall grade in civics.

"We get painted as nitpicking asses out to ruin students' lives," said the programs coordinator. "It's been a constant battle." All he wanted was for students to be prepared for the job market or college classes.

Astonishingly, parental protectionism does not even end in college. Graduates are surprising prospective bosses by bringing their parents with them on job interviews. Or dialing them in to hiring calls that turn into conference calls so the parents can negotiate salary and benefits packages on behalf of their offspring. The manager of staffing services at General Electric made an offer to one recruit last fall. The next day he got a call from the recruit's mother seeking to negotiate an increase in salary. The manager held firm.

"It's unbelievable to me that a parent of a 22-year-old is calling on their behalf," said the director of college relations for St. Paul Travelers, who was on the receiving end of calls from parents "telling us how great their children are, how great they'd be for a specific job." She views this generation of adults as "kamikaze parents," the ones who "already mowed down the guidance and admissions offices" and are now encroaching on the workplace. Sometimes parents call the recruiters wanting to know why their child was turned down for a job. Says a veteran staffing director, "That's something I haven't faced in 15 years" in the field.

Machinery of Heavy Lifting

There are names for the parents who do all the heavy lifting for their children. In the beginning—say, four or five years ago—school officials, among the first to feel their effects, would gather at meetings, roll their eyeballs, compare notes on the onslaught, and call them helicopter parents, because they hover and make a lot of noise, rescuing their children whenever difficulty arises. They might protest what they deem an unfair grade or demand to know what is being said in college-counseling sessions. At the very least, they want to know what the school is doing to help their child thrive. And if something occurs that they, or their child, don't like, they're apt to dial the headmaster or president directly.

"We started referring to helicopter parents in the 1970s," says James Fay, then a school principal in upscale Evergreen, Colorado, now head of the Love and Logic Institute he founded to educate parents about parenting. "The first day I was there, half the kids went to the phone in the office to whine to their parents that they forgot a field trip permission slip or something. I really clamped down on their getting rescued." But, he contends, as willing as parents were even then to solve problems that the children needed to solve for themselves, he is astonished at how helicopter parents have evolved; About five years ago, Fay surveyed seventeen hundred teachers in the United States about the most difficult aspect of teaching today. "I expected them to cite school violence; this was not long after the Columbine incident. But the number one thing they cited was parents who would not allow the kids to learn about the world in real ways. They want discipline in schools, but they don't want their kids to be held accountable for anything. These parents are constantly running interference and intimidating teachers to give kids better than they deserve. They're doing the homework for the kids, even lying for them. Today they are a jet-powered turbo attack model." So ferocious have parents become, Fay notes, that principals have told him they prefer working in an inner-city school "because they don't have to put up with so much of the entitlement stuff from parents."

Other educators see them as "snowplow parents": they work hard to clear the path for their kids, push obstacles out of the way, and make the traveling as smooth and safe as possible. They pasteurize parenting. From helicopters to snowplows, more than equipment has changed. There is a growing sense that a deleterious process is in operation and probably augurs trouble ahead. Accumulating snowbanks, after all, keep those on the road from seeing anything that is not positioned directly in front of them. Whether snowplows or helicopters, parents exert great force so that children do not have to solve problems, make decisions for themselves, or take responsibility for their course. The children also have no personal investment in or responsibility for the road down which they are guided.

"Parents are our worst enemy when their child isn't getting what they want. They whisper in the bleachers and send letters to administrators," says a soccer coach at an NCAA Division I university on the East Coast. For the first time ever, the team held a preseason meeting in the fall of 2006 for parents. "Our parent situation reached all-new levels last year. Some of our parents—of college athletes!—became a cancer which spread quickly to their children and quickly throughout our team. The goal of the meeting was to set PARENTAL STANDARDS OF BEHAVIOR, not player standards! We felt it was necessary to let the parents know how dangerous and destructive their behaviors can be to team chemistry and performance. So far, so good and they seem to be behaving themselves. One of the main themes of the meeting was that it is a privilege for their children to play NCAA Division I athletics, not their right."

Helicopters, snowplows ... the names for pushy parents are proliferating. But they all do the same thing: remove from their children opportunities for learning how to problem-solve. And so far there seems to be only one name for the children—teacup kids. Because, as we will see, without opportunities to experience themselves, to develop and call on their own inner resources, to test their own limits, to develop confidence in themselves as problem solvers, they are fragile and shatter easily.

"All Sorts of Crazy Stuff"

"It's not something you think is going to happen to you in your freshman year of college," says Marissa, "You think it's going to be this amazing party, with friends and all sorts of crazy stuff. I certainly had plenty of the crazy stuff. It just came in a different form."

In Marissa's freshman year at Yale, the girl who was best, who was cast from a very early age as The Achiever, slipped into suicidal depression. She lost interest in eating and gradually withdrew from her friends. She was constantly cold. Because her grades stayed high, no one thought anything was amiss. But when her five-foot-nine-inch frame withered to a mere hundred pounds, a dormmate finally noticed something was wrong and called Marissa's father, a physician. A nearby doctor was located who took one cursory look and "slapped on the label of anorexic" without bothering to find out what might be troubling her. She was weighed every morning "like I was a piece of produce." Her weight slipped further, and sterner measures were required. Marissa spent a chunk of her spring semester locked in the fluorescent haze of the Yale Psychiatric Institute. Day and night she was forced into "the fishbowl," a centralized glass enclosure, so the staff could assure themselves that she was swallowing her meds and drinking her calorie-dense cocktails. She wandered the wards with "a mind-blowing mix of local crazies and suicidal Yalies." It was the best thing that ever happened to her. Before she became a Yale honors graduate, before she became a Fulbright scholar with three years of self-guided travel, study, and anthropological work in South America, Marissa had to come back from emotional desolation and despair. Bred to be the quintessential upper-middle-class success machine, running a little too obediently on the expectations of others, Marissa had to find her own purpose, her own meaning, her own identity, her own voice, her own nerve. It took a taste of lockdown for her to stumble upon what so many in her generation are missing—a basic sense of self.

Psychological breakdowns are nothing new to adolescence or young adulthood. But what Marissa and so many peers are experiencing is not the breakdown characteristic of previous generations. What's significant about these kids, observers say, is that they commonly lack a fierce internal struggle toward a deeper state of authenticity. When they have a breakdown, it is not the product of introspection in which people seek to be aware of their own inner workings. It is not Kierkegaard's angst, a crisis of neurotic hyperawareness in an indifferent universe. No, it is more "the gray drizzle of horror," to borrow William Styron's stunning description of depression, a steady stream of performance pressure against an inner landscape of desolation.

Disconnected from themselves, they suffer unfocused anxiety and panic because they can't even identify their fears. Stricken students can be so robotic in their ability to perform, totally disengaged from themselves, that, like Marissa, nothing comes between them and their grades, not even a bout of hospitalization. They don't have a strong sense of self, because they have not been allowed to build one, not allowed to struggle, not encouraged to take the necessary time for reflection and introspection, for making experience their own and forging their own meaning. This, it must be stressed, is not due to any fault of their doing; it is the nature of the world they have inherited. It appears to be the logical end product of a culture that insists on engineering all the serendipity and spontaneity out of human experience and of parents who intrude on their every minute and motive. An order of curly fries in the school lunch line is such a taste of dietary disaster that these parents microplan every detail of their children's lives. Their concern has given rise to the belief that they—and only they—know what's good for their children and can secure their safety, that the children will be harmed in the absence of eternal, exhausting, intrusive—but, unfortunately, ultimately crippling— vigilance.

Rich Dad … Poor Kids

The hothouse is most intense among the most affluent. Their experience in building and maintaining the hothouse is instructive for everyone, however, as affluence and prosperity forge the dominant tone of American culture today.

Once upon a time, the most privileged youngsters often followed a time-honored tradition and went off to boarding school to acquire a good college-prep education, pick up some social skills, and get in some substantial rehearsal for independence. The adults had time to play. But somewhere in the 1990s, priorities shifted dramatically, children were given starring roles in the family drama, and preparation for adulthood lost ground to parental need for emotional closeness and control. Adults with means began following their kids to boarding school. They literally uproot themselves and the rest of the family and relocate near the campus. When one fourteen-year-old girl was accepted at a top boarding school in California, the family sold their house in the suburbs of New York City and moved to a ranch two miles from the new school. "We couldn't cope with the idea of her being here without us," the mother explained.

The hothouse approach to child rearing is becoming most intense among the most affluent in part because the affluent can afford to live on one salary. Indeed, demographers report, increasing numbers of women are dropping out of the workforce to become stay-at-home moms (SAHMs, they call themselves). For some, the impetus to stay at home comes from their partners. There are men who see it as a visible badge of their earning power to have a wife who doesn't need to work. The well-equipped nursery, the Bugaboo stroller (or a fleet of them), the nanny, the stay-at-home wife—according to the women who prowl and growl in the rarefied precincts of UrbanBaby.com, all are accoutrements of high-earning men whose competitive drive not only lands them a variety of luxuries but persuades them to make a public statement of them. Today's stay-at-home moms tend to be highly educated; their affluence enables them to be free all day every day to devote their formidable talents and know-how to their children. The new breed of hothouse mother, says one, "spends all day talking about parenting. There's a little bit of nostalgia thrown in for the pre-child-raising days." Often, they become volunteers for school activities—where not only do they get to apply their scrutiny but their influence serves to intensify the pressures on kids.

As one informed me: "The stereotypical mother in this town is college educated, married, upper-class or upper-middle-class, and taking time off from a successful career to raise and nurture her children." Suddenly stranded with no visible means of achievement, "she also measures her success through her children's successes." That encourages her to turn the school activities for which she volunteers into competitive events. Take the medieval fair held annually at an elementary school in her middle-size midwestern city.

Medieval Fest is a regular adjunct to the history curriculum when the second grade studies the Middle Ages. All three classes—representing about a hundred kids—participate in it. Instructions to parents outlining the event suggest they provide simple foods, such as raisins and nuts, and simple costumes, such as an inverted heavy-duty trash bag with strategically cut holes as a suit of armor for a knight.

Two years ago, when one mother got to the school gymnasium, "I discovered that the other mothers had spent weeks sewing elaborate gowns and costumes. My daughter was dressed as a simple jester. She felt left out by comparison." But it got worse. Last year the fest grew too sumptuous to be held in the humble precincts of a public school. "The parents made elaborate medieval meat dishes, when I'm sure that the kids would have preferred chicken McNuggets. These kids are seven and eight years old." The costumes got even more elaborate. The fair was moved to the Tudor-style clubhouse of a country club owned by one of the parents. It was fifteen minutes away, and the parents had to carpool to get the kids there. "It was ridiculous. The parent volunteers made everything more important and more elaborate than it needs to be. They compete as volunteers—making it a full-time career." Volunteering is supposed to be a support function, but in the hothouse of modern parenting it overtakes the event it was supposed to be helping. The history lesson is lost. The contributions of the kids themselves are overshadowed. And life in the Middle Ages becomes a competitive pageant of prosperity. Somewhere along the way, the educational value of the fair was sacrificed to the needs of high-powered parents to make the event worthy of their input.

Affluence Affords the High Price of Pressure

If she wants to slack off between runs, she can tune in to a TV channel dedicated just to her, to validate her approach to child raising and urge her on. Lest anyone think these women bear any resemblance to the stay-at-home mothers of previous generations, they call themselves, without any trace of irony, Alpha Moms, or Moms to the Max. They have won whatever the competition is to get to the top of the heap. They have top drive. They have top expectations. They can do it all, and they do it all for themselves and their kids. Not for all kids—just for their own kids. The very concept of Alpha Mom—and if your job is to be a mom, who wouldn't want to be alpha?—implies that there is such a thing as successful motherhood and that it is possible to perform the role with perfection; in fact perfection becomes absolutely necessary to be worthy of the title. "Maybe," the *New York Times* columnist Maureen Dowd lamented not long ago, "there would be more alpha women in the working world if so many of them didn't marry alpha men and become alpha moms armed with alpha SUVs, alpha muscles from daily workouts and alpha tempers from getting in teachers' faces to propel their precious alpha kids."

The hothouse is hottest among the most affluent because they can literally afford to put the most pressure on kids. They hire specialists with the aim of perfecting their children. Tutors, at five or six hundred dollars an hour, are brought on board even when the child is in preschool, and even in the summer; the affluent import tutors to their summer communities as performance enhancers who function as academic steroids. If the child is a little further along, they can shell out fifteen thousand dollars for what some tutoring and college-counseling services tout as their Ivy guaranteed admission program, or IGAP. Of course, it's best to start such "application management and strategies" programs early, preferably in ninth grade, so the kid can be steered right through to success in the college admission process. In the Ford-like assembly line production of successful college candidates, a child's own goals and interests are subordinated to the counselor's guarantee. And when the children finally settle into the dorm, their affluent parents are available to call them every morning to wake them up.

Population dynamics play a role. In New York City, where the number of parents with children is growing and wealth is concentrated, there are said to be fifteen applicants for every coveted slot in the top-tier nursery schools. As a result, parents hire educational consultants for their three-year-olds. They also enroll them in Japanese classes, swim classes, and art classes. Actually, said one observer of urban patterns, "the search for distinction starts in the womb."

The most affluent parents have the means, the power, and the know-how of the system's workings to influence it on behalf of their children. Unlike parents at lower income levels, they are not afraid to challenge the system and make it serve their interests, actions fed by their sense of entitlement as "full payers." They have the confidence and skills to tangle with high-ranking officials. Or to use their income to influence outcomes directly.

"Birmingham and Bloomfield Hills are tops in the state in the MEAP [Michigan Educational Assessment Program] testing," a Birmingham parent told me. All public school students, from elementary school through high school, are tested annually. "Of course we're number one," she observed." A large number of the students are being tutored. The parents are spending on private tutors. Many are tutored because their parents want them in an Ivy League school." "Ivy League" has become the top educational brand, the closest parents believe they can get to a guarantee of success.

The aggressiveness that affluent parents display on behalf of their children may also have its roots, at least in part, in the social philosophy affluence often bestows. The well-to-do tend to be politically and economically attuned to search for individual solutions to social problems. As a result, they may seek advantage for their own kids over general improvements that would help all kids, including their own. We are all prone to make errors of attribution regarding our successes and failures. We tend to internalize success, erroneously ascribing it to our own superior innate characteristics—often overlooking the powerful hand of luck or special opportunity—while attributing failure to general conditions or adverse circumstances. The affluent are at greatest risk of such self-serving biases—in fact, affluence may be the necessary condition for the attribution bias. It may intensify their motivation for acting on their own individualistic interests for their kids.

At colleges and universities across the United States, admissions and financial-aid administrators say it has become fairly common for parents with substantial six-figure incomes to seek financial assistance. "I have never seen so many families with incomes of $200,000 to $300,000 applying for need-based aid," one such administrator told the *Chronicle of Higher Education.* They look at their financial outlays and think they have need. But it's really about lifestyle choices they have made." The dean of enrollment at Kalamazoo College in Michigan received a three-page, single-spaced letter from a cardiologist explaining that his take-home pay of $17,000 a month might seem like a lot, but really wasn't.

Then, too, affluence has a way of expanding people's expectations about their life and their happiness. They want it all and often believe they deserve it all. Their rising expectations are applied to their kids as well as to the institutions that serve them. Ever-rising tuition costs fuel their expansive expectations. In making parents more consumer oriented, they drive a kind of demandingness that independent schools in particular are struggling to handle. Rising tuition costs, say administrators, make parents "harder to manage." As the cost of education necessities increases, children are viewed as prized possessions—and thus more precious, more worthy of monitoring and protection.

Globalization, says the Swarthmore College psychologist Barry Schwartz, has done two things that conspire to make people miserable. It has changed their pool of competitors, and it has changed people's aspirations, especially among the affluent. "There was a time before instant universal telecommunications when you were operating in your own little pond. You weren't competing with everybody. Those days are gone for the educated elite. You're competing against everyone, and increasingly that means everyone in the world, because there really are no natural boundaries to contain the set of people who might take your spot. There has always been competition, but it wasn't competition without bounds, the way it is now."

Aspirations have been ratcheted up enormously because "any magazine you open is giving you evidence of what your life could be like if only you tried a little harder. You no longer want a house that's a little bigger than your neighbor's house; you want it bigger than Bill Gates's house. You get to see everybody's house everywhere. Since we know our evaluation of how good things are is almost always in comparison with our expectations, the surest recipe for misery is high expectations. No experience can actually meet them."

What's more, "once you get told you can be anything you want to be, you want a job that pays you well, that's respected, that's fun, where you have good colleagues. You don't inherit the job your father had. Multiply that by romantic partners. You don't have to marry in your religion. You don't have to marry someone who lives in your town. A blond and blue-eyed movie star is possible." When experiences fail to live up to expectations, which is a certainty, "it is almost impossible to avoid concluding that it was your fault. You end up making a causal account of your failure that blames you rather than circumstance. So you have a significant contributor to the epidemic of depression. The competition for the goods and the escalation of expectations is really doing us in."

One thing money does is provide a sense of control. It matters little how much of that sense is an illusion. The ratcheting up of expectations has also inflated the sense of control the affluent believe they should enjoy. But against perpetual technological change, twenty-four-hour markets, economic volatility, and constant competition, it takes strong and sometimes desperate measures to impose a sense of control. What is a hothouse except an attempt to control the growing conditions of the young?

Reversal of Fortunes

Hey, wait a minute. This isn't the way life is supposed to be. Affluence traditionally insulated families from paying too much attention to their children and certainly relieved them of the necessity of putting pressure on them to succeed academically. As long as the kids didn't wrap themselves around a tree in an alcoholic haze, affluence itself would protect them. Sooner or later they would inherit the farm or the family business, or at least the stock portfolio. It's the upwardly mobile middle class that traditionally set its hungry sights on academic achievement as the route to general success in life, and it is the middle class that often gives their kids a healthy push down that path. But those are the old rules. Over the past two decades, the world has been turned upside down, or at least it feels that way to the adults. No one even knows what the new rules are, because they are constantly changing.

Behind this reversal of fortune stand two very important new developments: the radical transformation of everyday life by technological change and the emergence of the highly dynamic new economy via the globalization of markets. In the United States, these changes are set against a widening gap between the rich and the rest of us.

The speed and volatility of the marketplace leave no room for complacency; today's haves could be tomorrows have-nots. The rich have the most incentive to push the hardest because they, potentially, have the most to lose.

In many corners of the culture, the upper class now works harder than the middle class, the historic source of America's drive and strength. What is moving upper-class people to work longer hours than the working class is their realization that, given the dynamic uncertainties of a very fast and fluid economy, a relatively new development, they have the most to lose from a day at the beach and the most to protect, and even gain, by rolling up their sleeves.

Just as the affluent now work the hardest, they are the most worried about their kids—because they realize their children will have to work even harder to be where their parents are. They want their children to at least maintain the socioeconomic status they grew up in, but understand that it is getting increasingly difficult to do so while living in a precarious world. With formidable resources to push their kids, they often muster all that they've got. In trickle-down fashion, it becomes the new standard of parenting.

Here's only one irony: what they are pushing the children toward may not be worth the effort. It could be argued that the lifestyle that parents are struggling to launch their children into is a source more of stress than of freedom—a kind of Astroturf affluence, quite slippery, something that very much resembles the real thing but functions quite differently. According to the New York psychiatrist Maurice Preter, the affluence that has overtaken America does not deliver many of the traditional benefits of real affluence.

Working harder than ever just to maintain their socioeconomic status, the affluent, despite all the accoutrements of the good life, live in a state of near-chronic stress. They have few of the deep rewards affluence is supposed to bring: happiness, a sense of security, time to relax, time to spend with friends. "What's missing," Preter stresses, "is a social code unrelated to exchange of commodities." Studies persuasively show that Americans' circle of friends is dramatically shrinking. Families conduct almost all their socializing within the family unit, minimizing the exposure of children to adults other than their parents and thus limiting their knowledge of other perspectives. Activities intended to be restorative may be enjoyable in some ways, but they also wind up intensifying nuclear pressures and scrutiny. Preter calls it "ideological affluence" because it is no more than symbolic of true affluence and lacks its substantial social and emotional rewards. Ideological affluence is a lot like eating a gorgeous-looking cream pie made with artificial flavors and ersatz whipped cream. You keep devouring more in search of true flavor, but instead of being satisfied through intensity and authenticity of flavor, you wind up bloated, still unsatisfied, and unhappy.

It's not difficult to understand why all parents today are so on edge. The world shifted on our watch. We're the ones who've been blown sideways by the new technologies and ever more rapid speed of cultural change. There are real changed conditions of our lives. The technology changed completely; it didn't require just a retooling of the imagination—it continues to change at such a rapid pace it takes ongoing effort to keep up. The globalization of markets generates deep job insecurities and an endless supply of competitors; there are now no geographical limits to who can enter. The effects are still rippling through—and promise to ripple through continuously from here on in.

Nervousness about globalization has made parents so concerned about competitiveness they believe that they must do everything in their power to not let their kids fall behind. But they make the assumption that their kids have been hit, too. And meaning the best for their kids, they try to protect them.

The new insecurities of affluence and the growing economic divide for all create fertile terrain for hothouse parenting. Benefiting from affluence is no buffer against the sense that some pernicious new form of economic volatility will play out in the children's lifetimes, if not ours. This fact, locked away in the psyche of those most aware of current events, powers anxiety about the children and drives overwrought attempts to see that they are as well equipped as possible for success in whatever the future brings. "Because the adult workplace is so competitive today, we therefore think we have to equip our children with a competitive edge," one parent told me. "This couldn't be more true than about the metro Detroit area. My husband has worked as an executive for Ford Motor Company for twenty years, yet he comes home every night filled with anxiety about losing his job! It seems everyone around us is losing their jobs—maybe another reason we are so crazy!"

"It's easy to get sucked in," adds a parent in an affluent Connecticut town. "The parents are living vicariously through their children. And they want their children to eventually have the same lifestyle as they do. At some point you have to stand back and ask, 'But at what price?' If my child grows up and wants of his own accord to be a forest ranger, I could live with that. The parents around here would not, even if it reflected his own goals and his own interests." Parents elsewhere are saying the same thing. In talking to parent groups around the country, I found that the wealthier the community, the pushier the parents were—and the more anxiety they exhibited about their children's future socioeconomic status. Even when they suspected they were harming their kids by overinvolvement in their lives, they couldn't loosen their grip—"because then my kid will be at a competitive disadvantage to all the other kids and I'm terrified he'll be left behind."

The Age of Uncertainty

At bottom, hothouse parenting is the response of adults, fathers as well as mothers, to tremendous uncertainty and anxiety about what the next generation will need to thrive in the new economy. They know the rules have changed.

Having been knocked for a loop themselves by new technologies and often the need to retrofit themselves to the economy, they assume their children are facing the same prospects. Their solution is to intensify parenting, to start at or near birth with classes and programs to equip their child with as many skills as they can cram in, in the hope that at least some of them will provide a ticket to success. Because landing on the right side of the yawning economic divide is so critical, they judge the stakes so great that each child is essentially in competition with all the others. The sense of competition encourages parents to do all in their power to create an advantage for their own child. Affluent parents hover and clear the path for their kids, making demands of teachers, administrators, and coaches. The less affluent might vie to have their child singled out as special by being designated a genius, or an "indigo" child. Or they might seek neuropsychological testing to have their child declared "differently abled" and accorded academic accommodations that typically come down to taking their tests without time constraints, most importantly the SATs.

It is almost touching that in times of such anxiety and uncertainty, middle-class and affluent parents still see education as America's salvation. But their approaches reflect the desire, whatever way they can, to seek individual advantage, rather than to strengthen a system of public education for all. The almost exclusive focus on achievements that can be measured—such as reading skills—comes at the expense of more subtle abilities that can't be readily measured—creativity, willingness to experiment, social skills—but have a broad influence on development, on eventual success, and on quality of life. "The emphasis on performance is not developmentally meaningful and fails to furnish a philosophy of life," says Edward Spencer, associate vice president for student affairs at Virginia Tech. "College is treated as a credentialing factory rather than a place for developing the whole mind and the whole person."

Hothouse parents do exactly what everyone does when anxious. They tighten their grip. Anxiety narrows and shortens their range of focus, as it does for everyone. They exert pressure on their kids and hang on tight, overcontrolling them. It is the nature of anxiety to exaggerate dangers and apply hypervigilance.

Parental anxiety, however, is badly matched to the needs of children. In just the most obvious of instances, the children, unlike their parents, are digital natives, virtually born masters of the new technology that adults are still struggling with. Parental anxiety is also nonproductive. If there's one thing people need in a fast-changing world, it's the freedom to experiment and even fail, so that they can figure out what it takes to succeed, match that knowledge to their own interests, and find a way to make their own creative adaptations to the conditions of contemporary life.

Moreover, the ordinary obstacles and challenges that are swept from children's paths keep them from developing the skills they need to cope with life's uncertainties and vicissitudes. This might be fodder for stand-up routines were the consequences not so sad.

Intrusive parenting undermines children in the most fundamental ways. It spawns anxious attachment to the children. In doing so, it sets them up for lifelong fragility.

Despite all the parental pushing and overinvolvement, despite the six-hundred-dollar-an-hour top-of-the-line tutors, despite the accommodations and untimed SATs, despite constant surveillance down to the last curly fry, the kids who have virtually sacrificed their childhoods for a shot at the Ivy League are poorly prepared for changing a major or handling romantic rejection, or for the real world when they get there. "I see the interactions between parents and students," says a high school history teacher in New York's affluent Westchester County. "I wonder how much anxiety this parent is creating for the student by laying out, when they're in the sixth or seventh grade, that they need to get into Harvard. And then that parent seeks to relieve anxiety not by addressing the issue at hand, not by dealing with the anxiety and giving the child tools to cope with it, but by seeking out an accommodation. The child never learns to get past the anxiety."

Child Abuse by Any Other Name

There's abundant evidence that parental obsessiveness has reached the point of abuse. It's most obvious in children pushed to achieve their best in athletics; their pain typically declares itself in a frank, physical way that can prevent them from functioning at all and can even derail future development. Across the country, orthopedic surgeons and sports doctors report skyrocketing rates of overuse injuries in kids as young as eight—the kind that until a few years ago were seen only in adult athletes after years of playing professionally. More kids today are being urged to specialize in one sport at an early age and train year-round so they can engage in high-stakes competitions. Forget neighborhood pickup games; there's nothing casual or recreational about sports anymore; if you play, you play to win. That's how kids and their parents define success at sports.

And for such kids, summers are increasingly for suffering. It's an epidemic, say sports physicians. Dr. Sally Harris is one of them. Based in Palo Alto, California, she found that the number of overuse injuries virtually doubled from the summer and school year of 2005–6 to the summer of 2006. In 2003, the latest year for which national data are available, more than 3.5 million such injuries in children under age fifteen were treated in the United States, out of approximately 35 million children from six to twenty-one who participate in team sports. Parents not only push their kids to practice and encourage them to join traveling teams, especially if they are teens, but send the kids to highly specialized sports camps where the training can be superintensive. Many kids from affluent families fill their summer vacation by going to a succession of such high-powered programs and even squeeze in a few during holidays and breaks in the school-year schedule. "It's not enough that they play on a school team, two travel teams, and go to four camps for their sport in the summer," said one family sports medicine expert. "They have private instructors for that one sport that they see twice a week. Then their parents get them out to practice in the backyard at night."

Dr. James Andrews, a prominent sports orthopedist in Birmingham, Alabama, makes no secret of his astonishment. "You get a kid on the operating table and you say to yourself, it's impossible for a 13-year-old to have this kind of wear and tear.'" Like others, he regards it as "a new childhood disease." Concerned observers believe that coaches and parents are pushing bodies that are not ready for such stress. Muscles, bones, tendons, and ligaments get painfully inflamed or break down faster than young bodies can repair when pushed beyond their physical limits by the repetitive motions that incessant practice demands. Cortisone shots can relieve the pain but not heal the damage. When an orthopedic surgeon explained the nature of her child's injury to one mother, she broke down crying—not because her son was suffering but because the baseball-playing boy wouldn't be able to pitch for a whole year. "Sports are everything to us—that's the pronoun she used," the surgeon relayed.

Those who treat the pediatric injuries point the finger at an overaggressive culture of organized youth sports in league with overinvolved parents. The adults tend to push their kids back into competitive play before they've fully healed. For the kids, the gain is often more than pain.

Around the country, in affluent communities, parents are now paying their children if they achieve in sports. "It's amazing how many parents are doing this," a suburban Michigan mother told me. "In my community, the going rate is fifty dollars every time the child competes and gets first place or the team wins. It's easy to get caught up in this. My daughter is a swimmer, and she came right out and asked me why she doesn't get paid." The mother thinks "it's causing kids to rot from within, while parents are living their glory days through their kids."

Commerce is complicit in the pushing of children to the point of abuse. The highly competitive athletic shoe companies openly reward superspecialization in youngsters with cases of free merchandise and invitations to select sports camps that they run. They are hoping to discover and groom the next face of the sport. Adidas has its Jr. Phenom Camp for basketball players in middle school. If they are good enough, they might graduate to the Phenom 150 Camp when they enter high school. National scouting services the shoe companies hire leave no child unscrutinized and unevaluated; they comb the country looking for promising talent. Invitations can come with guarantees of media exposure and attention from college recruiters. As Reebok's senior director of grassroots basketball says, "We're going to find them, expose them and get them used to the grind at an earlier age. I believe in that theory." Not content to let Adidas and Reebok run away with all the middle schoolers, Nike recently made its own bid to put competitive pressure on ever-younger children by launching a new national tournament for sixth, seventh, and eighth graders. One scout said that he never hears parents complain when their kids show up on the lists of prospective talent. Instead, he hears from parents who think their kids should be ranked higher.

Before child rearing became a hothouse, sports-minded kids might have played baseball, basketball, and football all in one day. According to Dr. Lyle Micheli, head of sports medicine at Children's Hospital Boston, that was actually good for their bodies. Because the different sports make different demands on differing body parts, the bodies of those who played them developed in balance. Now, he says, "young athletes play sports supervised by adults who have them doing the same techniques, the same drills, over and over and over. There is no rest and recovery for the overused parts of their body. Parents think they are maximizing their child's chances by concentrating on one sport. The results are often not what they expected."

A Philadelphia orthopedist tells the story of a mother who recently asked her if there wasn't "some kind of shot or fix-it procedure I could do for her 11-year-old daughter's ankle so she could be ready for an upcoming regional competition. I told her that if it were the Olympic Games coming up, perhaps we could treat this situation differently. But as far as I understood, her upcoming competition wasn't the Olympics. At this point, the daughter is giggling—but the parent is in the corner crying. I said: This isn't Curt Schilling in the World Series. It's not worth not being able to run anymore for a plastic gold-plated medal."

Discussion Questions

1. What does the term *hothouse* mean in the context of plants? How do current education policies, practices, curricula, and parents make the lives of children like those of hothouse plants?

2. How did your parents help you to develop a healthy balance between dependence on and independence from them?

3. How did you know that your parents trusted you? What kinds of responsibilities were you given at various stages of growth as a child/adolescent?

4. Provide some examples of parental overbearing that you've witnessed among friends' parents or among parents you've encountered through your experiences in working with children.

5. What do you believe are some possible challenges of home schooling to children who experience it?

6. Why do some parents monitor/check every homework assignment their child does? What is a likely result of this intense scrutiny and overdependence by parents?

7. How are anxiety and mental health issues related to taking more responsibility for one's successes and failures during one's childhood and adolescence?

8. What are some examples of ways that you were held accountable for your behaviors/grades/actions as a child and adolescent?

9. How can you as a teacher encourage parents to permit their children to develop appropriate independence while they are in your classroom?

10. What is the value and significance of providing children and adolescents with developmentally appropriate academic and athletic activities throughout their childhoods to overall healthy mental states and satisfaction with life as an adult?

How to Reach Parents and Prevent Problems Before They Happen

By Maryln Applebaum

The Changing Face of Families

Educators tell me that students have changed. They say that children today are often disrespectful, irresponsible, and rebellious. I tell them that children have not changed, but childhood has changed. I believe that is the same with parents. Parents have not changed. They still love their children and want the best for their children, but parenthood has changed.

The face of the typical family unit has changed. When I was raising my two children, it was a mostly two-parent family world. People got married in their early twenties and had an average of two children. Most women stayed home and raised their children. Men went to work and were the breadwinners. Slowly over the years, this picture changed. More and more women joined the workforce. I vividly remember my own reentry into the workforce. I worked and still was in charge of taking care of the home activities, such as dishwashing, cooking, cleaning, getting the children ready for school, and finding adequate care for the children after school. I was exhausted at the end of the day. I still cared about my children

and their teachers and school, but I had less time available to go to their schools and be involved. This is often the case with today's parents.

I saw many instances of diverse types of parenthood in my career as a teacher and administrator. There were some two-parent families raising children. More and more, I found that I had single-parent families in which mothers or fathers had custody as well as parents with shared custody. I had grandparents who had either temporary or permanent custody. There were many blended families, and sometimes those blends changed in the course of the child's being in my schools. Parents married, divorced, remarried, and divorced. There were parents, stepparents, and step-grandparents coming to conferences and open houses. There were two-parent families in which both parents were same-sex parents. And there were parents who were separated not because of divorce but because of work. These were parents who were serving in the armed service and parents or stepparents whose spouses were working in another city, state, or even country.

Increasingly, there were parents who spoke little or no English. My own family growing up was like this. I entered kindergarten speaking absolutely no English. I did not even know that my name was Maryln because my name was said in a different language at home. Working with parents who speak little or no English presents its own challenges because many parents are like my parents and embarrassed to come to school even though they want to know what was going on. My own parents were not only embarrassed that they spoke no English but that we were living below the poverty line. When parents with little English-speaking ability do come to school, they may not understand what they hear. They may, in fact, hear something in such a way that that they get upset, and soon a situation can develop in which they become angry and the school perceives the parents as "hard-to-handle."

There are also parents with different parenting styles (Rudney, 2005). There are parents who are authoritative and always having to be in control. Their children rarely get to have a voice in decisions or choices. At the other end of the spectrum, there are parents who are so permissive that their children are in charge. These parents may be passive with their children, but often they may be aggressive in defending their children, refusing to see that their children have done anything wrong even when it is flaunting them in the face. There are parents who are nurturing, and there are parents who are neglectful.

There are parents who desperately wanted to have children, and there are parents who resent that they have children. There are parents who are good listeners, and there are parents who have no idea how to listen to their children. There are families that are TV families whose only time together is gathered around the television. They eat in front of the television. They talk on the phone while watching television, and they make all their important decisions in front of that television. At the other end of the spectrum, there are families who do not even own a television or a computer.

There are parents who are physically ill, mentally ill, alcoholic, or drug addicted (Rudney, 2005). Every parent is different. They are different even when they look alike. That is because every individual is different. Regardless of their differences, it has been my experience that all parents, in their own way, love their children.

Think about this. There is training to do most work, but for the most important work of all, to be a parent, there is absolutely no training. There is only the experience that each person has had growing up. Parents often vow to be different from their own parents, but without training, many fall back into patterns that they learned from their role models. Their parents also loved them and did the best they could do. Parents love their children and are doing the best they can, but without training, most parents are fated to repeat what they learned growing up, like it or not.

Throughout this book, whenever I speak of parents, I will be speaking about all types of family units and all types of parents.

What Parents Want From Teachers

Teachers Who Know and Care About Children

The number one thing all families want for their children in school is teachers who know and care about their children (Rudney, 2005). Mrs. Green was Jordan s mother. Jordan was an only child. The Greens had tried to conceive for four years when they finally had Jordan. Jordan was very tiny for his age and had had a series of childhood illnesses that had left their mark on this little family. Mrs. Green was concerned about Jordan's new elementary school. I asked her what she wanted for Jordan. She told me that she wanted to be sure that his teachers liked him. She said that if his teachers liked him, he would like them. She said he was so special to her and her husband, and she wanted him to be special to his teachers too, not just one of many students in the class.

Ali was a high school student. She had good grades and was one of those students who worried when assignments weren't turned in on time. Her parents never came to school. I often wondered about that. Ali got really ill and was hospitalized. When I visited her in the hospital, I met her mother and realized that she spoke limited English. An uncle was there who spoke really good English, and he was our interpreter. He explained to me that Ali was embarrassed to have her parents come to school, and that is why they did not come. They cared very much for Ali and were very proud of her good grades. Ali was like many other teens, who prefer that parents do not come to school even when they are fluent in English.

The point of these stories is that all parents want their children to be noticed and to be cared for. They want their children treated fairly and respectfully (Rich, 1998). It doesn't matter if their children are preschoolers, elementary students, or secondary students. They know their children will be part of a larger group, and they want to ensure that their children are not just a number, but someone who is special. They want teachers who care—really care—about their children. They want teachers to be knowledgeable, but first and foremost, they want to know that their children are cared for by their teachers.

Caring, Calm Classrooms

Parents want their children to be in classrooms in which teachers know and care about teaching (Rich, 1998). They want teachers who encourage their children to learn, teachers who set attainable learning goals, teachers who understand how to teach, and teachers who know how to reach students. They become upset when they hear that other children in the classroom disrupt the class and that children are not paying attention and learning.

Safety

Safety is another major concern of parents (Rich, 1998). Almost every parent at some time or another has seen video clips of school shootings. Parents fear that this can happen. Recently, in the Houston area, where I live, there were two terrorist threats. People who knew about these threats were worried. Some parents did not feel safe sending their children to school.

Parents also fear that their children will be victims of bullies and gangs. They want to know that their children are safe on their way to school, at school, and at the end of the day. That means that they are concerned for their children's safety not only while they are at school but also while they walk or ride the bus to or from school.

Communication With Parents

Most parents want to communicate with teachers (Rich, 1998). They want to hear how their children are doing. They do not like to be surprised. Mr. Kentrall told me a story about his son, Lanny. Lanny had Attention Deficit Hyperactive Disorder (ADHD). It was not diagnosed until Lanny got into middle school. The differences in middle school—which meant changing classes, walking through crowded hallways, having different teachers for different classes—contributed to Lanny's having problems focusing and paying attention. Mr. Kentrall took Lanny to a psychiatrist who diagnosed his son and started him on medication to help alleviate symptoms. When Mr. Kentrall attended the open house at the beginning of the school year, he met Lanny's teachers. They were very busy, but Mr. Kentrall came away with the impression that Lanny was doing fine. When the first report card came out, Lanny was failing math and history. Mr. Kentrall was stunned and angry. He wished he had known earlier so that he could have worked together with Lanny's teachers to help his son. He could not understand how Lanny's progress could change so quickly. Lanny's teachers did not communicate after the open house. If they had communicated, Mr. Kentrall would not have become so angry.

The ideal way to have prevented Mr. Kentrall from getting upset would have been for his teachers to stay in touch with him throughout that first grading period. At the school open house, his teachers could have told Mr. Kentrall positive points about Lanny and then also added any concerns about math and history. Later on during the same grading period, Lanny's teachers might have contacted Mr. Kentrall and updated him on Lanny's progress. Together, they might have worked out a plan so that Lanny did not receive failing grades. If they did not have time to call, they could have sent him an e-mail telling him options that were available to help Lanny.

Reasons Parents Do Not Come To School

Too Much to Do Barriers

It's difficult to reach and establish relationships with parents who do not come to school. There are many reasons that parents choose to not come to school. The most pressing reason is that they simply are so busy. They have great intentions but then have to work late, have to travel out of town for work, or may have so many other responsibilities that they just cannot come to school.

Language Barriers

There are parents who have limited English who sometimes do not come to school. This is often misinterpreted as lack of concern for their children (Yan, 2006). Cantu's parents came from another country. They spoke very little English. When they came to school and met with her teachers, they did not understand what was being said. They felt out of place and embarrassed. It seemed to them that everyone else knew what was happening. Even though they loved Cantu very much, they eventually stopped going and instead, asked her to tell them what was happening.

Single-Parent Barriers

More than thirty percent of all children in the United States live in single-parent homes (Lee, Kushner, & Cho, 2007). The single parent has increased responsibilities within the home. In an intact family, there can be a division of responsibilities. In the single-parent home, the responsibility belongs exclusively to that one parent. These responsibilities can be extremely time-consuming to the point of lack of parental involvement in the school. Students from single-parent families do not do as well in school academically as those from intact families (Lee et al., 2007). This may be because the single parent is so tired at the end of the day that it takes a lot of effort to ensure homework is done. It is just often easier to take the child's word that everything is fine.

Mrs. Carter has three children ages, fourteen, ten, and two years old. Her husband left when she was pregnant with the third child. She has not heard or received any financial support from him since he left. She has a great job as an executive secretary, and she is terrified of losing her job. When her company asks her to work longer hours, she does. Each night when she finally arrives home, she is exhausted but still has to deal with cooking dinner, getting the kitchen cleaned, packing lunches for the next day, doing emergency loads of wash, and trying to find time to be with each of her children. She wants more than anything to just put her feet up on the sofa and "veg out" for a few hours watching TV, and some evenings she feels lucky when she actually gets to do that. It's a huge sacrifice for her to come to school. It isn't that she doesn't love her children; it's just that she is so preoccupied with survival that it is difficult.

Negative Experiences Barriers

There are some parents who don't come to school because their own experiences in school were negative. I remember one parent telling me, "I hate being here. It reminds me of when I was a child." This parent went on to tell me that when he was a child, he was always in trouble. He was in and out of the principal's office. He said that now, he just doesn't want to go anywhere near the school.

Diversity Barriers

Parents may not come to school because they feel like they are a minority and are not sure if they will be valued or respected (Smrekar & Cohen-Vogel, 2001). Sadly, in some cases this may be true. Parents who are different in any way from the majority of teachers and the school population may feel that their opinions do not count, so why bother to go to school. These parents along with all parents and family types need to be valued for their diversity, and their voices need to be heard.

I told you earlier about my own parents who spoke almost no English. They were embarrassed to come to school for many reasons. Because we were living in a very low-income area, they were very aware that their clothing was different. We all wore the hand-me-downs from other family members and friends. In our community, stories had been shared of other parents who tried with their limited English to stand up for their children in school and were not well received.

Diversity even in these modern times plays an important role in whether or not families feel included. I have one family member who is Native American. He is a "gentle giant." He has been stopped at different times by the police for suspicious activity simply because he looks different.

Parents with physical or mental handicaps also feel different and may fear coming to school. These include parents in wheelchairs, parents missing limbs, parents with visual impairments, and parents with disorders like depression, anxiety, and Asperger's Syndrome which can impair effective communication.

Student Preferences

Students in elementary school generally have no preference about whether or not their parents come to school. Once they get into middle and high school, this sometimes changes. Their parents want them to be more independent, and the students want this independence. These parents become less involved and give their children the opportunity to handle things themselves. Some students carry this need to be independent quite far and become embarrassed or even resentful when their parents come to school. Parents who are struggling to maintain a relationship with their teens may find it easier to stay home.

Prevent Problems Before They Happen

The best way to prevent problems before they happen is to establish caring relationships with parents. It is very important to create situations in which parents want to come to school and want to be involved. This will affect all aspects of learning for their children including their achievement. Student achievement is higher when parents and educators work in partnership to help children (Lee et al., 2007). In Chapter 8, you will learn many strategies to create those partnerships. The partnership is the "marriage." Courtship comes before marriage, and the remainder of this chapter is filled with strategies to help you "court" parents so that they want to come to school, and they want to be in a partnership. Pick and choose the ones that work best for your school and your situation.

Start in the Neighborhoods

If parents won't come to the school, bring the school to them! Hold meetings in nearby churches in the parents' neighborhoods. Tell them about events happening in the school. Ask local clergypersons to help by making announcements at services and to encourage family members to attend meetings.

Have translators available for neighborhoods where English is limited. Train the translators to be motivational and inspiring. Ensure that they are individuals who are excited about motivating parents to become involved in school. Have them tell parents all the options open to them with English as their second language.

Make the meetings fun. Get food and door prizes donated from local vendors. Have fun activities for the whole family like face painting and games. Assign parent pals who can be translators for those with little or no English-speaking skills.

Make Home Visits

Home visits are an excellent way of building bonds between families and the school. They are time-consuming because it means meeting only one family at a time, and sometimes, it can even be potentially dangerous depending on the neighborhood. I made home visits when I had difficult students whose parents would not come to the school. The first time I ever did this was with the family of a student who was extremely defiant. I had invited the parents to come in to talk to me. They did not show up. I had phoned to speak to them, and they were always busy and going to call me back but never did. Finally, I sent a letter that I would be coming to visit. I followed it up with several messages on their voice mail. I believe that they were stunned when I showed up on their doorstep to talk to them about Jason. The first thing that I remember about that visit was the noise coming from their home. Their windows were open, and there was shouting and the sounds of chaos. They had three sons. The mother opened the door looking totally exhausted. Behind her, two of the boys were chasing each other through the house dressed in their dad's business clothing with shirts dragging over the floors. Two dogs were barking and chasing the boys. Jason, the oldest of the boys, was standing near his mom in total shock. He was stunned to see his teacher in his house. It reminded me of when I have bumped into any of my students at the supermarket or other stores, and they look at me as if to say, "What are you doing here? You are supposed to only be in the classroom!"

Jason's mom, Mrs. Donnelson, invited me into the house. We sat down in her kitchen while the boys and dogs were running around the house.

She told me that she felt like a total failure. I learned that she was a medical doctor who had given up her career to be a stay-at-home mom. She said she didn't come to school conferences or functions because she was terrified she would hear bad news about her boys. She talked and talked. I think she had been holding in her feelings for a long time. I gave her some tips on setting boundaries with the boys, and together, we came up with a plan for Jason. I also recommended some books that would help her manage her boys better. When I left, the house was still chaotic, but she was calmer. She had a plan. Jason's behavior slowly and steadily improved at school.

That was the first of many home visits I made. Almost all of the families I visited were embarrassed about some aspect of their lives, and that appeared to be what had prevented them from coming to school. There were families in which one of the parents was in jail, families in which both parents disappeared and the grandmother was raising the children, families living in extreme poverty. There was one family living in a two-room small home with no electricity and seven family members. This family spoke no English, so I took an interpreter with me. In every case, when families saw my efforts to reach out to them, they became more involved in the academic lives of their children, and it was reflected in their children's academic achievement.

Make Phone Calls

At the beginning of the school year, take time to call each family. Introduce yourself by telling them a few characteristics about yourself. Include your goals for the school year for each child. Have a smile on your face and enthusiasm in your voice. Invite them to share with you their concerns as well as their goals for their children. When you connect in a positive way at the beginning of the school year, it tells parents that you are upbeat and positive in nature. It also helps if you can tell them something positive about their children. It paves the way for a good school year and helps foster parental involvement.

If you call a family that does not appear to speak English, call again with a translator. I have used translators who are other teachers or trained parents to do this. They enjoy helping parents become connected.

Send Introduction Letters

An introduction letter can serve several purposes. It tells the parents a little bit about you and your goals for the coming school year. It also can be used for the purpose of getting parents involved. Be sure to get the letter translated for those families that cannot read English (see Figures 1.1 and 1.2).

Making Diverse Groups Feel Welcome

At one time, I owned several private schools. I made it a requirement that when parents wanted to enroll their children, they had to first visit and observe the classrooms. I often heard comments afterward about the diversity of the students. The truth is that I never thought about it. For me, a student was a student. I looked more at how diverse the individual students were in terms of learning needs then in terms of a child's appearance or socioeconomic status.

While that was my perspective, it is not necessarily the perspective of parents. Parents look for children who are similar to their own children. They look for other parents who are similar to them. They fear that their children will stand out in a negative way. It is important to make all parents and all children feel welcome. Here are some ways to welcome diverse populations and make them more comfortable.

Translation Buddies

Use parent volunteers to help translate information for parents who speak little or no English (Boult, 2006). Have them translate all letters to the parents' native tongue and also have them contact parents by telephone and speak to them in their native language.

My company does seminars throughout the United States. Sometimes, we are notified ahead that there will be an individual attending who is hearing impaired and has requested a sign-language interpreter. We always accommodate this need. It is interesting to me that while people think about making accommodations for those who are hearing impaired, people don't typically think of making accommodations for people who speak very little English, and do not understand what is being said. When you have parent nights, make sure that there is someone to greet parents in their own native language and translate for them things that are said.

At the beginning of the school year, identify the families who have second-language strengths. Use this information to pair up families based on language ability. For example, a family bilingual in Chinese and English would be paired with another family who spoke Chinese but little or no English. The bilingual family could then translate important school information into Chinese for their school buddies.

For matters of confidentiality, identify other faculty members who have strengths in other languages and have them serve as interpreters. The most important thing is to look for people who parents will trust when they are interpreting for them.

Telephone Tree

Have bilingual parents contact other parents who are not fluent in English to tell them about events occurring in the school and to invite them. Parents sign up for this at the beginning of the year, and then you contact the volunteers when you need help. This is a great strategy to get all parents to come to school, not just for parents who have limited or no English. It is especially effective for passive parents who do not attend functions. It benefits both the volunteers who make the calls because they can do it on their own time at home, and it is a benefit to parents who receive the calls. You can have a prepared script for parents to use when making the calls to ensure there is no miscommunication.

Books

Books are a great resource for parents. Some parents are passive and have a hard time coming to school but enjoy reading and learning. Refer them to books on different topics that are relevant to your school. Secondary schools may offer books on occupations, colleges, and obtaining scholarships. Both elementary and secondary schools can have a recommended list that includes books on communicating with children, getting children to do their homework, and other relevant topics. Find books in languages other than English that bilingual parents can read and share with their children at home.

Wish Lists

Create a wish list for your class and have it translated into the languages of each of your families. Send it home with students. Knowing what teachers need for their classrooms can help build communication between all parties involved. It is a great way for more passive parents to be involved. They may not want to come to school, but they can still feel like they are contributing.

Parents Share Cultures

Find ways to include diverse parents in your classroom. Parents come and share about their holidays. They can also come and share about objects and artifacts from their cultures. It is a great way to open the door to teaching a social studies, geography, or history lesson. You can tie it in to other lessons too in other subjects. It makes parents feel welcome while also benefiting the class. Keep in mind that in secondary school, students whose parents are speaking may be absent that day. Mrs. Rawana was excited about speaking at her son's social studies class. She had signed up when she went to his conference. When the day came for her to go to his school, he said he didn't feel well. She went and spoke to his class. When she came home, he was magically feeling better. He told her several days later that he just didn't want to be there. He was afraid of what his peers would say. Fortunately, they all spoke highly of his mom and what she had shared. This is not always the case. Children can be critical and even cruel about the parents and families of their peers.

Opening The Doors To The School For All Families

Picnics

Picnics are great ways for families to get many parents to the school. It is a safe, easy way to have fun and help parents feel comfortable with school. Depending on the budget, schools can provide the food or families can bring their own food.

Fashion Shows

Fashion shows are a fun way of getting families to come to school. Get local stores involved to provide the clothing. Parents will come to schools to see their children participate in a fashion show. Involve the parents and have them also be models. They will tell their friends, and the more the entire neighborhood realizes that your school is a warm, and friendly school, the more it will encourage further family participation.

Thoughts for the Day

I send out daily a thought for the day that is a strategy or inspiration for teachers. Teachers have told me that they pass these thoughts on to their parents. That is another way of helping family members better understand both how important they are in the lives of their children and also gives them strategies for handling childhood issues. You

are welcome to subscribe to my thought for the day at www.atiseminars.org or to come up with your own saying or thought for the day. This can be posted on the wall for parents to see, or better still, copied and sent home on a special colored paper every day. Another option is to forward it through e-mail to parents.

Helping Hand Projects

It has been my own experience that even parents who typically do not come to school or get involved in other ways will help others in times of need. Several years ago, a major hurricane struck in Louisiana, and thousands of people fled to Houston. The schools were filled with students whose homes in Louisiana had been destroyed. Schools and teachers sent home notes that they needed support for these families. Children who had little or no clothing poured into Houston-area schools. Family members contributed whatever they could to help those families, including clothing. It created a sense of community to come together to help someone else.

You can use this same theme with your families. Find a cause, something that all the students and family members can help with. Let them all know ways they can help and acknowledge and thank them for coming together as a school community to help others.

Babysitting

I have talked with many families over the years who tell me that they would come to school, but they have no one to watch their children. Provide babysitting for families to enable parents to come to school with their children.

Convenient Times

Schedule all family functions at times that are easier for parents. Have evening functions early in the evenings so that it does not interfere with bedtimes of children. When planning, always think of what will work best for families.

Food

Have you ever heard the saying, "If you feed them, they will come!" The food served does not have to be fancy. It does have to be filling and good. Many times, family members rush to their children's schools after a long day at work. Food provides incentive to get parents to make the journey to their children's schools.

Door Prizes

Have lots of door prizes when parents come to the school (Bergmann et al., 2008). Invite community businesses to donate the door prizes. Have students make door prizes to be given away. It's fun for parents to win prizes and adds an extra incentive to get parents to come to school.

Discussion Questions

1. What do you think most parents/caregivers could tell you about their children that you wouldn't discover within the first two months of school?

2. What would you want to know about children whom you teach that only their parents/caregivers could tell you?

3. What are some strategies for eliciting information from parents/caregivers about their children?

4. What strategies does the author suggest that teachers use to elicit information from parents/caregivers about their goals for their children?

5. Why is communicating clearly with parents/caregivers about your homework philosophies and policies so critical to students' academic successes in your classroom?

6. What suggestions do you have for parents/caregivers for helping their children with homework?

7. What information do you want parents/caregivers to know about your classroom policies, procedures, and rules to ensure cooperation from students?

8. What are some strategies for connecting with immigrant parents?

9. What are the advantages of making home visits?

10. Why would some parents/caregivers not be interested in making connections with the school?

Parent Conferences

An Ounce of Prevention That Prevents a Pound of Problems

By Maryln Applebaum

Conferences are an excellent way to begin a partnership with parents to ensure that conflicts do not later arise. Here is a story that helps to illustrate the importance of fostering each unique teacher–parent relationship.

When two people get married, they do not generally get to choose their in-laws. Instead, they choose each other. When you begin teaching each school year, you receive "your" students. They are your students for better or for worse throughout the school year. You are "married" to them. Just as spouses do not get to choose their in-laws, you too do not get to choose your new "in-laws," the parents of your students. To be most successful with your students, you too have to establish a warm and caring relationship with your "in-laws." They are part of the marriage too, for better or for worse, for the entire school year. It is your job to ensure that it is for better, and not for worse. When it is worse, there will be hard-to-handle situations and hard-to-handle people.

Conferences are opportunities to build partnerships and foster communication. The conference is the first real time set aside to get to know each other. Even though you may have met the parent before, it was probably a quicker meeting. It's like the first time that married couples get to spend time with their in-laws. Everyone is looking each other over, hoping for the best, and feeling a little nervous. Conferences can be viewed as an ounce of prevention that prevents a pound of problems.

Set the Scene: The Focus Factor

Set up your classroom so that it is a warm and welcoming place. Also, keep in mind the "focus factor." In order for both you and the family members to communicate, create a room that is calm and relaxing. You may want to have calming music playing in the background. Add some natural lighting to "warm up" the room. You can do this by adding a floor or table lamp. The calmer your room, the more parents and you will be able to focus on what is being said.

Have Comfortable Seating

Make sure the seating is comfortable for both you and the parent (Jordan, Reyes-Blanes, Peel, Peel, & Lane, 1998). Have the parent sit across from you at a table or sit side by side. Make sure that the chairs are the same height. If you tower over parents, there are some parents who might be immediately on guard rather than comfortable. Avoid student desks and seats. They are often not as comfortable because they are so small. It can be quite embarrassing for a parent who has a large frame to have to sit in a tiny chair that feels like it may break at any moment. That is not a good way to foster a parent partnership.

Dress for Success

Wear clothing that is attractive, conservative, and professional. Mrs. Landon attended a conference at her son Kyle's school. His teacher, Miss Staffield, had on a T-shirt, casual pants, and sandals. Her hair was unkempt and her T-shirt was stained. The slacks were frayed at the cuffs with big threads hanging out over sandals. Her socks looked like they once were white but were now grayish. Miss Staffield walked over to a table to get some papers for the conference slouching as she walked as though she did not have a care in the world. They sat down at a table to talk, and Mrs. Landon noticed Miss Staffield had a big earring on her tongue. Mrs. Landon tried to listen to what Miss Staffield was saying to her about her son, but she kept staring at the tongue earring and thinking about this teacher's total appearance.

It is important to remember when preparing for a conference that there are people who do judge people by how they look. Think carefully about what you will wear. Take extra time with your appearance. Dress for success. The success will be becoming a team with parents of your students.

Be Prepared

Get lots of rest ahead of time so that you are alert and prepared for anything. You never know what questions or statements you will hear. Mr. Jacobs was a teacher having his first conference of the school year with Mr. and Mrs. Bender. Mr. Jacobs told them that their son had a problem with misbehavior. He said that it was interfering with their son's learning and that the youth had a hard time paying attention. Mrs. Bender kept looking off into space as Mr. Jacobs spoke. Her husband said, "He probably takes after my wife. She is schizophrenic and sometimes hears voices." And then, Mr. Bender leaned forward and said, "There's more. We think our son is evil and has come into the world to do bad things to others." Mr. Jacobs sat there nodding his head as he listened. Mr. Bender went on to say his father had killed himself. He said that sometimes he felt like doing this. While Mr. Bender listened, he tried not to show any reaction. That was a new one for him! He did know that he had to win those parents over or they would continue to believe their son was bad or evil. Their son had a problem paying attention at times, and he could be mischievous, but Mr. Bender did not believe that he was evil. He resolved to get them to work with him as a team. While his parents may still have had preconceived beliefs about their son, their son did do well in Mr. Bender's class. His parents became more and more cooperative as the school year progressed.

Send Family Profile Sheets Home

Some students live with their parents, and others live in other arrangements. It's important for you to know who is coming to the conference and that person's relationship to the student. Sometimes a teacher has assumed that an older parent was a grandparent. Nowadays there are all types of families, and you need to be prepared. You also need to know the surname of the parent or guardian who is coming to the conference. Do not assume that it is the same as the child's name.

A great way to do this is to send family profile sheets home with students (Mariconda, 2003; (see Figure 7.1). Students interview their parents and complete the information on the sheets. They bring the sheets back to school. The sheets contain names of family members as well as other pertinent data. A fun thing to do is to have students bring in a photo of the person coming to the conference or draw a picture of the person. This becomes part of the student portfolios, and parents enjoy seeing their own photos or the drawings their children made representing them.

The Conference

Because conferences are so important, you need to be completely prepared (Jordan et al., 1998). They can make or break your relationship with families and this in turn, can make or break your relationship with students.

Carefully Plan Important Issues

Plan ahead what you hope to accomplish (Mariconda, 2003). Decide what information you need to discuss with the parent. You may have a long list. Choose only two or three of the most important concerns to be addressed. It is important not to overwhelm the parent.

Check Your Negatives at the Door

If you have strong negative feelings about the student, make sure that you cool off before you meet the parent. It is important that you are objective when you meet with the parent. Parents can sense when you are negative about them or their children.

Role-Play Ahead of Time

If you do have students who are more difficult and you are concerned about the conference and how to say the right thing to parents, role-play the situation ahead of time (Million, 2005). You can do this with another teacher or even with the principal or assistant principal if it's a really important conference. If you do role-play with another person, be sure it is one who can keep confidentiality. You can also role-play in front of a mirror. The more you practice the words you want to say, the easier it will be the day you actually meet.

Use the Behavior Notebook

If the student has a behavior problem, be sure to have the behavior notebook previously discussed in Chapter 4. The misbehaviors are listed and signed by the student. This is concrete evidence that clearly demonstrates to a parent that there is a problem. It is hard to argue with a child's writing and signature documenting the problem.

Accommodate Parent Times Whenever Possible

When sending home notes for the conference, strive to accommodate the parent's schedule whenever possible (Stevens & Tollafield, 2003). It will help gain cooperation and show parents that you care. Most parents work. Some can take time off from work and others cannot. Keep this in mind when setting up schedules. There are some caring parents who may cancel several times because of crises at work that are beyond their control. Stay patient and reschedule. Ask them to give you several times of day that work best for them, and then try to find the time that works best for you so that it is a mutually agreed upon time.

Figure 7.1

The Family Profile

Student's name _____

Family member's name _____

Relationship to student _____

Favorites

Color _____

Animal _____

Book _____

Food _____

Hobby _____

Subject in school _____

Restaurant _____

Who were your "heroes" when you were growing up? _____

_____

_____

_____

What is your favorite motto or saying? _____

_____

_____

_____

We ar looking forward to meeting you at the parent–teacher conference.

Even the most well-intentioned parent can miss a conference. Their schedules are often jampacked. Send a reminder of the time, date, and place to the parent again a couple of days before the conference.

Include directions on how to find your classroom and where to park. Wandering through schools can be like wandering through a maze if you do not know where to go. Parents may get frustrated before they ever arrive in your classroom because they were lost within the school. This is something you do not want to happen. When you provide clear directions on how to find your classroom and where to park, you can help prevent problems before they happen. Make sure to have your name on the door so that it easier to locate your room once parents are in the correct corridor.

Have a Comfy Waiting Area

Sometimes parents come earlier than they anticipated to the conference. Set up several chairs in the hallway outside your door. Have a sign indicating that you will be with them soon. If it's possible, have some cookies, crackers, or pretzels for a snack with a little sign saying, "Welcome. Feel free to have a snack. I'll be with you soon."

Include a bin with a sampling of student textbooks for parents to view while they are waiting for you to begin. When they do come into the classroom, be sure to apologize for any inconvenience that a wait may have caused.

Do Not Disturb

Arrange for no interruptions during a conference. It is disturbing to be interrupted at a crucial moment. Privacy is a big issue for parents. They may start talking about their child and totally stop when someone walks into the room. This needs to be a time in which you are not disturbed. Add a "Do Not Disturb" sign outside the door to your classroom while you are meeting with parents.

Have a Welcoming Classroom

Make your classroom parent friendly. Have student work on display. Include every student in your class. Parents generally will look around the classroom to find their children's work. Have "welcome parent" signs up in several places and in several languages as discussed in Chapter 1. Have the students make the signs. Involve the students in ideas for what the signs should say and how they should be decorated. Some students will tell their parents about the welcome signs before the parents come. This opens the doors to having your classroom be a warm and friendly place.

Welcome Parents

The best decoration is your own smile as you welcome parents. My own personal experience with my two children is a living testimony to this. My daughter was several years older than my son and started school before he did. When I went to her parent–teacher conferences I always heard comments such as, "She is a delight to have in class," and "Wish we had more like her." When my son started kindergarten, I was excited to meet his teacher. I was assigned times for the two conferences. My daughter's conference was first. I went in and met her teacher and saw some of her work and heard over and over again, "She is a delight to have in my classroom." I proudly left that room feeling wonderful. I walked down a flight of stairs to the kindergarten classrooms. I had on a big name tag that said, "Maryln Appelbaum." I walked into the kindergarten classroom and saw the teacher was speaking to another parent. I walked over near them so she could notice my name and know that I was Marty's mother. I could see that she noticed my name tag, but she avoided eye contact. When she was through speaking to the other parent, I walked over to her and proudly said, "Hi, I'm Maryln Appelbaum, Marty's mom." She gave me a withering look and sarcastically said, "Yes, I know." I felt devastated. Before she could even say another word to me, I too felt like I knew two things about this teacher! The first was that I hated her! I felt humiliated. The second thing I knew beyond a shadow of a doubt was that I was not going to like anything she said, and if she could be that rude, that it was probably all lies anyhow. That was the power of the lack of a warm greeting! It later turned out that my son misbehaved whenever he had close work because he had a vision problem and could not see the work. But by then it was too late. My first impression was the lasting impression. And it is the same with the first impressions of all your parents, so take time to sincerely greet them warmly. It makes anything you have to say more palatable.

Greet parents warmly (Jordan et al., 1998). Shake hands and introduce yourself, "Hi, I'm Pat McMartin, Troy's teacher, and I'm really glad to meet you, Mrs. Clay." Try to appear unhurried even if you ran a bit late. All parents want to feel that you are not going to rush through what you have to say. They want to feel important and that their child is important to you. Do set time limits when you welcome them so that they know that there will be an ending time.

Have a Work Portfolio

Work portfolios are excellent concrete ways to show parents exactly what their children are doing (Wilford, 2004). This is effective for both elementary and secondary students. Have one for each student. Involve the students in choosing the work to be placed in the portfolio. Include a note from the student to the parent in the portfolio. Have students write individualized notes to their parents. Almost all parents smile when they see the unique handwriting of their children addressed to them.

Include a blank page in the portfolio for parents to return a positive note to their children. When children come back into the classroom, they will see that their parents did attend the conference and their parents' letters. Make sure to tell parents to keep the letters to their children upbeat and positive.

Use Systematic Observations

Prepare for the conference by planning time to observe each student (Wilford, 2004). Observe students during different times of day to see how they behave during varying times. You may discover that different conditions produce different types of behaviors and learning.

Mrs. Thompkins was concerned about Stephanie's erratic behavior and learning. She decided to do some observations to get a fuller picture of how Stephanie functioned. She did this while teaching other students. She carried a little notebook in her pocket and wrote down the times of day and the varying behaviors. She discovered that Stephanie was easily distracted and then had problems focusing. She kept her notes as part of a file so that she could give more specific examples of Stephanie's behavior at the conference with Stephanie's family (see Figure 7.2).

Key Points to Enhance Conferences

Listen, listen, and listen some more. Find out how the parent is thinking and feeling about the student. It will help you understand the student's behavior. Use the skills you have learned in this book. Sometimes, students are doing fine in school, yet parents may have other worries about their children. Everything that happens

Figure 7.2

Examples of Systematic Observation
Stephanie W., October 3rd
9:00   Concentrates on seat work
9:01   Look around room
9:02   Gets up and walks to pencil sharpener
9:03   Sits back down and look around

in children's lives generally has an effect on how children react when they come to school. If the parent is worried about the child's behavior, follow through and find out why the parent is worried.

Kathy Jorgens was Kiley's teacher. Kiley was a quiet child who studied hard and got good grades. When Kathy Jorgans met with Kiley's parents, she was surprised to learn that they were very concerned about Kiley's eating habits. They suspected that she might have an eating disorder. She listened to their fears and then made some suggestions for them to get help for Kiley.

Be careful to not be judgmental. Do not criticize parents either directly or indirectly. They will become offended and shut down. It doesn't have to be your words. It can be the looks you give them that reflect your criticism or blame.

Do not get ahead of parents. Just like children may process information more slowly or more rapidly, so, too, do parents. Check for understanding before going on to new points. You can do this by saying, "So now that we have found a solution for _____, how about if we move on to _____." This opens the door for the parent who is processing the information more slowly, to tell you that he or she still has something to address. Some parents may be repetitive about the information, wanting to stay focused on just one thing when you want to move on. If that is the case, and you feel very sure that the parent understands, say, "If it's OK with you, I would like to move on to the next topic. I'm worried

we will run out of time and not be able to cover everything. If you want, we can make a new appointment to meet again."

Stay calm and focused throughout the conference. Your attitude is contagious. When you are calm, it will help the parent to also be calm.

Stay aware of the parent's facial expressions, gestures, and voice. These all will provide you with clues to the parent's emotions. Mr. Smith, William's father, said that he totally understood about William's misbehavior. He smiled as he listened. But Mrs. Cordan, William's teacher, noticed that Mr. Smith's arms were crossed across his chest and his facial expression was one of anger even as he smiled.

The Five-Step Approach to Telling Parents Negative News

1. Establish a Connection

Start the conference by telling parents something positive about their child (Million, 2005). That is a must. Saying something positive serves several functions. First, it lets them know that you care. Parents don't care how much you know until they know how much you care. Second, it tells them that you really know their child. They know that their child is just one of many students. When they hear something positive that they know is true, it tells them that you have taken time to get to know their child. Third, when you tell them something positive that they know to be true about their child, they typically nod their heads to indicate "yes" in agreement with you. It starts the conference on a positive note of agreement rather than disagreement.

Jenny Brody was Zachery's teacher. He was a difficult student constantly challenging her authority as a teacher. When she met with Zachery's parents, she started off the conference by telling them that Zachery really enjoyed P.E. and that he was really good at it. His dad nodded his head, "yes," and then said, "Zachery has always loved sports." You too need to find something positive to say about each student and get parents to nod their heads "yes." This starts the conference out with the parents agreeing with you.

2. Establish Yourself as Knowledgeable

It is important that parents respect you so that they will listen to the things you tell them. This is especially true when you are going to tell them something negative about their children. An excellent way to do this is to tell them something you do with their children that "works." It may be the only thing you do that works, but it does work. When parents hear that you have something that you do that works, they often look at you with new respect. Many parents do not like to admit that they have problems in the home with their children when they are confronted with misbehavior. They may even say things like, "My child never does that at home." However, they still want to know that there is someone who does know how to manage their children in a positive manner that is effective.

3. Ask for Parent Involvement

Children's parents want to be seen as colleagues (Stevens & Tollafield, 2003). They want to be involved. The truth is that they share a common goal with you, and that is to improve their children's learning and behavior—to prepare their child for the future.

Ask them questions like these:

"How do you think we should handle this?"
"Do you have any ideas?"
"What works for you at home?"

When you ask parents for their input, it opens the doors to cooperation. Two-way communication is a must (Haviland, 2003). Parents need to feel that they have a voice. When parents give their input, they know that their viewpoints are encouraged and respected. It opens the doors to teamwork so that you and the parents can work together on behalf of their children.

4. Come Up With Solutions

Brainstorm solutions. Write them down. Together, choose the best and come up with a plan. Think through the plan to ensure that it is something that will be effective (Stevens & Tollafield, 2003). Write the plan down. Include all the resources you and parents will need. You may want to recommend a specific book for parents to use at home. Jessie's teacher recommended that his parents read a book that had helped her with classroom management. She wanted the parents to read the book so that they could use some of the same strategies.

Some of the resources may be people. Together, you may decide that it would be good for the student to see the school counselor. You may even decide that the child needs to see a physician. You could decide that the child needs a peer with whom to study.

5. Follow Through

A plan is only as good as the follow-through. End the conference with a plan to follow through and methods to communicate to determine progress. You may pass daily notes, use e-mail, or meet again in a month to talk about progress.

When the conference is ended, it is a good idea to give the parents a form documenting everything that was discussed (see Figure 7.3).

A week later, send home another conference follow-up that reviews in more detail the issues

Figure 7.3

Conference Documentation

Student's name _____

Date of conference _____

Name of individual who attended conference _____

Relationship to student _____

Issues discussed _____

_____

_____

_____

_____

_____

_____

_____

_____

_____

_____

_____

Action plan _____

_____

_____

_____

_____

_____

_____

_____

_____

_____

_____

Teacher's signature _____

_____ _____, 20_____

discussed and the action plan. It helps serve as a reminder to parents. It is amazing how soon some parents can forget. They get busy with their lives. When they receive the conference follow-up, it is a reminder that there is a plan and that they have a part in the plan (see Figure 7.4).

Figure 7.4

Follow-Up for Conference

Dear _____,

Thank you so much for attending the conference concerning

_____ held on _____ _____, 20_____.

It was great to meet and speak with you. I am looking forward to working with you as a team for your child.

As a positive reminder for both of us, I am outlining the suggestions and plans we made at the conference.

_____

_____

_____

_____

_____

_____

_____

_____

_____

_____

_____

_____

_____

Thanks again for coming. It was a pleasure meeting you. I look forward to working together with you.

Sicerely yours,

_____

_____ _____,20 _____

Checklist.

Many people have a grocery list when they go shopping. They do this so that they will not forget anything important. Do this for conferences so that you too will remember everything that is important (see Figure 7.5).

Figure 7.5

Checklist for Parent Conferences

Before the conference

- ❏ Did you plan for the conference and know what you would discuss?
- ❏ Did you try accommodate parent times for the conference?
- ❏ Did you "cool down" any negatice feelings?
- ❏ Did you do systematic observation of students?
- ❏ Did you send home family profile sheets?
- ❏ Did you arrange an area outside your classroom for the parent to
- ❏ wait?
- ❏ Did you have a snack in the waiting area?
- ❏ Did you decorate the room so that it is neat and attractive?
- ❏ Did you arrange comfortable seating for the conference?
- ❏ Did you prepare student protfolios?
- ❏ Did you treat the parent like a VIP?

During the conference

- ❏ Did you help the parent to feel welcome?
- ❏ Did you tell the parent something positive about the child?
- ❏ Did you tell the parent something you do that works?
- ❏ Did you involve the parent in coming up solutions?
- ❏ Did you encourage the parent to participate in the conference?
- ❏ Did your comments indicate interest and respect for the student?
- ❏ Did you both come up with an action plan for the child?
- ❏ Did you brainstorm solutions?
- ❏ Did you plan for following up the conference?
- ❏ Did you give the parent a conference documentation form?
- ❏ Did you close the conference on a positive note?
- ❏ Did you use power listening?
- ❏ Did you use power persusion when and if it was needed?

Follow-Up

- ❏ Did you follow-up your conference with a notation of what was covered and suggestions made?

Discussion Questions

1. What concerns and fears do you have about conducting conferences with parents/caregivers?

2. What fears or concerns might parents/caregivers feel about having a conference with a teacher?

3. What are some inventive strategies for encouraging reluctant parents/caregivers to attend conferences?

4. How can teachers improve conference attendance of parents/caregivers who are recent immigrants?

5. Which materials should teachers have available to show parents at conferences?

6. What are the advantages of including your students in parent/teacher conferences?

7. What materials should teachers have available for parents/caregivers at conferences?

8. What are some educational terms that might confuse parents/caregivers, and how can teachers clearly explain those terms so that parents/caregivers understand them?

9. What steps can be taken to ensure that the suggestions made at a conference are implemented following the conference?

10. What are the essential purposes of parent/teacher conferences?

11. What are some strategies for sharing negative issues with parents?

Does Homework Improve Learning?
A Fresh Look at the Evidence

By Alfie Kohn

Because the question in the title of this chapter doesn't seem all that complicated, you might think it has a straightforward answer. You might think that open-minded people who review the evidence should be able to agree on whether homework really does help.

If so, you'd be wrong. "Researchers have been far from unanimous in their assessments of the strengths and weaknesses of homework as an instructional technique," according to an article published in the Journal of Educational Psychology. "The conclusions of more than a dozen reviews of the homework literature conducted between 1960 and 1989 varied greatly. Their assessments ranged from homework having positive effects, no effects, or complex effects to the suggestion that the research was too sparse or poorly conducted to allow trustworthy conclusions."

When you think about it, any number of issues could complicate the picture and make it more or less likely that home work would appear to be beneficial in a given study. What kind of homework are we talking about? Fill-in-the-blank worksheets or extended projects? In what school subject(s)? How old are the students? How able

and interested are they? Are we looking at how much the teacher assigned or at how much the kids actually did? How careful was the study and how many students were investigated?

Even when you take account of all these variables, the bottom line remains that no definite conclusion can be reached, and that is itself a significant conclusion. The fact that there isn't anything close to unanimity among experts belies the widespread assumption that homework helps. It demonstrates just how superficial and misleading is the declaration we so often hear to the effect that "studies show" homework is an important contributor to academic achievement.

Research casting doubt on that assumption goes back at least to 1897, when a study found that assigning spelling homework had no effect on how proficient children were at spelling later on. By 1960, a reviewer tracked down seventeen experimental studies, most of which produced mixed results and some of which suggested that homework made no difference at all. In 1979, another reviewer located five more studies. One found that homework helped, two found that it didn't, and two found mixed results. Yet another review was published a few years later that described eight articles and seven dissertations from the mid-1960s to the early 1980s. The authors, who included a longtime advocate of traditional educational policies, claimed the results demonstrated that homework had "powerful effects on learning." But another researcher looked more carefully and discovered that only four of those fifteen studies actually compared getting homework with getting no homework, and their results actually didn't provide much reason to think it helped.

"The literature reviews done over the past 60 years … report conflicting results," one expert concluded in 1985. "There is no good evidence that homework produces better academic achievement." Four years later, Harris Cooper, an educational psychologist, attempted to sort things out by conducting the most exhaustive review of the research to date. He performed a metaanalysis, which is a statistical technique for combining numerous studies into the equivalent of one giant study. Cooper included seventeen research reports that contained a total of forty-eight comparisons between students who did and did not receive homework. About 70 percent of these found that homework was associated with higher achievement. He also reviewed surveys that attempted to correlate students' test scores with how much homework they did. Forty-three of fifty correlations were positive, although the overall effect was not particularly large: Homework accounted for less than 4 percent of the differences in students' scores. Worse, most of the studies included in the review had such serious "methodological shortcomings" as to raise doubts about the validity of any conclusion based on them, according to two experts.

Cooper and his colleagues published a review of newer studies in 2006. Those that compared students with and without homework found a stronger association with achievement than the earlier studies had, but these new experiments measured achievement by students' scores on tests that had been designed to match the homework they had just done. As for more recent studies looking for a relationship between achievement and time spent on homework, the overall correlation, was about the same as the one found in 1989.

But several new studies weren't included in Cooper's recent review, and they "do not support the notion that students who spend more time on homework have higher achievement gains than do their classmates." Still another study—the same one that found younger students are spending a lot more time doing homework these days (see pp. 6–7)—confirmed that the time commitment was "not associated with higher or lower scores on any [achievement] tests." (By contrast, the amount of time children spent reading for pleasure was strongly correlated with higher scores.)

Taken as a whole, the available research might be summarized as inconclusive. But if we look more closely, even that description turns out to be too generous. The bottom line, I'll argue in this chapter, is that careful examination of the data raises serious doubts about whether homework enhances meaningful learning for most students. Of the eight reasons that follow, the first three identify important limitations of the existing research, the next three identify findings from these same studies that lead to questions about homework's effectiveness, and the last two introduce additional data that weaken the case even further.

Limitations of the Research

1. At best, most homework studies show only an association, not a causal relationship. Statistical principles don't get much more basic than "correlation doesn't prove causation." The number of umbrellas brought to a workplace on a given morning will be highly correlated with

the probability of precipitation in the afternoon, but the presence of umbrellas didn't made it rain. Also, I'd be willing to bet that kids who ski are more likely to attend selective colleges than those who don't ski, but that doesn't mean they were accepted because they ski, or that arranging for a child to take skiing lessons will improve her chances of being admitted. Nevertheless, most research purporting to show a positive effect of homework seems to be based on the assumption that when students who get (or do) more homework also score better on standardized tests, it follows that the higher scores were due to their having had more homework.

There are almost always other explanations for why successful students might be in classrooms where more homework is assigned—let alone why these students might take more time with their homework than their peers do. Even Cooper, a proponent of homework, concedes that "it is equally plausible," based on the correlational data that comprise most of the available research on the topic, "that teachers assign more homework to students who are achieving better … or that better students simply spend more time on home study." In still other cases, a third variable—for example, being born into a more affluent and highly educated family—might be associated with getting higher test scores and with doing more homework (or attending the kind of school where more homework is assigned). Again, it would be erroneous to conclude that homework is responsible for higher achievement. Or that a complete absence of homework would have any detrimental effect at all.

Sometimes it's not easy to spot those other variables that can separately affect achievement and time spent on homework, giving the impression that these two are causally related. One of the most frequently cited studies in the field was published in the early 1980s by a researcher named Timothy Keith, who looked at survey results from tens of thousands of high school students and concluded that homework had a positive relationship to achievement, at least at that age. But a funny thing happened ten years later when he and a colleague looked at homework alongside other possible influences on learning such as quality of instruction, motivation, and which classes the students took. When all these variables were entered into the equation simultaneously, the result was "puzzling and surprising": Homework no longer had any meaningful effect on achievement at all. In other words, a set of findings that served—and, given how often his original study continues to be cited, still serves—as a prominent basis for the claim that homework raises achievement turns out to be spurious.

Several studies have actually found a negative relationship between students' achievement (or their academic performance as judged by teachers) and how much time they spend on homework (or how much help they receive from their parents). But researchers who report this counterintuitive finding generally take pains to explain that it "must not be interpreted as a causal pattern." What's really going on here, we're assured, is just that kids with academic difficulties are taking more time with their homework in order to catch up.

That sounds plausible, but of course it's just a theory. One study found that children who were having academic difficulties actually didn't get more homework from their teachers, although it's possible they spent longer hours working on the homework that they did get. But even if we agreed that doing more homework probably isn't responsible for lowering students' achievement, the fact that there's an inverse relationship seems to suggest that, at the very least, homework isn't doing much to help kids who are struggling. In any event, anyone who reads the research on this topic can't help but notice how rare it is to find these same cautions about the misleading nature of correlational results when those results suggest a positive relationship between homework and achievement. It's only when the outcome doesn't fit the expected pattern (and support the case for homework) that it's carefully explained away.

In short, most of the research cited to show that homework is academically beneficial really doesn't prove any such thing.

2. Do we really know how much homework kids do? The studies claiming that homework helps are based on the assumption that we can accurately measure the number and length of assignments. But many of these studies depend on students to tell us how much homework they get (or complete). When Harris Cooper and his associates looked at recent studies in which the time spent on homework was reported by students, and then compared them with studies in which that estimate was provided by their parents, the results were quite different. In fact, the correlation between homework and achievement disappeared when parents' estimates were used. This was also true in one of Cooper's own studies: "Parent reports of homework completion were … uncorrected with the student report." The same sort of discrepancy shows up again in cross-cultural research (parents and children provide very different accounts of how much help kids receive) and also when students and teachers are asked to estimate how much homework was assigned. It's not clear which source is most accurate, by the way—or indeed whether any of them is entirely reliable.

These first two flaws combine to cast doubt on much of the existing data, according to a damning summary that appears in the Encyclopedia of Educational Research: "Research on homework continues to show the same fundamental weaknesses that have characterized it throughout the century: an overdependence on self-report as the predominant method of data collection and on correlation as the principal method of data analysis."

3. Homework studies confuse grades and test scores with learning. Most researchers, like most reporters who write about education, talk about how this or that policy affects student "achievement" without questioning whether the way that word is defined in the studies makes any sense. What exactly is this entity called achievement that's said to go up or down? It turns out that what's actually being measured—at least in all the homework research I've seen—is one of three things: scores on tests designed by teachers, grades given by teachers, or scores on standardized exams. About the best thing you can say for these numbers is that they're easy for researchers to collect and report. Each is seriously flawed in its own way.

In studies that involve in-class tests, some students are given homework—which usually consists of reviewing a batch of facts about some topic—and then they, along with their peers who didn't get the homework, take a quiz on that very material. The outcome measure, in other words, is precisely aligned to the homework that some students did and others didn't do—or that they did in varying amounts. It's as if you were told to spend time in the evening learning the names of all the vice presidents of the United States and were then tested only on those names. If you remembered more of them after cramming, the researcher would then conclude that "learning in the evening" is effective.

In the second kind of study, course grades are used to determine whether homework made a difference. The problem here is that a grade, as one writer put it long ago, is "an inadequate report of an inaccurate judgment by a biased and variable judge of the extent to which a student has attained an undefined level of mastery of an unknown proportion of an indefinite amount of material." Quite apart from the destructive effects grades have on students' interest in learning, their depth of understanding, and their preference for challenging tasks, the basis for a grade is typically as subjective as the result is uninformative. Any given assignment may well be given two different grades by two equally qualified teachers—and may even be given two different grades by a single teacher who reads it at two different times. The final course grade, moreover, is based on a combination of these individual marks, along with other, even less well-defined considerations.

As bad as grades are in general, they are particularly inappropriate for judging the effectiveness of homework for one simple reason: The same teacher who handed out the assignments then turns around and evaluates the students who completed them. The final grade a teacher chooses for a student will often be based at least partly on whether, and to what extent, that student did the homework. Thus, to say that more homework is associated with better school performance (as measured by grades) is to provide no useful information about whether homework is intrinsically valuable. Yet grades are the basis for a good number of the studies that are cited to defend that very conclusion. The studies that use grades as the outcome measure, not surprisingly, tend to show a much stronger effect for homework than studies that use standardized test scores.

Here's one example. Cooper and his colleagues conducted a study in 1998 with both younger and older students (from grades 2 through 12), using both grades and standardized test scores to measure achievement. They also looked at how much homework was assigned by the teacher as well as at how much time students spent on it. Thus, there were eight separate results to be reported. Here's how they came out:

YOUNGER STUDENTS

Effect on grades of amount of homework assigned	No sig. relationship
Effect on test scores of amount of homework assigned	No sig. relationship
Effect on grades of amount of homework done	No sig. relationship
Effect on test scores of amount of homework done	No sig. relationship

OLDER STUDENTS

Effect on grades of amount of homework assigned	No sig. relationship
Effect on test scores of amount of homework assigned	No sig. relationship
Effect on grades of amount of homework done	No sig. relationship
Effect on test scores of amount of homework done	No sig. relationship

Of these eight comparisons, then, the only positive correlation—and it wasn't a large one—was between how much homework older students did and their achievement as measured by grades. If that measure is viewed as dubious, if not downright silly, then one of the more recent studies conducted by the country's best-known homework researcher fails to support the idea of assigning homework at any age.

The last, and most common, way of measuring achievement is to use standardized test scores. Purely because they're standardized, these tests are widely regarded as objective instruments for assessing children's academic performance. But as I've argued elsewhere at some length, there is considerable reason to believe that standardized tests are a poor measure of intellectual proficiency. They are, however, excellent indicators of two things. The first is affluence: Up to 90 percent of the difference in scores among schools, communities, or even states can be accounted for, statistically speaking, without knowing anything about what happened inside the classrooms. All you need are some facts about the average income and education levels of the students' parents. The second phenomenon that standardized tests measure is how skillful a particular group of students is at taking standardized tests—and, increasingly, how much class time has been given over to preparing them to do just that.

In my experience, teachers can almost always identify several students who do poorly on standardized tests even though, by more authentic and meaningful indicators, they are talented thinkers. Other students, meanwhile, ace these tests even though their thinking isn't particularly impressive; they're just good test takers. These anecdotal reports have been corroborated by research that finds a statistically significant positive relationship between a shallow or superficial approach to learning, on the one hand, and high scores on various standardized tests, on the other. What's more, this association has been documented at the elementary, middle, and high school levels.

Standardized tests are even less useful when they include any of these features:

- If most of the questions are multiple choice, then students are unable to generate, or even justify, their responses. To that extent, students cannot really demonstrate what they know or what they can do with what they know. Multiple-choice tests are basically designed so that many kids who understand a given idea will be tricked into picking the wrong answer.
- If the test is timed, then it places a premium not on thoughtfulness but on speed.
- If the test is focused on "basic skills," then doing well is more a function of cramming

forgettable facts into short-term memory than of really understanding ideas, making connections and distinctions, knowing how to read or write or analyze problems in a sophisticated way, thinking like a scientist or historian, being able to use knowledge in unfamiliar situations, and so on.

- If the test is given to younger children, then, according to an overwhelming consensus on the part of early-education specialists, it is a poor indicator of academic skills. Many children under the age of eight or nine are unable to demonstrate their proficiency on a standardized test just because they're tripped up by the format.
- If the test is "norm-referenced" (like the Iowa Test of Basic Skills, Terra Nova, Stanford Achievement Test, and others used widely in classrooms and also by researchers), then it was never designed to evaluate whether students know what they should. Instead, its primary purpose is to artificially spread out the scores in order to facilitate ranking students against each other. The question these tests are intended to answer is not "How well are our kids—or our schools—doing?" but "Who's beating whom?" We know nothing about academic competence in absolute terms just from knowing what percentage of other test takers a given child has bested. Moreover, the selection of questions for these tests is informed by this imperative to rank. Thus, items that a lot of students answer correctly (or incorrectly) are typically eliminated—regardless of whether the content is important—and replaced with questions that about half the kids will get right. This is done in order to make it easier to compare students to one another.

My purpose in these few paragraphs has been to offer only a brief summary of the reasons that informed educators and parents would never regard a standardized test score as meaningful information about the quality of a student's thinking—or about the quality of a school. (In the latter case, a high or rising average test score may actually be a reason to worry. Every hour that teachers spend preparing kids to succeed on standardized tests, even if that investment pays off, is an hour not spent helping kids to become critical, curious, creative thinkers.) The limitations of these tests are so numerous and so serious that studies showing an association between homework and higher scores are highly misleading. Because that's also true of studies that use grades as a stand-in for achievement, it should be obvious that combining two flawed measures does nothing to improve the situation.

I'm unaware of any studies that have addressed the question of whether homework enhances the depth of students' understanding of ideas or their passion for learning. The fact that more meaningful outcomes are hard to quantify does not make test scores or grades any more valid, reliable, or useful as measures. To use them anyway calls to mind the story of the man who looked for his lost keys near a streelight one night, not because that was where he dropped them but just because the light was better there.

If our children's ability to understand ideas from the inside out is what matters to us, and if we don't have any evidence that giving them homework helps them to acquire this proficiency, then all the research in the world showing that test scores rise when you make kids do more schoolwork at home doesn't mean very much. That's particularly true if the homework was designed specifically to improve the limited band of skills that appear on these tests. It's probably not a coincidence that, even within the existing test-based research, homework appears to work better when the assignments involve rote learning and repetition rather than real thinking. After all,

"works better" just means "produces higher scores on exams that measure low-level capabilities."

Overall, the available homework research defines "beneficial" in terms of achievement, and it defines achievement as better grades or standardized test scores. It allows us to conclude nothing about whether children's learning improves.

Cautionary Findings

Assume for the moment that we weren't concerned about basing our conclusions on studies that merely show homework is associated with (as opposed to responsible for) achievement, or studies that depend on questionable estimates of how much is actually completed, or studies that use deeply problematic outcome measures. Even taken on its own terms, the research turns up some findings that must give pause to anyone who thinks homework is valuable.

4. Homework matters less the longer you look. The longer the duration of a homework study, the less of an effect the homework is shown to have. Cooper, who pointed this out almost in passing, speculated that less homework may have been assigned during any given week in the longer-lasting studies, but he offered no evidence that this actually happened. So here's another theory: The studies finding the greatest effect were those that captured less of what goes on in the real world by virtue of being so brief. View a small, unrepresentative slice of a child's life and it may appear that homework makes a contribution to achievement; keep watching and that contribution is eventually revealed to be illusory.

5. Even where they do exist, positive effects are often quite small. In Cooper's review, as I've already pointed out, homework could explain only a tiny proportion of the differences in achievement scores. The same was true of a large-scale high school study from the 1960s. And in a more

recent investigation of British secondary schools, "the payoff for working several more hours per week per subject would appear to be slight, and those classes where there was more homework were not always those classes which obtained better results." As one scholar remarked, "If research tells us anything" about homework, it's that "even when achievement gains have been found, they have been minimal, especially in comparison to the amount of work expended by teachers and students."

6. There is no evidence of any academic benefit from homework in elementary school. Even if you are untroubled by the methodological concerns I've been describing, the fact is that after decades of research on the topic, there is no overall positive correlation between homework and achievement (by any measure) for students before middle school or, in many cases, before high school. More precisely, there's virtually no good research on the impact of homework in the primary grades—and therefore no data to support its use with young children—whereas research has been done with students in the upper elementary grades, and it generally fails to find any benefit.

The absence of evidence supporting the value of homework before high school is generally acknowledged by experts in the field, even those who are less critical of the research literature (and less troubled by the negative effects of homework) than I am. But this remarkable fact is rarely communicated to the general public. In fact, it's with younger children, where the benefits are most questionable (if not absent), that there has been the greatest increase in the quantity of homework!

In 1989, Cooper summarized the available research with a sentence that ought to be e-mailed to every parent, teacher, and administrator in the country: "There is no evidence that any amount of homework improves the academic performance of elementary students." In revisiting his review a

decade later, he mentioned another large study he had come across. It, too, found minuscule correlations between the amount of homework done by sixth graders, on the one hand, and their grades and test scores, on the other. For third graders, the correlations were negative: more homework was associated with lower achievement.

In 2005, I asked Cooper if he knew of any newer studies with elementary school students, and he said he had come across exactly four, all small and all unpublished. He was kind enough to offer the citations, and I managed to track them down.

The first was a college student's term paper describing an experiment with thirty-nine second graders in one school. The point was to see whether children who did math homework would perform better on a quiz taken immediately afterward that covered exactly the same content as the homework. The second study, a master's thesis, involved forty third graders, again in a single school and again with performance measured on a follow-up quiz dealing with the homework material, this time featuring vocabulary skills. The third study tested sixty-four fifth graders on social studies facts.

All three of these experiments found exactly what you would expect: The kids who had drilled on the material—a process that happened to take place at home—did better on their respective class tests. The final study, a dissertation project, involved teaching a lesson contained in a language arts textbook. The fourth graders who had been assigned homework on this material performed better on the textbook's unit test, but did not do any better on a standardized test. And the third graders who hadn't done any homework wound up with higher scores on the standardized test. Like the other three studies, the measure of success basically involved memorizing and regurgitating facts.

It seems safe to say that these latest four studies offer no reason to revise the earlier summary statement that no meaningful evidence exists of an academic advantage for children in elementary school who do homework. And the news isn't much better for children in middle school or junior high school. If the raw correlation between achievement (test scores or grades) and time spent on homework in Cooper's initial research review is "nearly nonexistent" for grades 3 through 5, it remains extremely low for grades 6 through 9. The correlation only spikes at or above grade 10.

Such a correlation would be a prerequisite for assuming that homework provides academic benefits, but I want to repeat that it isn't enough to justify that conclusion. A large correlation is necessary, in other words, but not sufficient. Indeed, I believe it would be a mistake to conclude that homework is a meaningful contributor to learning even in high school. Remember that Cooper and his colleagues found a positive effect only when they looked at how much homework high school students actually did (as opposed to how much the teacher assigned) and only when achievement was measured by the grades given to them by those same teachers. Also recall that Keith's earlier positive finding with respect to homework in high school evaporated once he used a more sophisticated statistical technique to analyze the data.

All of the cautions, qualifications, and criticisms in this chapter, for that matter, are relevant to students of all ages. But it's worth pointing out separately that no evidence exists to support the practice of assigning homework to elementary students. No wonder many Japanese elementary schools in the late 1990s issued 'no homework' policies." That development may strike us as surprising, particularly in light of how Japan's educational system has long been held out as a model, notably by writers trying to justify their support for homework. But it's a development that seems entirely rational in light of what the evidence shows right here in the United States.

Additional Research

7. The results of national and international exams raise further doubts about homework's role. The National Assessment of Educational Progress (NAEP) is often called the nation's report card. Students who take this test also answer a series of questions about themselves, sometimes including how much time they spend on homework. For any number of reasons, one might expect to find a reasonably strong association between time spent on homework and test scores. Yet the most striking result, particularly for elementary students, is the absence of such an association. Even students who reported being assigned no homework at all didn't fare badly on the test.

Consider the results of the 2000 math exam. Fourth graders who did no homework got roughly the same score as those who did thirty minutes a night. Remarkably the scores then declined for those who did forty-five minutes, then declined again for those who did an hour or more! In eighth grade, the scores were higher for those who did between fifteen and forty-five minutes a night than for those who did no homework, but the results were worse for those who did an hour's worth, and worse still for those did more than an hour. In twelfth grade, the scores were about the same regardless of whether students did only fifteen minutes or more than an hour. Results on the reading test, too, provided no compelling evidence that homework helped.

International comparisons allow us to look for correlations between homework and test scores within each country and also for correlations across countries. Let's begin with the former. In the 1980s, thirteen-year-olds in a dozen nations were tested and also queried about how much they studied. "In some countries more time spent on homework was associated with higher scores; in others, it was not." In the 1990s, the Trends in International Mathematics and Science Study (TIMSS) became the most popular way of assessing what was going on around the world, although its conclusions can't necessarily be generalized to other subjects. Again, the results were not the same in all countries, even when the focus was limited to the final years of high school (where the contribution of homework is thought to be strongest). Usually it turned out that doing some homework had a stronger relationship with achievement than doing none at all, but doing a little homework was also better than doing a lot. This is known as a "curvilinear" relationship; on a graph it looks like an upside-down U.

But even that relationship didn't show up in a separate series of studies involving elementary school students in China, Japan, and two U.S. cities: "There was no consistent linear or curvilinear relation between the amount of time spent on homework and the child's level of academic achievement." These researchers even checked to see if homework in first grade was related to achievement in fifth grade, the theory being that homework might provide gradual, long-term benefits to younger children. Again they came up empty-handed.

What about correlations across cultures? Here we find people playing what I'll later argue is a pointless game in which countries' education systems are ranked against one another on the basis of their students' test scores. Pointless or not, "a common explanation of the poor performance of American children in cross-cultural comparisons of academic achievement is that American children spend little time in study." The reasoning, in other words, goes something like this:

Premise 1: Our students get significantly less homework than their counterparts across the globe.

Premise 2: Other countries whup the pants off us in international exams.

Conclusion: Premise 1 explains premise 2.

Additional conclusion: If U.S. teachers assigned more homework, our students would perform better.

Every step of this syllogism is either flawed or simply false. We've already seen that premise 1 is no longer true, if indeed it ever was (see p. 8). Premise 2 has been debunked by a number of analysts and for a number of different reasons. Even if both premises were accurate, however, the conclusions don't necessarily follow; this is another example of confusing correlation with causation.

But there is now empirical evidence, not just logic, to challenge the conclusions. Two researchers looked at TIMSS data from 1994 and 1999 to compare practices in fifty countries. When they published their findings in 2005, they could scarcely conceal their surprise:

> Not only did we fail to find any positive relationships, [but] the overall correlations between national average student achievement and national averages in the frequency, total amount, and percentage of teachers who used homework in grading are all negative! If these data can be extrapolated to other subjects—a research topic that warrants immediate study, in our opinion—then countries that try to improve their standing in the world rankings of student achievement by raising the amount of homework might actually be undermining their own success, ... More homework may actually undermine national achievement.

In a separate analysis of the 1999 TIMSS results that looked at twenty-seven U.S. stages or districts as well as thirty-seven other countries, meanwhile, "there was little relationship between the amount of homework assigned and students' performance." And the overall conclusion was also supported by TIMSS data showing that "Japanese junior high school students performed at the top but did not study as much as their peers in other countries."

8. Incidental research raises further doubts about homework. Reviews of homework studies tend to overlook investigations that are primarily focused on other topics but just happen to look at homework, among several other variables. Here are two examples:

> First, a pair of Harvard scientists queried almost two thousand students enrolled in college physics courses in order to figure out whether any features of their high school physics courses were now of use to them. At first they found a very small relationship between the amount of homework students had in high school and how well they were currently doing. Once the researchers controlled for other variables, such as the type of courses kids had taken, that relationship disappeared. The same researchers then embarked on a similar study of a much larger population of students in college science classes and found the same thing: Homework simply didn't help.

Second, back in the late 1970s, New Jersey educator Ruth Tschudin identified about three hundred "A+ teachers" on the basis of recommendations, awards, or media coverage. She then set out to compare their classroom practices to those of a matched group of other teachers. Among her findings: The exceptional teachers not only tended to give less homework but also were likely to give students more choices about their assignments.

It's interesting to speculate on why this might be true. Are better teachers more apt to question the conventional wisdom in general? More likely to notice that homework isn't doing much good? More responsive to its negative effects on children and families? More likely to summon the gumption to act on what they've noticed? Or perhaps the researchers who reviewed the TIMMS data put their finger on it when they wrote, "It may be the poorest teachers who assign the most homework [because] effective teachers may cover all the material in class." (Imagine that quotation enlarged and posted in a school's main office.)

This analysis rings true for Steve Phelps, who teaches math at a high school near Cincinnati. "In all honesty," he says, "the students are compelled to be in my class forty-eight minutes a day. If I can't get done in forty-eight minutes what I need to get done, then I really have no business intruding on their family time." But figuring out how to get it done isn't always easy. It certainly took time for Phil Lyons, the social studies teacher I mentioned earlier who figured out that homework was making students less interested in learning for its own sake, and then watched as many of them began to "seek out more knowledge" once he stopped giving them homework. At the beginning of Lyons's teaching career, he assigned a lot of homework "as a crutch, to compensate for poor lessons. ... But as I mastered the material, homework ceased to be necessary. A no homework policy is a challenge to me," he adds. "I am forced to create lessons that are so good that no further drilling is required when the lessons are completed."

Lyons has also conducted an informal investigation to gauge the impact of this shift. He gave less and less homework each year before finally eliminating it completely. And he reports that

> each year my students have performed better on the AP economics test. The empirical data from my class combined with studies I've read convinced me. Homework is an obvious burden to students, but assigning, collecting, grading, and recording homework creates a tremendous amount of work for me as well. I would feel justified encroaching on students' free time and would be willing to do the grading if I saw tangible returns, but with no quantifiable benefit it makes no sense to impose on them or me.

The results observed by a single teacher in an uncontrolled experiment are obviously not conclusive. Nor is the Harvard physics study. Nor is Tschudin's survey of terrific teachers. But when all these observations are combined with the surprising results of national and international exams, and when these in turn are viewed in the context of research literature that makes a weak, correlational case for homework in high school—and offers absolutely no support for homework in elementary school—it gradually becomes clear that we've been sold a bill of goods.

People who never bought it will not be surprised, of course. "I have a good education and a decent job despite the fact that I didn't spend half my adolescence doing homework," said a mother of four children whose concern about excessive homework eventually led to her becoming an activist on the issue. On the other hand, some will find these results not only unexpected but hard to believe, if only because common sense tells them that homework should help. But just as a careful look at the research overturns the canard that "studies show homework raises achievement," so

a careful look at popular beliefs about learning will challenge the reasons that lead us to expect we will find unequivocal research support in the first place. The absence of supporting data actually makes sense in retrospect, as well see in Chapter 6 when we examine the idea that homework "reinforces" what was learned in class, along with' other declarations that are too readily accepted on faith.

It's true that we don't have clear evidence to prove beyond a reasonable doubt that homework doesn't help students learn. Indeed, it's hard to imagine what that evidence might look like—beyond repeated findings that homework often isn't even associated with higher achievement. To borrow a concept from the law, however, the burden of proof here doesn't rest with critics to demonstrate that homework doesn't help. It rests with supporters to show that it does, and specifically to show that its advantages are sufficiently powerful and pervasive to justify taking up children's (and parents' and teachers') time, and to compensate for the distinct disadvantages discussed in Chapter 1. When a principal admits that homework is "taking away some of the years of adolescence and childhood" but then says that requiring it from the earliest grades "give[s] us an edge in standardized testing," we have to wonder what kind of educator—indeed, what kind of human being—is willing to accept that trade-off even if the latter premise were true.

Most proponents, of course, aren't saying that all homework is always good in all respects for all kids—just as critics couldn't defend the proposition that no homework is ever good in any way for any child. The prevailing view—which, even if not stated explicitly, seems to be the premise lurking behind our willingness to accept the practice of assigning homework to students on a regular basis—might be summarized as "Most homework is probably good for most kids." I've been arguing, in effect, that even that relatively moderate position is not supported by the evidence. I've been arguing that any possible gains are both minimal and far from universal, limited to certain ages and to certain (dubious) outcome measures. What's more, even studies that seem to show an overall benefit don't prove that more homework—or any homework, for that matter—has such an effect for most students. Put differently, the research offers no reason to believe that students in high-quality classrooms whose teachers give little or no homework would be at a disadvantage as regards any meaningful learning.

But is there some other benefit, something other than academic learning, that might be cited in homework's defense? We turn now to that question.

Discussion Questions

1. Why do you think assigning homework is such a common and traditional practice?

2. Do you think it's parents or teachers who are more interested in children receiving homework? Why would each group be interested in children having homework?

3. What guidelines do you know of that exist for assigning homework? Are those guidelines based on research or merely tradition?

4. What do you believe that homework actually does to assist students in their learning?

5. Should homework be merely an extension of material covered during the day or should assignments add to content or encourage elaboration on information learned during the day?

6. After reading this article, what evidence exists in support of homework? What evidence dispels the notion that homework is beneficial?

7. Should homework be graded?

8. Is there any way to accurately determine that homework improves learning? Grades? Standardized test scores?

9. Does research support the idea that homework is better for high school students than for elementary students? Explain.

10. Describe your philosophy of homework and how you plan to implement it in your class.

Dealing With Feelings

Intervention Strategy A

By Meryl Englander

Reacting to Emotional Outbursts

The children came rushing into the room with the ring of the morning bell. It was a beautiful day and Ms. Austin was refreshed and anticipated a productive day. The second graders quickly quieted and Ms. Austin was about to announce the first activity when she noticed that Jose was curled up under his seat. She hurriedly walked over, feeling a bit piqued at such nonsense. She asked, "What are you doing, Jose?" Jose, choking on his sobs, shouted, "Get away from me! You hate me! My mother hates me! The priest hates me and the police hate me!" With this, Jose burst into loud crying.

Ms. Austin quickly glanced out the window and noted a teacher was on the playground. She said to the class, "I think that we ought to have an early recess today. Go out to the playground and tell Mr. Smith that I asked him to keep an eye on you. Barra, you and Tonya get the kickball and get a game going."

The children excitedly left the room thankful for their unexpected good fortune. Ms. Austin turned to Jose, who was still sobbing under the desk. She knelt down so as to be at his level and said quietly and gently, "Jose, tell me about it." She then waited and in a few minutes Jose began to talk.

There are a number of alternative ways that a teacher might respond to such a situation. He might react punitively to the obviously inappropriate behavior of crawling under one's desk. Or, he may counterattack Jose's impudent command "Get away from me!", or the teacher might sympathetically indicate, "I don't hate you, Jose, and I'm sure the others don't either," or the teacher may simply ignore Jose because this is neither the place, time, nor circumstances for dealing with an upset child. The teacher tasks this morning are to teach reading, writing, and arithmetic. That's what the class objectives and lesson plans call for on this day. Ms. Austin was not trained for psychological therapy. Furthermore, if left alone, Jose will certainly recover. In a matter of minutes he probably will be back in his seat and they can go on as if this unfortunate incident had never happened.

Roadblocks to Communication

To be more explicit we can identify at least 12 ways that Ms. Austin may respond:

1. Ordering. "Stop that nonsense. Sit up in your seat like you are supposed to."

2. Warning. "If you stay under your seat crying you'll not get your work done. Then you will have to stay in during recess.

3. Moralizing. "Big boys don't cry every time something doesn't go their way. You have to accept whatever happened, stick out your chin and be tough."

4. Advising. "Now dry your tears, sit up straight and start work. Things will look better after you do your work."

5. Teaching. "Well, crying won't solve your problem. Let's look at the facts. Priests and policemen are trained to help people."

6. Labeling. "Jose, you are just acting like a baby."

7. Criticizing. "You ought not to say that about your mother. Besides, you look silly all scrunched down there under your seat. You'll get all dirty."

8. Interpreting. "Oh, you just got out of bed on the wrong side. No matter what happens on some days everything looks bad."

9. Praising. "Why, Jose, you are such a fine boy. No one could hate you. You are one of the nicest children in class."

10. Reassuring. "Jose, I don't hate you and I am sure that the others don't either. Dry your tears and smile, everything will turn out all right."

11. Questioning. "Why do you say that? What happened? Did you do something bad? Did your mother say something that upset you?"

12. Diverting. "Oh, let's talk about something pleasant. It is too beautiful a morning to be sad. It is so nice today we are going to read a funny story about a boy who found a dog. You can be first reader."

These are logical, common alternatives. In fact, Gordon (1974) points out that such statements are offered by 90 to 95 percent of the teachers when confronted with troubled students. He calls them roadblocks to communication. Although they fit many of our conceptions of the role of the teacher or a kindly adult, they are roadblocks because when used they deflect communication from the real issue.

Furthermore, roadblocks are belittling. As you reread them you will note that each in some way denies Jose the right to have feelngs, to express his feelings, and to direct his own life. You have no trouble sensing that some of the alternatives are bad: ordering, threatening, humoring, criticizing, labeling. However, there are others that seem right. One would think that either praise or reassurance would always have positive helpful effects. Likewise, it is logical that if we are going to help we need the facts, so what is wrong with questioning? Finally, as educated adults isn't it our task to advise, teach, be logical and solve student problems? Let's look more closely at the nature of praise, questions, and advice.

Praise

Praise has a better reputation than it deserves. As Farson (1966) points out, praise is believed to induce motivation, improve personal relations, reassure people of their worth, free people to be creative, and open up communication. In fact, however, praise tends to threaten people, separate the participants, differentiate the one who praises as superior, and terminate ongoing communication. Perhaps because people have been "had" by praise so many times it can easily come across as phony and manipulative.

Before considering support for the above contentions let us make certain that we have a common notion of the meaning of the concept, praise. Farson (1966) defined praise as a verbal statement that makes a positive evaluation of an object, event, or person, but otherwise contains little supplementary information. For example, statements like "You are a good boy," or "I like you," or "Excellent paper," fit this definition. Differentiate that from responses like "Good, good! You kept your eye on the ball," or "Okay, that's right, you multiply both sides of the equation by equal values, great!" or "That is better, you quietly formed the line without pushing each other—I appreciate that." These latter responses refer to explicit behaviors, events, or products. They can be used as productive feedback which will be discussed in Chapter 8, under "Selective Reinforcement." Describing a behavior, event, or product with an honest indication of support in contrast to global person-oriented compliments has positive effects.

Does praise backfire? For evidence that it does, observe someone who has been praised or reflect on occasions when you have been praised and you will note something peculiar. The reaction is negative. These are symptoms of anger. The recipient of praise not only becomes uncomfortable but often becomes defensive, denies the value of his contribution and derogates himself: "Aw, it really isn't a big deal." "I was just lucky." or "You are just saying that."

Why the defensiveness? Perhaps we learned at an early age not to trust praise. For example, a colleague was having breakfast one Sunday morning with his wife and five-year-old daughter. The mother said, "How sweet you look, Sherrie." Sherrie clouded up and after a moment hesitantly asked, "But?" Not understanding the mother inquired, "But—what?" Sherrie retorted, "But what? When you say something nice you always say but, and then say something bad."

Another reason for resenting praise is that in accepting praise one takes on the responsibility of being praiseworthy. If one accepts at face value "You are very good at arithmetic," one then has a status that must be carefully maintained. Being

"very good at arithmetic" has no boundaries. An error becomes a betrayal of that status. Thus, one is constricted by the praise. Once praised the individual is at risk; errors betray one's praiseworthiness.

In addition, when one is praised it is apparent that he has been evaluated. Most of us don't relish the idea of being judged and graded. It is particularly bad because if for some unknown reason later performances are not praised it leaves open the question of why. Was this latter performance not up to par, not praiseworthy? This has a double bind because we then feel we have to please someone else. It is, thus, potentially degrading, particularly if we find ourselves fishing for praise.

When one person praises another the process implies a hierarchy. For example, when one says, "That is a very good painting" and the artist graciously responds, "Thank you," the implication is that the former is superior, one capable of making a judgment on the artist's work. It implies that the painting isn't good until the critic says it is.

Questions

Doesn't the teacher need to ask questions to get the needed information if she is going to help students? In the case of behavioral problems and in particular with feelings the answer is, No! Our task is to help the student deal with his feelings and his perceptions of the factors behind the feelings.

Questions tend to work at cross purposes with these ends in a number of ways.

First and foremost, questions put the responsibility and control at the wrong place, in the hands of the teacher. If the teacher asks a question and the student replies, he then waits for the next question. Out of this develops undesirable expectations: the teacher is collecting information and when she has it all put together she will provide a solution. Since the teacher is asking the questions and thereby controlling the nature and direction of the communication it becomes the teacher's problem. Thus, questioning leads to dependency and a passing of the problem from the student to the teacher. These are undesirable consequences. We want students to learn to own their feelings and problems and to be responsible for seeking solutions. We can accept student feelings and give support, but we need to take care not to take over student rights and obligations.

Questions tend to work toward closure. Almost by definition questions dictate the topics and the nature of the answers. This restricts the student's input and the range of issues to be considered. Contrariwise, dealing with feelings ought to be an opening up, an awareness of feelings and their antecedents.

When one asks questions it is from his own perspective. The questions seek information that the questioner senses is relevant. In many instances the probes go in the wrong directions, focusing on irrelevant issues while bypassing critical information.

Finally, the exploration of feelings and their antecedents is a rather fragile process. Probing and questioning may touch on sensitive areas that the student is not ready to open up. Questions tend to invade privacy. Thus, instead of helping we may frighten or anger the student, causing her to clam up, become defensive, feign indifference, or deepen the feeling. Questioning is too crude an instrument to use when helping someone sort out feelings.

To sum up, when dealing with feelings the fewer the number of questions the better.

Advice

As teachers, we have a strong propensity to be logical and to impart knowledge and advice. To some extent this is our task in the cognitive domain. However, in the affective domain where we are dealing with personal matters and trying to help students clarify feelings, it is out of place.

First, when one gives someone else information or advice, the implication is that the adviser is knowledgeable, that the recipient is not. In reality that which a teacher can give a student about appropriate behavior, values, and feelings is most often already known. When a teacher tells a student what she already knows, defensiveness and hostility are aroused. The student stops listening because she feels put down. At best, the teacher's views are discarded because "he doesn't understand." The generation gap is nowhere as visible as it is when the issue is behavior and feelings and the elder says, "If I were you I would …" We are not the other person and in no way should we impose our solutions on their problems.

Finally, the solution, ideas, or interpretation may be good but not right for the issue at hand. In the teacher's eagerness to resolve the situation, to explain to students what ought to be, he may easily overlook pertinent aspects of the situation. Thus, the advice, admonishments, or information may be right for some situations but erroneous from the perspective of the student.

Roadblocks in Action

In order to obtain a better perspective let's take a look at another episode. This situation occurred in a secondary school:

Cry for Help

It was some time after school and most of the students and teachers had already left for the day. However, it was not unusual for a few students to be around for special projects or individual conferences with teachers. Therefore, when

Mr. Gentle walked out of the office and started toward his room it didn't seem too unusual that Jill should come up and start to walk along. As they walked Mr. Gentle made several perfunctory remarks about the end of the day and the weather and noted to himself that Jill seemed to be jittery. All at once Jill burst out, "Mr. Gentle, I'm worried about drugs." Mr. Gentle stopped, looked quizzically at Jill and remarked, "I don't know what you mean." Jill, who was upset but in control of herself, barely squeaked out, "Well, you know—uh, sometimes me and my friends smoke a little marijuana—sometimes for kicks."

"Um humm."

"Well … ah … mm … well a friend of mine, um … her dad is a doctor and she works for him in his office and ah … he umm … he has some drugs there and my friend well she ah … she gets some drugs and she uh or aaa … we take them to see what would happen and aa … Mr. Gentle, I think that I am hooked … that is all I think about." (This last bit comes in a rush with some overtones of panic.)

Suppose that Mr. Gentle had responded in one of the following ways when the first mention of drugs was made:

Mr. G.: That is against the law you know. You kids keep that up and you will have serious trouble. The police are bound to pick you up and then your parents will be very embarrassed. (warning)
Mr. G: You ought not do that. It's bad for your health, but more important it leads to other things—bad company. You might become addicted to heroin or something. Drugs are bad business. (moralizing)

Mr. G: Oh, I can't believe that. You are such a fine girl. Why Jill, you are one of the smartest students I have. You are beautiful and have such a bright future ahead. (praise)

Do you think that such comments would have diverted Jill and her friends from using marijuana? Do you think that if Mr. Gentle had responded as above that Jill would have openly continued with what was really bothering her, with the disclosure of the more serious problem? Is it likely that Jill, and her friends, would continue to confide in Mr. Gentle? Would they feel that he was trying to understand them, to be someone they could trust?

At this point the task is to provide an accepting, open atmosphere to allow and encourage Jill to tell what was on her mind. She is upset. The first thing she needs to do is to share these feelings, to get them out so she can look at them, deal with them. This occurs best under conditions under which she can share feelings with someone she can trust.

Let us assume that Mr. Gentle did respond as indicated in the original scene, that is, "Um-humm," which is just an indication that "I'm listening." Jill, as we noted, then exposed the more serious problem. The question remains—what kind of response might Mr. Gentle now give to help Jill? Before going on to some alternatives not yet discussed, let's continue to inspect the possible effects of Gordon's list of communication roadblocks.

Mr. G: I think that things will be all right. You probably haven't had enough to become addicted. You think about it all of the time because you feel guilty or perhaps that it is exciting. Now, just stop doing it and I'm sure that everything will be okay. (reassurance)

Mr. G: I can't imagine a doctor not keeping better track of his drugs. How does she get away with it? What is your friend's name? What drugs are you using? Are you hallucinating? What other symptoms do you have? (questioning and probing)

Mr. G: I'm glad that you brought this to me. First thing is to stop doing it. If necessary stop seeing your friend. The longer you wait, the worse it becomes. After you stop, if you have any symptoms no matter what time, day or night, call me. Meanwhile I'll try to find out some information. (teaching, advising)

These latter communication alternatives may relieve the anxiety that Jill is feeling about the drugs, but at best she has simply transferred her problem over to Mr. Gentle. With all of his wisdom he has assured Jill that all will be okay. His questioning and suggested remedies carry the implication that now that Mr. Gentle is on the scene, everything is going to be all right. She may feel better, and if he has a strong need to nurture and protect others he may feel some satisfaction. However, a disservice has been performed. The good feelings will be short-lived. Jill has given up her right to control and influence her own life. In accepting Mr. Gentle's reassurance she has subjected herself to a subordinate role and will remain a child. Finally, the probabilities are high that she will continue with the kind of behavior that created the original problem. She has not learned much except that Mr. Gentle is a nice person, someone whom you can go to if you have a problem. If it goes this way, Jill will have a nagging feeling that she is a helpless little girl, quite different from the adult she aspires to be. The feeling of anxiety of an unfulfilled self will return. Unfortunately, such conditions are more

likely to result in an increase of drug use, contrary to our wishes.

Mr. Gentle's feeling of gratification for having helped someone in need may also deteriorate as he contemplates the problem for which he is now responsible. Will Jill and her friends kick their interest in drugs? Might they overdose? Should he contact the doctor or the police and protect himself and perhaps save the lives of the youngsters at the risk of betraying their trust? To become involved in other people's problems can be risky. However, the risks can be minimized and the help maximized if the intervention is accomplished with care.

The Resolution of Personal Problems

Since emotions are allegedly aroused by self-concept difficulties, they signify a problem for the individual. That is, a personal problem exists for an individual when his concept of self is jeopardized by perceived events. When the problem is resolved the emotional state will return to normal. If we can help the student solve the problem then the emotional effects will dissolve. The discussion of communication roadblocks suggests that the logical means of sympathy, advising or telling, will not achieve the desired end. Fortunately, alternatives that have proven helpful are available. The alternative strategies will become apparent as we study the nature of problems, the importance of problem ownership, and interpersonal relationships that facilitate problem solving.

The Nature of Problems

Guba and Lincoln (1981) define a problem as a discrepancy between what a person wants and what she has. A problem is manifested by the statement, "I want ..., but the conditions are such that ..." When the desires refer to those qualities on which self-esteem is based (competence, control, acceptance, and virtuousness) the individual's integrity is threatened and she develops an emotional reaction.

The process of solving personal problems is a multiple-phase process. The first step is for the individual to become aware of her feelings and the reason for the feelings. Feelings are a signal that something is wrong—there is a problem. The second step is to develop from this awareness of feelings and their causes an indication of what conditions exist and what is wanted. Third, it is necessary to identify what one can do to get what is wanted. The fourth step is to put the course of action in behavioral terms so that it can be explicitly identified.

In order to put the problem-solving sequence in perspective let's consider a simple situation. A student blurts out the following comment: "I feel terrible; I have to leave this school and my friends and go to Chicago. My dad's got a new job and my ma says we gotta move." Our task is not to comfort him but to help him solve his problem and in so doing help him develop the confidence and skills to control his own life by solving his own problems. If we are going to help this student our first task is to assist him in clarifying his feelings. He may be sorrowful about leaving his friends or the comfort of the school, he may be worried about making new friends, he may be fearful of his physical safety in a city, or he may be angry at his parents for changing residence without consulting him. When the feelings are clarified so that he knows what he is feeling and why then we can address desires. Let's assume that through discussing the issue with you he concludes that he is sad because he anticipates that he will be isolated and friendless in his new residence. Only with this recognition can he now specify what he wants, the kind of friends and activities that he values. Once he knows what he wants he can draw on his experiences to identify some strategies for making friends. Finally, he can specify some

places where he will go, and what he might say and do in order to become involved with a new group. As simple as this process is, without experience and help from others, people do not use it.

Unfortunately, most people impulsively act out their emotions. As we noted in Chapter 3 when discussing the conflict cycle, such acting out is often disconcerting to other people and they in turn respond negatively. Acting out short-circuits the logical resolution of personal problems. The process of helping students is to initially focus on their immediate feelings, and as these dissolve, the identification of wishes and actions is more reasonable. Before moving on to the necessary communication skills to achieve these ends, however, the issue of problem ownership must be resolved.

Problem Ownership

Gordon (1974) points out significantly that problem ownership is a critical factor in the helping relationship. Although an individual may suggest or obtain help from others, people should resolve their own problems. In order to clarify ownership let's look at these problem statements:

1. I want students to do their own work, but people are copying answers from others. I become angry when I see cheating.
2. I want to play kickball but the other kids never choose me.
3. It is important that everyone scores well on the achievement tests, but the parents in this district won't give any support at home.
4. I want my daughter to be qualified for college, but you teachers don't make any academic demands on the student.
5. The parents don't care if the kids learn or not.

Number 1 is a teacher problem. Number 2 belongs to the student, but number 3 is an administrative problem. The fourth problem belongs to a parent. Item number 5 isn't a problem because what is wanted from the parents is not stipulated; it is just a statement of a perceived condition.

A rule of thumb suggests the following: A person owns a problem when some condition exists contrary to what is wanted by that person, and the discrepancy arouses feelings. Problem ownership is important because the owner should be the one who stipulates the feeling and what is wanted, and selects the action to be taken to resolve the problem. There are several reasons for this point. First, people tend to resist accepting someone else's solution for their problems. Second, an individual ought not be held responsible for consequences of actions dictated by someone else. Third, if others repeatedly solve a youngster's problems, then she never learns the process of analyzing feelings and wants, and thence planning appropriate action. Learning to solve problems takes practice. Finally, if one person solves another's problems a dependency is developed. Such a dependency inhibits maturity and fosters an undesirable relationship.

To resist the temptation to solve someone else's problems takes self-control. We have powerful motives to advise, moralize, and share our wisdom. Students who are upset come looking for someone to take over. People caught in the web of a problem often seek comfort. Beware of communication roadblocks. The goal of education is maturity and independence. Teachers can facilitate such development through helping relationships.

The Generation Gap

When asked to discuss their relationships with adults, students offer three criticisms:

1. Adults don't listen to us so they don't know what we want and feel. They don't identify our point of view.

2. Adults don't respect our judgment. They don't think our ideas are of any value.

3. Adults are phony. They pretend we are the important ones but it is just a game because in the end they want it their way. They have double standards; one for them and a different one for us.

Much of student behavior is retaliation based on these beliefs.

If we expect students to mature and act responsibly then we must eradicate these criticisms by altering the nature of the relationships on which they are based. The way we respond to their concerns is important to this end.

The Helping Relationship

What kind of teacher is most helpful? It is fair to assume that it is not the teacher who controls by manipulating others through harassment, giving false praise, moralizing, threatening, or even giving advice. It is not the teacher who is judgmental, cajoling, sarcastic, stereotyping, or who knows best what is to be done. Likewise, it is more than just being a nice person. Tender loving care by itself is equally detrimental to development.

Gazda et al. (1984) describe a number of conditions and offer exercises for developing skills critical for helping students deal with their feelings and resolve personal problems. These conditions of positive communication were identified and tested in numerous observations of counselors and teachers as they interacted with students. The five selected conditions by which one can help others to deal with their feelings and resolve problems are warmth, confirmation, empathy, respect, and genuineness.

Experience suggests that you will develop the needed skills for arranging these conditions most readily if you become knowledgeable of their respective characteristics, observe models as they work with students, experience the give and take of such communication through role playing, and receive feedback regarding your own communication with students. Every teacher who wishes to honestly and humanistically interact with students should develop these skills.

The characteristics of the selected five conditions will be presented here. Although the conditions will be described separately, when in operation they blend together and are integrated into a natural relationship. Just as the fundamentals of a proper golf swing seem awkward in the beginning, so too will some of these ways of communicating with a troubled student.

Warmth. Warmth and caring are more easily appreciated and discerned than defined. However, it does embody concern, nonjudgmental acceptance, openness, and reaching out. Warmth is established primarily through such physical moves as gestures, posture, tone of voice, and facial expression. A warm person is affective, responsive, and communicates caring. Warmth is contrasted to indifference, glad-handed salesmanship, disapproval, and sympathy. On a continuum the end points may be summed up thus:

Responses that Reflect Warmth: Degrees of Caring

Coldness or indifference	Warmth
Gestures and facial expression are omitted or coldness is exhibited by frowns, turning and leaning away. Stiff posture or standing over a student communicates rigid authoritarianism.	Undivided attention exhibited by a relaxed approaching straight ahead posture. Avoid staring, but face to face eye contact facilitates communication. Tender physical touching may be helpful, depending on individuality and emotional situations (e.g., never touch an angry person).

Practice with someone on such situations as the following. Concentrate on generating warmth and caring through physical nonverbal behavior.

Student: I hope that I am in your class next year, you are so nice.

Student who has low grades: I am going to drop out of school when I'm sixteen, join the armed service and get an education there. Then maybe I'll come out and go to college and be a doctor or something.

Student: I hate this school and everybody in it.

A fellow teacher: I'm not going to put up with these brats any longer! They act like animals.

Student: I try and try but I always get bad grades. I'm just dumb or something.

Confirmation. Communication often goes astray because the meaning of the message as intended by the speaker was not the same or even close to the one interpreted by the listener. We have a very complex language in which many words have multiple meanings. In addition, a simple word can change the whole meaning of an expression. Confirmation is simply paraphrasing or in some other way making certain that both the speaker and listener are agreed as to the meaning of the message.

Particularly in disagreements, people tend to concentrate more on what they are going to say than on what the other person is saying. Thus, when feelings are involved there often is an important difference between what one person thinks he said and the other thinks he heard. Disagreements can often be solved if that difference is dissipated through confirmation. If you strive to confirm the other person's message, it will help you as a listener and communicate to others that you are trying to understand.

Confirmation is not repeating verbatim everything the other person says. It is more like an occasional, "As I understand your point, it is …" or

"Let's see if I can summarize what you are saying"; or an interpretation, "Is it fair to say that you want …?" Confirmation is a form of paraphrasing that should be less frequent that the speaker's statements. It is noticeably more critical during the beginning and closing phases of a dialogue than during the time that the subject details are being discussed.

See if you can paraphrase and thereby confirm that you understand each of the following:

Student: This school isn't as good as where I went last year. The kids here aren't friendly. I used to have a lot of friends.

Student: Marijuana don't hurt you none. It's no worse then all of the smokin' and drinkin' that grown-ups do. My dad and his friends drink all the time and it don't hurt 'em.

Parent: My daughter needs more discipline. I've just thrown up my hands. We can't do anything with her. It is up to you to make her behave at school. It's your problem. You have my permission to spank her. She just won't listen to me.

Principal: You teachers don't understand the position you put me in. If you foul up, the parents call me. If someone's child is delayed in arriving home, the mother calls me. By that time most of the teachers have left. If you are going to keep a student after school you have to let me know.

Empathy. Empathy is a two-step process. First, it involves an awareness or sensitivity to the other person's feelings. Second, it includes a tentative communication to the other person of this awareness. Empathy is a difficult but critical tool for communication and problem resolution. Gazda et al. (1984) indicate it as the key condition for developing helpful communication. More than anything else empathy tunes into and thereby helps clarify and relieve the emotional stress felt by others. The continuum of empathy may be characterized by these end points.

Responses that Reflect Empathy: Identifying and Indicating Perceived Feelings

Unempathetic	Empathetic
Judging or criticizing a person without in any way acknowledging even surface feelings. Shifting topic away from that behind the other's feelings. Condemning a person for his feelings (e.g., "You shouldn't be angry just because …)"	Being aware of nonverbal facial and other cues that indicate emotion. Accurately indicating surface feelings expressed by other person. Tentatively identify inferred feelings underlying behavior.

The task of identifying someone's feelings is not as easy as we might suspect. People seem to learn at a relatively young age to cover over their feelings. By the time students reach high school age, as little as 10 percent of their true feelings are expressed in words. Thus, we need to look for nonverbal cues and contextual information as a basis for inferring feelings and then be tentative in indicating what we perceive. Despite people's learned tendency to cover up feelings they respond positively and are more clear headed when someone helps in a supporting way to clarify the felt emotions. The pain of emotion is eased and people are then better able to resolve the underlying problems if another person supportively listens and indicates an awareness of the feeling. Empathetic listening releases the energy of emotion and thereby enables troubled people to get at the I want and I will do aspects of problem solving.

Several examples are presented here to help clarify the properties and processes of empathy. No one, except perhaps the person experiencing the emotion, can indicate with certainty the true feelings, causes, and desires. Therefore, there are no right or wrong answers per se. You are encouraged to compare your own responses to these situations with those given here and with those of others who are reading this material.

Empathy Exercises

In this exercise a situation will be established that ends with a student statement. Illustrative inferences are given regarding the student's feelings, and the basis for the feeling followed by an empathetic statement designed to help the student clarify the feelings.

The teacher has just said to Jon, a second-grader who is a very poor reader: "If you don't pay closer attention you will never learn to read."

Jon replies, "I don't care. I don't care if I never learn to read. It makes no difference to me."

a. Inferred feeling: Discouragement.

b. Inferred reason: Repeated failure.

c. Empathetic statement: "You feel pretty discouraged because you don't read well."

The teacher walked into the room and noted its general messy appearance, particularly the litter on the floor. He turned to Oscar, one of about a dozen students present, and said: "Oscar, you and some of the other students pick up the paper and leaves off the floor."

Oscar replied: "I ain't going to do no menial work. That is beneath me."

a. Inferred feelings: Humiliation.

b. Inferred reason: Requested behavior incongruent with perceived status.

c. Empathetic statement; "You feel put down because you think that a boy your age shouldn't have to clean up the floor."

Kris came to the teacher during recess and whined, "Nobody likes me. They call me names and never let me play."

a. Inferred feelings: Loneliness.

b. Inferred reason: Rejection by peers.

c. Empathetic response: "You feel hurt because it seems like the other children don't like you."

In this episode the student had skipped chemistry a total of 60 times out of 76 class meetings. He was given a grade of C. The student's response: "Damn that teacher, she gave me a C! She thinks so little of me that she gave me a C!

a. Inferred feeling: Anger

b. Inferred reason: I should have failed the class. She insulted me by giving me an undeserved C grade.

c. Empathetic response: "It is painful to be passed on, no matter what you do."

Respect. To some extent respect is a measure of trust, but more explicitly, respect embodies believing in the other person's abilities, rights, and responsibility to manage her own affairs. Respect is an attitude that communicates: "I'm here to help you, I care what happens to you but I believe that you are fully capable of controlling your own life." Notice that this use of the term respect is contrary to the notion of respect as fear. One cannot demand respect out of power. It is something given to another person as a belief in her ability and responsibility to act correctly on her own behalf. When a teacher says "I respect you," the meaning is synonymous with "I believe in your integrity, willingness, ability, and desire to properly govern your own life. You are worthy and have the potential to do whatever is necessary." Generally speaking, people do not get into difficulties beyond their capabilities of working out solutions and alternative behaviors.

**Responses that Reflect Respect:
Trusting Others to Care for Themselves**

Low respect	High respect
Responder attempts to impose his own values and solutions to student problems. Teacher focuses attention on himself as a model. Teacher dominates conversation by asking questions and giving advice. Teacher ignores or challenges the accuracy of the student's perceptions of the situation.	Being open and supportive to student's ideas. Teacher encourages student to act in his own behalf. Teacher is nonevaluative of student or his behavior and the apparent consequences. Teacher strives not to make prediction with a tone of certainty or superiority.

The following examples are designed to clarify the meaning of respect. As in the case with the empathy examples the situation is established by a student remark. High- and low-respect responses will be given for your consideration. Once more, you are encouraged to discuss these examples and responses with others.

Amy: I'm so mad at my parents. They never listen to me or let me do what I want. I think that I'm going to run away.

High-respect response: You must be finding things pretty tough at home. Would you like to explore some alternatives open to you?

Low-respect response: Oh, the worst thing you can do is run away. Terrible things happen to runaways.

Shawn: The principal says that I gotta apologize to Mr. Brown. I called him a bitch because that is what he is. Besides he did me wrong by saying I'm lazy. He owes me an apology. I shouldn't have to apologize to him.

High-respect response: This sounds like a difficult situation. How do you think that you can best handle it at this point?

Low-respect response: You won't get very far in life if you are disrespectful to your superiors.

Brad: I should be going to high school next year. I'm a year behind just because I had a no-account first grade teacher and I had to take it over. I don't see why I can't go to high school like I'm supposed to.

High-respect response: I think that I understand your view. Let's see if we can develop a plan to help you get what you want.

Low-respect response: Well, look at the bright side of it. You'll be a year older than others in your class and that will give you an advantage.

Ann: I want to be in the best reading group. My mom said that I'm a good reader. My best friend, Kristi, is in that group. So, that is where I should be.

High-respect response: You would like to be in Kristi's reading group. Tell me more about why you would rather be in that group than the one you are in. Then we will look at their materials and see if that would help you be a good reader.

Low-respect response: I started school in the low reading group but because I worked real hard I soon was promoted to the top group. It just takes hard work.

Genuineness. Genuineness involves risk taking, an openness that perhaps is best summed up by the term honesty. Thinking has to do with cognition, feelings with values and emotions. To be genuine is to share your feelings, your position. Genuineness has to do with owning and exposing one's own biases, views, and feelings but not imposing them on others.

With respect to discipline problems and interpersonal disagreements the genuine teacher approaches the situation in search of causative factors rather than blame. The focus is toward describing situations rather than the evaluation of student behavior in terms of teacher criteria. Genuineness is the antithesis of pretending. Pretending is saying and doing things because they are proper rather than the way one feels. Genuineness is also the antithesis of using role and status as a defense for behavior (e.g., "I didn't want to do it but since I'm a teacher I had no choice."). When students accuse adults of being phony the essence is that the adults are not perceived as being genuine.

Responses that Reflect Genuineness:

Low genuineness	High genuineness
Hiding one's feelings or using them to hurt others. Phoniness and facade. Responding according to preconceived role in contrast to one's own feelings.	Expression of feelings used to facilitate a positive relationship and to clarify student's goals and feelings.

The following examples are designed to enable you to become more familiar with the nature of genuineness. As before, each episode will be established by a student comment.

Sara: I hate you! I hate you with a passion!

High-genuineness response: I'm sorry to hear you say that. Frankly, it bothers me if students don't like me.

Low-genuineness response: I don't like you either. Unfortunately for you, I'm the teacher and you do as I say or you are in trouble.

Carla: I know that I am supposed to be ready to work. But I always forget my material. Gee, I have a lot of other things I have to do. I'm sorry. I just forgot.

High-genuineness response: You have a lot on your mind but you should know that I'm finding it very difficult to be patient.

Low-genuineness response: You are just making excuses. If you do that once more you will lose one full grade. We'll see if that helps your memory.

Parent: How come my child got a C on his report card? He will never get into a college with C grades. You just gave him a C because you don't like him.

High-genuineness response: I resent the charge that I grade on personal feelings. Let's look at the evidence from Charlie's work.

Low-genuineness response: I don't give low grades, students earn low grades on their own. I would give every student an A if I could.

Student confronted with evidence of cheating: Everybody in this class cheats. Your tests are unfair. If you were a better teacher we wouldn't have to cheat.

High-genuineness response: Don't lay your behavior on me. If the tests and teaching are unfair, I want to correct them, so we'll discuss them in class. Meanwhile, you are responsible for your own misbehavior.

Low-genuineness response: You impudent scoundrel. How dare you accuse me of being unfair.

Summary: A New Role for the Teacher

We have said that feelings and emotions are a product of an incongruency between the self-concept and a situation as experienced by the individual. This set of circumstances constitutes a personal problem for the individual.

A personal problem is a state of affairs in which an individual is confronted with significant evidence that she is different from what she supposed herself to be in terms of competence, control over herself and others, acceptance by others, or her own value system. The discrepancy may become apparent as a result of a message from another person, a reflection of one's own behavior, or some objective information like a test score. Whatever the source of information, if it is significantly at odds with some important aspect of the self-concept, an emotion or feeling will be aroused and the individual will be moved to act.

Discussion Questions

1. What are some comments you've heard from authority figures in your lifetime that demonstrate their inability to listen to your needs?

2. Describe three situations you've experienced in your past as a child or as an adult that match some of the twelve roadblocks mentioned by Englander.

3. Why are the roadblocks so commonly used by adults?

4. Why is praise so commonly used by teachers? What are the dangers of using praise?

5. Why is questioning children a poor listening strategy?

6. How can we encourage children to take greater ownership of their difficulties and problems?

7. How have you seen adults handle the *generation gap* successfully?

8. Describe empathetic responses that you have heard.

9. What are some alternatives to using roadblocks when children speak to you?

Section Three

Punishment and the Alternatives to Encourage Change in Behavior

Introduction

Punishment and the Alternatives to Encourage Change in Behavior

By Dave F. Brown

Punishment has a long tradition in the United States. Unfortunately, punitive behaviors have the opposite effect on students—more disruptive actions—rather than what teachers expect to obtain as a result of punishing children—cooperative behavior. Many teachers falsely believe that they control their students. Nothing could be further from the truth! Teachers don't make students do anything—children must unilaterally agree to be cooperative. Children cooperate with teachers because they take upon themselves to act appropriately. Children are much more likely to act cooperatively when teachers encourage students to internalize behaviors, teach appropriate strategies for dealing with frustration, and provide alternative coping behaviors.

An essential aspect of developing healthy relationships is encouraging and guiding children to take responsibility for their behaviors. To accomplish this result, the authors in this third section offer suggestions for

- identifying the history behind and inaccurate rationale for using punishment;

- understanding that alternatives to traditional punishment exist;
- clarifying the definitions of consequences and punishment;
- understanding internalization and strategies for encouraging its development;
- comprehending the connections between reward and punishment;
- developing classroom-management strategies that encourage cooperation; and
- identifying alternatives to punishment that encourage students to change behaviors.

Breaking the traditional punitive culture of schools requires a sound rationale as well as a reasonable set of strategies for encouraging children to change their behavior through alternative means. The articles in this section will aid teachers in helping students develop an internal locus of control that places more responsibility for cooperative behavior and self-monitoring on students—where it ultimately belongs.

Bribes and Threats

By Alfie Kohn

If you punish a child for being naughty, and reward him for being good, he will do right merely for the sake of the reward; and when he goes out into the world and finds that goodness is not always rewarded, nor wickedness always punished, he will grow into a man who only thinks about how he may get on in the world, and does right or wrong according as he finds either of advantage to himself.

—Immanuel Kant, *Education*

Once we have reassured ourselves that virtually all problems in a classroom are the fault of the students, and once we have decided that our role is mostly to "manage" their behavior until it becomes acceptable to us, there are remarkably few practical options available. The cards to be played, so to speak, have already been dealt. That is why the methods outlined in discipline programs typically amount to variations on two or three basic themes. These themes, moreover, are just as pervasive in classrooms where the teacher has never read a book or attended a workshop on classroom management; the formal programs just refine and systematize the application of these same interventions.

Coercion

The most basic way to get what you want from someone, assuming you have more power than he does, is just to make him do it.

Technique number one, then, is straightforward coercion: without regard to motive or context, past events or future implications, the adult simply forces the child to act (or stop acting) in a certain way.

- Problem: Chris and Pat, who are sitting next to each other, are making an unusual amount of noise. Maybe one is annoying the other, or maybe the two are simply talking together, oblivious to everything else going on in the room. Solution: The teacher points to one of the students and then to a distant chair. "Chris, sit over there."[1]

• Problem: Petrified clumps of chewing gum are appearing under tables and desktops throughout the school. Solution: Ban the stuff. The adult in charge simply decrees that there will be no more gum chewing in school.

• Problem: Kids are coming to school in outrageous clothes, offensive to certain adults or perhaps just so expensive as to suggest that an elaborate status contest is underway. Solution: Tell students what they may and may not wear (dress code), or compel them all to wear the same thing (uniforms).

To make, sense of this technique, and the ones that follow, it may help to consider the following framework. As educators, our responses to things we find disturbing, our approach to both academic and nonacademic matters, might be described as reflecting a philosophy of either doing things to students or working with them. As with any dichotomy, there are limits to this classification scheme. But I believe it is a useful exercise to take any of our policies and try to decide whether it more nearly resembles "doing to" or "working with." (Alternatively, one could start with these concepts and then try to think of real practices that exemplify them.)

In any case, simple coercion is the purest illustration of "doing to." The students in each of these examples are treated as objects rather than

subjects. Adults decide unilaterally when there is a problem and what is to be done about it.

And the effect? Consider Chris and Pat. When the teacher separates them, does either student come away with any understanding of, or concern about, how his or her actions may affect other people in the room? Have the two learned how to negotiate a solution, attend to social cues, or make the best of sitting next to someone who is not a friend? Hardly. But they, like the other students watching, have learned one important lesson from this intervention. That lesson is power: when you have it (as the teacher does, at the moment), you can compel other people to do whatever you want.

The Meaning of Punishment

The second major disciplinary technique is punishment, which is easy to confuse with coercion. Two features, however, have to be present for an intervention to qualify as a punishment: it must be deliberately chosen to be unpleasant, such as by forcing the student to do something he would rather not do or preventing him from doing something he wants to do; and it must be intended to change the student's future behavior. A punishment makes somebody suffer in order to teach a lesson.

Our predilection for euphemism has allowed us to avoid seeing punitive practices for what they are. Thus, we incarcerate students but describe it as "detention." We exile them from the community and refer to it as "suspension." We forcibly isolate small children and call it by the almost Orwellian name "time out." And then there is the most ambitious euphemism of all, which allows adults to punish children in any number of ways but describe what they are doing as merely imposing "logical consequences." (These last two labels are discussed in the next chapter.)

---

[1] Or perhaps, "Chris, you need to sit over there." The invocation of what someone "needs" to do usually has much less to do with that person's needs than with the preferences of the speaker.

The techniques for punishing go on and on. We humiliate students by what we say to them in front of their peers. We send ominous notes home to parents. We withdraw privileges, which sometimes seem to have been dangled in front of students for the express purpose of being snatched away at our pleasure. We remand students to the principal's office, give them bad grades, saddle them with extra work, and even (in some states) resort to physical violence.

These punishments are not equivalent; some of them carry uniquely destructive effects. Corporal punishment, the worst of all, has long ago been renounced by most Western nations. As researchers have documented for decades, using force on children teaches them that aggression is acceptable, to say nothing of its other psychological effects (e.g., Straus 1994, Hyman 1990). Sending a student to the principal's office for punishment, meanwhile, tends to turn the principal into an ogre in the eyes of the students. Giving them additional (or longer) assignments when they have done something wrong sends a powerful message to everyone that learning is aversive, something one would never want to do.

Let's leave aside the specifics, though, and consider punishment as a category. Quite a few writers have cautioned that it does little good to threaten a punishment if the threat isn't credible, or to use one that isn't actually aversive to the recipient. But assume we have punished "properly." When I address a group of educators or parents, I like to dramatically extract an imaginary gun from behind the podium, wave it around, and threaten to shoot anyone who talks during the presentation. I ask whether this threat will keep the room quiet, and of course, there is little doubt about the answer.

So: does punishment work? In this example, everyone finds the prospect of being shot sufficiently disagreeable, my aim is good, and I have been convincing about my willingness to pull the trigger. (I have had a very bad week.) The answer, then, is that punishment can be quite effective indeed—but only to get one thing: temporary compliance.

Reflect for a moment on the limits of such an accomplishment. Punishment generally works only for as long as the punisher is around. But this is not just because it loses effectiveness over time, like a medication. It's because the student is led to focus on avoiding the punishment itself. A child who hears "I don't want to catch you doing that again … or else!" may quite reasonably reply (if only to herself), "Fine. Next time you won't catch me."

Another way to put this is to say that punishment, even at its most successful, can only change someone's behavior. It can't possibly have a positive effect on that person's motives and values, on the person underneath the behavior. The fact that teachers continue to punish the same students over and over suggests that the problem with this strategy runs deeper than the way a particular punishment has been implemented.

The Price of Compliance

Perhaps your response to these arguments is something like the following: "Hey, don't knock temporary compliance. When a student acts intolerably—when other kids are prevented from learning—I'll settle for whatever stops it."

My answer is threefold. First, if you have to keep returning to the same strategy, then it isn't particularly effective, even for a limited goal like stopping a particular behavior. Not long ago, a teacher told me how a colleague of hers had had enough of a student and, as she had so often done throughout the year, told him he was to report to the principal's office. In one of those moments of blistering clarity (for those ready to receive them), the boy turned to the teacher on his way out the door and said quietly, "This has never helped before. Why do you think it's going to help now?"

Second, punishment doesn't just fail to solve problems: it generally makes them worse. Researchers have found, for example, that children who are severely punished at home are more likely than their peers to act out when they are away from home. I have yet to find an educator who is surprised by this finding, which suggests that we have all noticed something similar going on in schools. The problem is that we have trouble acting on this recognition.

Several years ago, I spotted a sign taped to a wall in a 6th grade classroom in Idaho. It read: THE BEATINGS WILL CONTINUE UNTIL MORALE IMPROVES. The good news is that the sign was intended ironically. The bad news is that something similarly illogical underlies any use of punishment, even if the beatings are only figurative and regardless of whether the objective is to enhance morale or to achieve something else. The more you punish someone, the more angry that person becomes, and the more "need" there is to keep punishing. If this is not an example of a vicious circle, then that term, has no meaning.

Finally, and perhaps most significantly, punishment creates a new set of problems, proving worse in many respects than doing nothing at all:

- *It teaches a disturbing lesson.* Like simple coercion, punishment models the use of power—as opposed to reason or cooperation—and this can profoundly affect a child's developing value structure. Specifically, the child learns that when you don't like the way someone is acting, you just make something bad happen to that person until he gives in: Do this or here's what I'm going to do to you. Much of what is disturbing about some children's behavior suggests

that they have learned this lesson all too well—possibly from us.

- *It warps the relationship between the punisher and the punished.* Once an adult has come to be seen as an enforcer of rules and an imposer of unpleasant consequences, the child is about as happy to see that person coming as an adult is to see a police car in the rearview mirror. The caring alliance between adult and child, so vital to the latter's growth, has been significantly compromised.

This fact, by the way, also helps to explain why punishment typically exacerbates exactly what it is meant to improve. To help an impulsive, aggressive, or insensitive student become more responsible, we have to gain some insight into why she is acting that way. That, in turn, is most likely to happen when the student feels close enough to us (and safe enough with us) to explain how things look from her point of view. The more students see us as punishers, the less likely it is that we can create the sort of environment where things can change.

Imagine that Randy sticks out his foot just as Kenny is passing by his desk, causing Kenny to fall on his face. And imagine that the teacher punishes Randy by making him sit all alone in a room while everyone else is off doing something enjoyable. Let's look in on Randy and try to guess what's going through his mind. Maybe, as the teacher who punished him would like to think, he's reflecting on what he did, saying to himself thoughtfully, "Gee, now I understand that hurting people is wrong …."

Right. And maybe next year teachers will be paid as much as professional athletes.

Back in the real world, the chances are that Randy is angry and bitter, feeling picked on unfairly. He's blaming Kenny for his troubles and possibly planning a spectacular revenge at a time and place where he won't get caught. Also, he probably feels resentful of, and alienated from, the teacher who put him there. Don't expect him to come up to that teacher later, feeling a little embarrassed, and say, "I know it wasn't cool to trip him and stuff, and I feel kinda bad, but God, it's like Kenny is your favorite! It's like everything he does, he's Mr. Perfect. And that just makes me really mad, OK?"

Such an explanation doesn't excuse hurting someone, of course, but how can you expect to make any headway with Randy if you don't know that this is how he experiences the classroom?, And how can you expect to know this if your relationship with him has been eroded as a result of defining yourself as a punisher? The point here, again, is that punishment shouldn't be avoided just because it s mean or disrespectful, but also because it makes it harder to solve problems.

- *Punishment actually impedes the process of ethical development.* A child threatened with an aversive consequence for failing to comply with someone's wishes or rules is led to ask, rather mechanically, "What do they want me to do, and what happens to me if I don't do it?"—a question altogether different from "What kind of person do I want to be?" or "What kind of community do we want to create?"

Think about such a shift in the context of this commonly heard defense of punishment:

When children grow up and take their places in society, they're going to realize that there are consequences for their actions! If they rob a bank and get caught, they're going to be put in jail. They'd better learn that lesson right now.

The fatal flaw in this argument is that we want children not to rob banks—or do various other things that are unethical or hurtful—because they know it's wrong, and also because they can imagine how such actions will affect other people. But when disciplinarians talk about imposing "consequences" for a student's action—and inducing him to think about those consequences ahead of time—they almost always mean the consequences to him. The focus is on how he will get in trouble for breaking the rule. This fact, so fundamental that it may have escaped our notice entirely, is a devastating indictment of the whole enterprise. Just as some people try to promote helping or sharing by emphasizing that such behaviors will eventually benefit the actor (see Kohn 1990a), so the reason for the child to behave "appropriately" is the unpleasantness he will suffer if he fails to do so.

By contrast, ethical sophistication consists of some blend of principles and caring, of knowing how one ought to act and being concerned about others. Punishment does absolutely nothing to promote either of these things. In fact, it tends to undermine good values by fostering a preoccupation with self-interest (McCord 1991). "What consequence will I suffer for having done something bad?" is a question that suggests a disturbingly primitive level of moral development, yet it is our use of punishment that causes kids to get stuck there!

You say you're concerned about the real world, where some people do awful things? So am I. In the real world, getting children to focus on what will happen to them if they are caught misbehaving simply is not an effective way to prevent future misbehavior because it does nothing to instill a lasting commitment to better values or an inclination to attend to others' needs. Most people who rob banks assume they won't get caught, in which case there will be no consequences for their action, which means they have a green light to go ahead and rob.

In fact, if an auditorium were filled with bank robbers, wife batterers, and assorted other felons, we would likely find, as Thomas Gordon (1989, p. 215) has remarked, that a significant majority of them were regularly punished as children. They weren't encouraged to focus on how others were affected by what they were doing. They were trained to think about what would happen to them if some more powerful person, for any reason or no reason, didn't like it. In other words, the problem is more likely to be too much discipline than too little, at least as that word is typically used.

Why We Punish

So why do we do it? Why do we continue to rely on punishment if it makes things worse in the classroom (and elsewhere)? Here are some answers that make sense to me, many of which I've heard from educators around the country.

- It's quick and easy. Lots of thought and skill are required to work with students to figure out together how to solve a problem. There's no trick to just making something bad happen to a child who fails to do what you say.

- It obviously works to get temporary compliance, while its relation to the various long-term harms described here is harder to see. Result: it keeps getting used.

- Most of us were raised and taught in environments that were, to some

degree, punitive, and we live what we know. Hence the phenomenon known as "How did my mother (or father or teacher) get in my larynx?" The flip side of this is that many of us don't know what else to do.

- It's expected by various constituencies: administrators, colleagues, and even the students themselves. From parents, we can often count on hearing, "What are you going to do to the kid who did this to my kid?" (This is an invitation for us to ask whether the goal is to get revenge or solve the problem.)

- It makes us feel powerful. A defiant student has issued a challenge that many adults feel obliged to answer by making sure they wind up on top. There's no better way to win the battle—and, indeed, this rationale implicitly assumes the existence of an adversarial encounter—than by using one's power to make the student unhappy. Thus, when that teacher was asked why she thought sending the student to the principal's office yet again was likely to help, the question may have been misconceived: perhaps it wasn't intended to help at all but simply to let that teacher feel triumphant. "I'm on top again; I'm back in control."

- It satisfies a desire for a primitive sort of justice, a rarely articulated but deep-rooted belief (at least, among some people) that if you do something bad, something bad should happen to you—regardless of the long-term practical effects.

• We fear that if students aren't punished, they will think they "got away with" something and will be inclined to do the same thing again—or worse. Apropos of Chapter 1, it's interesting to ponder the hidden beliefs about children, and about human nature, that animate this fear.

• Finally, punishment continues as a result of a false dichotomy—an unnecessary either/or—that is lodged in many of our brains. On the one hand, we can punish; on the other hand, we can do nothing, let it go, give the kid another chance. Thus, until we have made the wrongdoer suffer, we haven't really taken any action. We haven't gotten serious; we've been permissive, or "soft," Any attempt to get to the bottom of the problem by working with the student is therefore just a fancy version of doing nothing.

Once, in a workshop, as I laid out the arguments against punishment, I noticed a middle-aged man, a junior high school guidance counselor, starting to turn red with rage. Finally he could stand it no longer and shouted, "You're telling me if a kid comes up to me in the hall and calls me a son of a bitch, I'm supposed to let it go!"

Now, part of this man's reaction may have come from the need to triumph over the student, to show him who's boss. He might have been afraid that refraining from punishment would leave him feeling that the student had got the better of him. But at bottom I suspect that this counselor had made room in his head for two, and only two, possible responses: punitive action and inaction. If his repertoire was limited to these options, then there was no way other than punishment to communicate that what the student

had said was unacceptable. Thus, not to punish is tantamount to losing one's only mechanism for making a judgment, one's only way of indicating that it's not OK to talk to someone like that. Until this false dichotomy (punishing versus doing nothing) is identified and eradicated, we cannot hope to make any progress in moving beyond punitive tactics.

Any of these reasons, then, might explain why we continue to punish. But none of them proves that it's necessary, much less desirable, to do so. None of them offers any reason to think that punishment is effective at helping students to become caring, responsible members of a community. And none of them changes the fact that the obedience produced by punishment comes at a terrible price.

Rewards

What if, instead of threatening my audience with a gun, I had offered them money for doing something? Suppose I had announced that I wanted everyone in the room to cross his or her legs, and that my assistants were clandestinely scattered throughout the room to monitor their compliance. (This is one of many things that punishments and rewards share: both require surveillance.) Keep your right leg on top of the left one until the session is over and you'll get $2,000, I tell them. Will they do it?

Someone would have to be awfully defiant, or awfully rich, to turn down such an offer. The question, then, is "Do rewards work?" And the answer should sound familiar: Sure! Rewards work very well to get one thing, and that thing is temporary compliance. The third technique of classroom management, alongside coercion and punishment, is dangling rewards in front of students for doing what we demand. Instead of "Do this—or here's what I'm going to do to you," we say, "Do this—and you'll get that." Instead of leading a student to ask herself "What do they want me to do, and what happens to me if I don't do it?" her question becomes "What do they want me to do, and what do I get for doing it?" The latter question, of course, is no closer to the kind of thinking we wpuld like to promote.

"Do this and you'll get that" is at the heart of countless classroom management programs, including some that energetically promote themselves as positive or enlightened. These books can be summarized in four words: Punishments bad, rewards good. Although it is tempting to regard a strategy based on the use of carrots to get compliance as more humanistic than one based on sticks, these two approaches are far more similar than different. They are two sides of the same coin—and the coin doesn't buy very much.

Because I have written an entire book on the subject of rewards (Kohn 1993a), there isn't any need to rehearse all the arguments and evidence here. Instead I will make just a few points to indicate why rewards belong in the category of things to move beyond.

The key to understanding why positive reinforcement isn't really so positive is to recognize the distinction between the goody itself and its status as a reward. It's the difference between money and merit pay, between having a popcorn party with your class and telling your class that they will get a popcorn party *if they're good this week.*

Carrots seem more desirable than sticks because people like getting carrots. Kids usually love the stickers and stars, the A's and praise, the parties and pizza and payments. But what no one likes is to have the very things he needs or desires used to manipulate his behavior. Rewards, in the unforgettable phrase of Edward Deci and Richard Ryan (1985, p. 70), are just "control through seduction." In the long run, control of any variety is aversive—and we should expect

that, ultimately, rewards wouldn't work much better than punishments.

And as a matter of fact, they don't. At least two dozen studies have shown that when people are promised a reward for doing a reasonably challenging task—or for doing it well—they tend to do inferior work compared with people who are given the same task without being promised any reward at all. Other research has shown that one of the least effective ways to get people to change their behavior (quit smoking, lose weight, use their seatbelts, and so on) is to offer them an incentive for doing so. The promise of a reward is sometimes not just ineffective but counterproductive—that is, worse than doing nothing at all.

Most relevant to our subject here is the finding that children who are frequently rewarded tend to be somewhat less generous and cooperative than those who aren't rewarded (Fabes, Fultz, Eisenberg, May-Plumlee, and Christopher 1989; Grusec 1991; for other research, see Kohn 1990a, pp. 202–203). Some teachers and parents find that result shocking. Others understand it immediately: Rewards, like punishments, can only manipulate someone's actions. They do nothing to help a child become a kind or caring person.

In fact, what the rewarded child has learned is that if he is generous he will get something. When the goodies are gone, so is the inclination to help. By the same token, a student who does what we want in order to receive some reward can't really be described as "behaving himself." It would be more accurate to say that the reward is behaving him.

Some educators are genuinely concerned about helping students become caring people—and genuinely misguided in believing that a program in which the adults "catch children doing something right," and offer them the equivalent of a doggie biscuit, will help that to happen. It won't. But in lots of classrooms and schools, such reward-based programs aren't really intended to help students become "responsible" or "good citizens"; these are just code words for blindly following someone else's rules. The point is not altruism but compliance.

When rewards are used for the purpose of eliciting mindless obedience, it soon becomes clear just how similar they are to punishment. Another form of evidence comes from noticing that the teachers and principals who have a reputation for enjoying power and needing to be in control are often the people most enamored of behavior management systems that feature rewards and praise. This is not a coincidence; indeed, research has confirmed a link between a tendency to control and a reliance on praise (e.g., Deci, Spiegel, Ryan, Koestner, and Kauffman 1982).

But we don't need studies to tell us about this connection. All we may need to know is that rewards and praise play a central role in Assertive Discipline. "Positive recognition … must become the most active part of your classroom discipline plan," says Lee Canter (Canter and Canter 1992, p. 57). For educators who recoil from a program as coercive as this one, yet have always assumed that positive recognition is beneficial, trying to reconcile these two ideas can be profoundly unsettling.

Educators who genuinely seek to help students become more excited about learning or more confident about their abilities should reflect carefully on what distinguishes the sort of positive feedback likely to have those effects from the sort that backfires (Kohn 1993a, chap. 6). If that distinction is sometimes murky in practice, there is one area where the damaging effects of praise ought not to be surprising, and that is where expressing approval is intended as a verbal reward—and, to that extent, as a way of manipulating students' future behavior.

Consider how many teachers gush over the way a child has acted, telling her how pleased or proud they are: "I like the way you found your seat so quickly and started working, Alisa!" The most important word in this sentence is *I*. The teacher is not encouraging Alisa to reflect on how she acted, to consider why one course of action might be better than another. Quite the contrary: all that counts is what the teacher wants, and approval and attention are made conditional on doing it. Truly, this sort of praise is not about bolstering self-esteem; it is about "control through seduction." No wonder it is an integral part of the same discipline programs that include punishment.

Things get even worse when such comments are offered in front of others (e.g., Canter and Canter 1992, pp. 143–145): "I like the way Alisa has found her seat so quickly …" Here the teacher has taken rewards, which are bad enough, and added to them the poison of competition. Children are set against one another in a race to be the first one praised. This sort of practice does Alisa no favors; one can imagine how the other kids will treat her later: "Look, it's Miss Found-Her-Seat Dork!" Over time, singling children out like this works against any sense of community in the classroom.

What's more, public praise is a fundamentally fraudulent interaction in its own right. The teacher is pretending to speak to Alisa, but is actually *using* her, holding her up as an example in an attempt to manipulate everyone else in the room. Even apart from its long-term effects, this is simply not a respectful way to treat human beings. And needless to say, seeing a *group* of students used in this manner is just as disturbing (e.g., Slavin 1995, p. 135).

Similar to public praise in its divide-and-conquer approach is the use of collective rewards. Here the teacher holds out a goody to the whole class if everyone does what he demands, the point being to make the students pressure their peers to obey (Canter and Canter 1992, pp. 69-71; Jones 1979). Thus, the children become unwitting accomplices of the teacher, doing his dirty work for him. Should the teacher ultimately opt not to provide the goody, woe to the child who is regarded as the reason for this decision. Once again we glimpse the punitive underbelly of reward systems.

But these are only particularly egregious examples of what goes on whenever teachers make something—be it attention or food— conditional on students' compliance. Like punishments, rewards warp the relationship between adult and child. With punishments, we come to be seen as enforcers to be avoided; with rewards, as goody dispensers on legs. In neither case have we established a caring alliance, a connection based on warmth and respect. Like punishments, rewards try to make bad behaviors disappear through manipulation. They are ways of doing things to students instead of working with them.

Make no mistake: the issue is not which reward or punishment we use, or how such a program is implemented, or what criteria are used to decide who gets a goody or a consequence. Such questions occupy school faculties for meeting after meeting, and they are massive exercises in missing the point. The problem rests with the very nature of these basic tools of traditional discipline. For all the reasons discussed in this chapter, schools will not become inviting, productive places for learning until we have dispensed with bribes and threats altogether.

Discussion Questions:

1. Why is the use of punishment such a strong tradition in the U.S.? Describe some of the punishments you've seen in schools that seem inappropriate to you.

2. What are some alternatives to punishment that you've experienced or know about that teachers use?

3. What are the purposes of punishment?

4. Describe corporal punishment and where you know it's used.

5. What do you think students learn from receiving punishment?

6. What actually occurs as a result of punishment; that is, what do students learn from it?

7. What is the relationship between rewards and punishment?

8. Which punishments are guaranteed to work?

9. Are any punishments effective at encouraging students to alter their behavior?

10. How can teachers and parents encourage children to change their behavior (internalize)?

Punishment Lite

"Consequences" and Pseudochoice

by Alfie Kohn

> The would-be progressives … thought that there were good ways and bad ways to coerce children (the bad ones mean, harsh, cruel, the good ones gentle, persuasive, subtle, kindly), and that if they avoided the bad and stuck to the good they would do no harm. This was one of their greatest mistakes.
>
> —John Holt, How Children Fail

A growing number of educators are in the market, quite literally, for alternatives to the coercive, traditional kind of discipline. They have misgivings about programs in which adults are essentially urged to assert their will over children, to wield rewards and punishments until students obey without question. Many of these educators have eagerly signed up for new classroom management programs that bill themselves as more modern and humane.

One of the central purposes of this book, as you may have noticed by now, is to inquire whether these "New Disciplines," with names like Cooperative Discipline and Discipline with Dignity, represent a real departure from what they claim to replace. Whether we are talking about their view of human nature (Chapter 1), their assumptions about where the fault lies when things go wrong in a classroom (Chapter 2), or what we are ultimately trying to achieve (Chapter 5), there is reason to believe that these programs are different only in degree, rather than in kind, from the more traditional approach. Notwithstanding the rhetoric they employ, the New Disciplines suggest a subtler, somewhat nicer way by which we can continue to do things to children—as distinct from working with them in a democratic environment to promote their social and moral development.

Rewards Redux

The first clue to the nature of the New Disciplines comes from the fact that many of these programs use rewards to control behavior, as described at the end of the last chapter. A glance at any book with "classroom management" in the title will confirm the pervasiveness of this approach. Dreikurs, to his credit, offered

Alfie Kohn, "Punishment Lite: 'Consequences' and Pseudochoice," *Beyond Discipline: From Compliance to Community*, pp. 37–53. Copyright © 2006 by the Association for Supervision and Curriculum Development (ASCD). Reprinted with permission.

an incisive analysis of the dangers of praise, recommending in its place a kind of nonevaluative feedback that he called "encouragement" (Dreikurs et al. 1982, pp. 108–112; Dreikurs and Grey 1968, p. 57), although he sometimes seemed inconsistent on this point. Some of the books derived from Dreikurs's work contain brief passages in which the idea of rewarding or praising children for being good is viewed with the appropriate skepticism (Nelsen 1987, p. 13; Albert 1989, p. 66).

Yet Cooperative Discipline, whose author's misgivings about rewards seem to be limited to the fact that children will keep demanding more of them, is peppered with Skinnerian gimmicks, such as handing out "stars and stickers … [and] awards" (Albert 1989, pp. 102, 111), writing the names of well-behaved students on the chalkboard (p. 38), publicly praising someone "who's on task" in order to get another student to comply (Albert 1995, p. 44), and even pinning ribbons on children (Albert 1992a, p. 38).

Likewise, Discipline with Dignity, far from "overlook[ing] the importance of positive reinforcement," as Canter (1988, p. 72) claims, fairly bubbles with enthusiasm about extrinsic inducements. These include a list of ten different "classroom privileges [that] should be earned, not given," such as field trips, free time, being a hall monitor, and so on (Curwin and Mendler 1988, p. 56). Also recommended: a "merit/demerit system to encourage successful cooperation"—which, moreover, is turned into a competition so that only "the table that most successfully worked together as a team gets a merit" (p. 59)—and exemptions from homework for good behavior (p. 78). Teachers are also urged to "catch a student being good" every few minutes and praise that child (p. 97)—a very specific echo of Assertive Discipline (e.g., Canter and Canter 1992, p. 60).

Repackaged Punishment

The New Disciplines may depend on rewards but their central claim is that, unlike their old-fashioned counterparts, they reject the use of punishment. Sometimes sounding for all the world like William Glasser, Thomas Gordon, or Haim Ginott, the purveyors of these programs eloquently denounce the practice of punishing children, declaring that it "provokes hostility and antagonism" (Albert 1989, p. 79) and a desire "to get even very soon" (Nelsen 1987, p. 67), that it is "ineffective for long-term change" (Curwin and Mendler 1988, p. 69) and "outdated" (Dreikurs and Grey 1968, p. 47).

So far, so good. But the programs influenced by Dreikurs present as an alternative to punishment the idea of imposing "logical consequences" on children when they do something wrong. Logical consequences are said by various writers to differ from punishment in any of three basic ways: They are (1) motivated by a desire to instruct, (2) reasonable and respectful in their application, and (3) related to the act of the wrongdoer.

Before examining each of these criteria more closely, it's instructive to observe that even the people who have built their careers on the ostensible benefits of logical consequences sometimes acknowledge that what they are proposing can be pretty tough to distinguish from old-fashioned punishment. The authors of one discipline guide for parents (Dinkmeyer and McKay 1989, p. 85) admit that "the line between punishment and logical consequences is thin at times." Another writer (Albert 1989, p. 79) concedes that, after all, the message in both cases is essentially the same: "when you do this, then [that] will happen." And Dreikurs himself (Dreikurs and Grey 1968, p. 58) observed at one point that "tone of voice alone often distinguishes one from the other."

Another reason to question the distinction between punishment and logical consequences is supplied (inadvertently) by Assertive Discipline. In this program, the names of disobedient children are conspicuously recorded—and, later, checked off—on a clipboard. This is quite simply a threat, since further misbehavior brings down on the child's head a variety of punishments, which have already been listed on the wall in order of severity. What's interesting for our purposes is that Canter explicitly disavows the label of punishment, preferring to refer to forcible isolation, a disapproving note to the child's parents, and a trip to the principal's office as—you guessed it—"consequences" (Canter and Canter 1992, p. 82).

Thomas Gordon, who devised the influential approach to working with children known as Parent Effectiveness Training (P.E.T.), was forced to conclude that "Dreikurs's concept of logical consequences is … nothing less than a euphemism for external control by punishment; it's another act of punitive discipline" (Gordon 1989, pp. 31–32). But let's look more closely at the claim that there really is a difference between logical consequences and punishment. Many teachers and principals have signed up for New Discipline programs precisely because they have been promised a nonpunitive technique for getting student compliance.

First, users of Discipline with Dignity are informed that the recipient of a logical consequence "may feel lousy," but that "there's an instructional intent" to making him feel that way (Curwin and Mendler 1991, Part 2; also see 1988, p. 71). The problem here, of course, is that any punishment, regardless of its severity or negative effects, can be rationalized in exactly the same manner. Presumably, many of the "more than three million American children [who] are physically abused each year in the name of discipline" (Lewin 1995) are told that punishment is necessary to "teach them a lesson" or is "for their own good."

Dreikurs offers a different version of this criterion, specifying the nature of the instructional intent. Whereas punishments underscore the authority of the adult doing the punishing, logical consequences are supposed to be geared to preserving the "social order" more generally, so that children "learn to respect the established rules" (Dreikurs and Grey 1968, pp. 71–72). Apart from the remarkable conservatism of Dreikurs's world view—more about which in the next chapter—there is not much reason to think that the distinction here will mean much to the average student. The teacher is the representative of the social order, the person who imposes a consequence for failing to respect the established rule. It is difficult to imagine that anyone will feel less put off by being made to undergo something unpleasant just because the teacher's goal has broader social ramifications.

The second set of criteria for defining logical consequences concerns their lack of harshness. The person who invokes them should be friendly and avoid scolding or judging (Dreikurs and Grey 1968, pp. 74, 77, 128); she should act in a "respectful" fashion and make sure the consequence itself is "reasonable" (Nelsen 1987, p. 73; also see Albert 1989, p. 79). Thus, if a student tips his chair back, it is supposedly a logical consequence for him to be forced to stand for the rest of the period (Albert 1989, p. 78). Is this more reasonable than making him stand for, say, the rest of the week? Unquestionably. It is also more reasonable to paddle a child than to shoot him, but this does not offer much of an argument for paddling.

Likewise, is it more respectful if we announce in a matter-of-fact tone that the student will be forced to stand up, as opposed to screaming this at him? No doubt—but again, the nature of what we are doing remains pretty much the same. A punishment does not change its essential nature merely because it is less harsh or invoked in a softer tone of voice. Someone who wants to know whether a given intervention is punitive can find the answer not in a book on discipline but in the child's face.

Imagine the face, for example, of the 2nd grade student who Dreikurs tells us is guilty of "talking out of turn, squirming, and so on" and who is ordered not only to leave the room but to spend time back in a kindergarten class. Dreikurs approves of this response so long as it does not seem "arbitrary": to ensure that it is a consequence rather than a punishment, the teacher need only strike the right tone by saying that she wonders whether he is "ready to continue in second grade" and suggesting that "it might be better for [him] to try and go back to kindergarten for a while" (Dreikurs and Grey 1968, pp. 143–44). If there is a difference between doing this to a child and engaging in old-fashioned punishment, it is at best a quantitative rather than a qualitative difference. What Dreikurs and his followers are selling is Punishment Lite.

(IL) Logical Consequences

The third and most widely cited distinction between punishments and logical "consequences" is that the latter are related to what the child did wrong; there must be some connection between the child's action and the adult's reaction. By definition a "consequence" fits the crime (Dreikurs and Grey 1968, pp. 73–74; Nelsen 1987, p. 73). This is really the linchpin of Dreikurs's system because of his core belief that "children retaliate [when they are punished] because they see no relationship between the punishment and the crime" (Dreikurs et al. 1982, p. 117). If this premise is wrong, then the whole house of cards—the distinction between consequences and punishments, and the rationale for the former—comes crashing down.

I believe it is wrong. To contrive some sort of conceptual link between the punishment and the crime may be satisfying to the adult, but in most cases it probably makes very little difference to the child. The child's (understandable) anger and desire to retaliate come from the fact that someone is deliberately making her suffer. That person is relying on power, forcing her to do something she doesn't want to do or preventing her from doing something she likes. The issue here is not the specific features of the coercive action so much as the coercion itself: "You didn't do what I wanted, so now I'm going to make something unpleasant happen to you." This power play invariably enrages the person who is being discomfited, in part because she is forced to confront her helplessness to do anything about it. We would not expect her anger to vanish just because of modest modifications in the implementation.

Now consider the following examples of "logical consequences" commended to us by Dreikurs and some of the New Discipline practitioners, and ask whether they would not meet any reasonable definition of punishment:

- If a child leaves his toys lying around at home, his mother is advised to hide them and, when asked, lie to the child by saying, "I'm sorry. I put them somewhere, but I don't remember right now." Dreikurs continues:

  Eventually, of course, the mother "finds" the toys, but not until the child had experienced the discomfort of being without some of his favorite playthings for a period of time. In another method—though not, for the fainthearted—the parent "accidentally" steps on one of the child's favorite toys which has been left around (Dreikurs and Grey 1968, p. 96).

- Instead of sitting quietly, two 1st graders are using their hands to rehearse a dance they will be performing later. The teacher makes them come to the front of the room and tells them they must demonstrate the dance to the rest of the class. "Though the children were obviously embarrassed, it was a result of their own action and not a result of any arbitrary judgment by the teacher," we are told (Dreikurs and Grey 1968, pp. 142–143).

- A kindergarten girl who has bitten other children is required to wear a sign that reads "I bite people." This consequence, we are told, "shows ingenuity ... and also courage" (Dreikurs and Grey 1968, p. 169).

- If a student makes a spitball, the teacher should force him to make 500 more spitballs so that his throat becomes "increasingly parched" (Albert 1989, p. 34).

- For various infractions, students are to be prevented from going to the library or from eating lunch in the cafeteria, told to sit in the principal's area, forced to miss a class field trip, or required to write an essay on how they "intend to stop breaking this rule" (Curwin and Mendler 1988, pp. 72, 81).

- If students have been noisy, the teacher should give an unannounced test with "the most difficult questions she can think of. When the papers are returned, there should be as many low marks as are possible to give, though the results are not placed in the grade book" (Dreikurs and Grey 1968, p. 135).

- Children who do not comply with the teacher's wishes are isolated in a time-out area so they will "experience a few uncomfortable moments." More such moments are added for "repeat offenders" (Albert 1989, p. 77). However, the place where children are forced to sit by themselves can be made less punitive by calling it "the 'happy bench'" (Nelsen, Lott, and Glenn 1993, p. 124).

- "Each student who violates a rule [must] write his own name on the blackboard"—or, in another approach, must have his name

written there by an elected class "sheriff" who is "responsible for keeping the behavioral records" (Curwin and Mendler 1988, p. 76).

- If a student has been disturbing the class, the teacher should "discuss the situation with the class" to "evoke group pressure" that will make him change his behavior—or alternatively, wait for a peaceful moment and then facetiously say to the student, in front of everyone, "You've been quiet for some time, wouldn't you like to say something?" (Dreikurs et al. 1982, p. 124, 132).

These are only a few examples of the scores of suggestions offered by the New Discipline theorists; still others appear in books intended for parents. Even though many, if not all, would seem to be indistinguishable from punishments—and in some cases, rather cruel ones—we are reassured that we have done nothing more in each instance than to impose a logical consequence. In essence, the New Disciplines give us permission to "punish with impunity," in Marilyn Watson's apt phrase; they relieve us of a bad conscience and of the need to think about real alternatives to the paradigm of control.

Take another look at the case against punishing people (pp. 24–30): The punisher is only controlling the behavior—or trying to do so—rather than influencing the person who behaves. Temporary compliance will be purchased at the cost of making the student even angrier, and therefore making the problem worse in the long run. The relationship between the punisher and the punished is ruptured.

Attention is focused on avoiding the punishment, not on the action—and on how one is personally affected, not on the way others feel or what is the right thing to do.

Every one of these arguments applies to the use of so-called logical consequences. Consider the last point. The Discipline with Dignity program says we should be concerned with "developing an internal orientation" in students by asking them, "What do you think will happen if you do this [bad thing] again?" (Curwin and Mendler 1991, Part 2). In practice that usually means "What do you think will happen to you?" The video for this program shows us successful applications of this question, in which students predict that they will get in trouble. The likely result of this strategy, however, is less an internal locus of control (as contrasted with being at the mercy of unpredictable forces) than a focus on self (rather than on others).

Do logical consequences "work"? One is naturally suspicious of unfalsifiable claims of success, such as this one: "Truly appropriate consequences will have a beneficial effect on students whether they let on or not" (Albert 1989, p. 82). But what Dreikurs observes about punishment can just as well be said of consequences: "the fact that the results were good does not make it a correct procedure" (Dreikurs and Grey 1968, pp. 164–165). Leaving a small child to cry himself to sleep can force him to learn how to console himself, but the emotional cost may be high. Likewise, even if a consequence did succeed in eliminating a misbehavior—which is by no means a likely outcome—we may have reason to doubt its wisdom.

More of the Same

Apart from the suggestions labeled as logical consequences, the New Disciplines offer a variety of other techniques for dealing with students who don't act the way we want. Once again, they bear a striking similarity to old-fashioned punishment. It's not surprising, for example, that someone who cheerfully tells us to become more "authoritarian" would recommend that when a student objects to something we say, we should just keep repeating our original "request ... like a broken record" (McDaniel 1982, p. 247). But it may be surprising that a program called Cooperative Discipline, which claims to support a democratic, self-esteem-enhancing classroom, would offer exactly the same advice (Albert 1989, p. 75; also see Cline and Fay 1990, p. 83).

Of course, to say the same thing to (or at) a student over and over is to ignore what the student has to say. That advice is consistent with Dreikurs's suggestion that we should make a point of paying no attention to any student who does something "negative" (Dreikurs et al. 1982, pp. 34–37). And in case that doesn't work, we should play tit for tat: If a student has interrupted you, just wait until the next time he starts to answer a question and then cut him off abruptly and talk to someone else (Dreikurs and Grey 1968, pp. 148–149). One may be struck by how childish these responses are, or perhaps how likely they are to backfire in light of how they make students feel. But most of all, one is struck by how little they differ from the traditional punitive model.

The same may be said of an old standby used on young children: time out. This term originally was short for "time out from positive reinforcement," a practice developed to suppress certain behaviors in laboratory animals. Quite frankly, that fact alone gave me pause when I began to think about the topic, but before passing judgment I wanted to hear the opinions of educators whose work I already respected—particularly those with considerable experience in early childhood education.

The consensus seemed to be that sending someone away and forcing him to sit by himself does nothing to resolve whatever the problem was. It "cannot give a child new standards of behavior, insight into how one's actions affect others, or strategies for coping with an uncomfortable or painful situation," as Lilian Katz (1985, p. 3) has observed. The adult is not asking, "Why have you

…?" or even saying, "Here's why you might …" She is simply telling the child, "Do it my way or leave."

Yes, it's true that exiling a disruptive child can make everyone else feel better, at least for a while. But this means that time out acts as "a wedge that pushes persons into opposite directions. Some are feeling relieved at the same time that another person is feeling oppressed" (Lovett 1985, p. 16).

Adele Faber and Elaine Mazlish (1995, pp. 115-116), who have adapted some of their sensible parenting strategies for classroom use, ask us to put ourselves in the place of a child who is forcibly isolated: "As an adult you can imagine how resentful and humiliated you would feel if someone forced you into isolation for something you said or did." For a child, however, it is even worse, since she may come to believe "that there is something so wrong with her that she has to be removed from society." And Vivian Paley (1992, p. 95) adds that such feelings ultimately reverberate through the classroom:

> Thinking about unkindness always reminds me of the time-out chair. It made children sad and lonely to be removed from the group, which in turn made me feel inadequate and mean and—I became convinced—made everyone feel tentative and unsafe. These emotions show up in a variety of unwholesome ways depending on whether one is a teacher or child.

Let me be clear that there is nothing objectionable about having a safe, comfortable place where a child can go to calm down or just be alone for a few minutes. That's a terrific idea—so good, in fact, that adults can set a powerful example by taking some time by themselves to cool off when they feel angry. Children should be given this option, and when emotions are running high, they can be gently (and, if possible, privately) reminded that it exists. What Katz and Paley and the rest of us are talking about, though, is a situation where the child is ordered to leave the group, where, in the words of one fervent proponent, it is "a direction, not a negotiation" (Charney 1991, p. 95). In practice, that means it's a punishment—and for many children, a remarkably hurtful one.

However, for teachers who remain unconvinced that time out should be eliminated, I offer these suggestions for minimizing the damage. First, use time out only as a last resort, in extraordinary situations. Second, do everything in your power to make it less punitive. The National Association for the Education of Young Children (1986) offers the following reasonable and important recommendations:

- Time out does not mean leaving the child alone, unless he or she wants to be. After the child has calmed down, the adult and child can talk about the child's feelings.
- Children should not be threatened with or afraid of a time out.
- Time out should not be humiliating. There should not be a predetermined time, chair, or place.

The last of these suggestions is particularly significant. If a teacher has established a "time-out chair"—or, worse, a formula for the number of minutes a child must spend in it—then the results are likely to be no better than we would expect with any other technique designed to make children unhappy.

Heads I Win, Tails You Lose

Discussions of how to impose "logical consequences" and other punishments are often connected to the issue of choice. As we saw in

Chapter 2, there is a relationship between insisting that students do, in fact, choose their behavior and making them suffer a punitive consequence for what they have "chosen."

But consider for a moment the question of whether students should be allowed to make choices. In the abstract, almost everyone says yes. Even Lee Canter (1988, p. 72), citing Dreikurs, agrees that "it is through choice that students learn about responsibility." But what exactly is meant by "choice"? That's the question we need to ask anyone who claims to endorse the concept. In practice, the word may be misleading; it may be used to describe situations in which students actually have very little opportunity to make meaningful decisions.

What is described as a choice may, in any of three distinct ways, actually be a pseudochoice.

1. "Obey or suffer." Canter (quoted in Hill 1990, p. 75) elaborates as follows on his idea of letting students make decisions: "The way you teach kids to be responsible is by telling them exactly what is expected of them and then giving them a choice" as to whether they comply.

Here we have a rather peculiar understanding of the word responsible, which looks suspiciously like a euphemism for "obedient" (set Appendix 2). But Canter's pronouncement also contains a sharply limited view of "choice," which amounts to either (a) doing "exactly what is expected" by the teacher or (b) facing the consequences.

Consistent with a pattern we have already noticed, the philosophy and techniques of Assertive Discipline are echoed in the New Disciplines, notwithstanding the claims of the latter to be substantially different. If a child is late returning from recess, for example, Dreikurs suggests that in the future we give her "a choice of returning with the others or standing by the teacher during recess until it is time to return to class" (Dreikurs et al. 1982, p. 123).

But children may not even get to recess in the first place if teachers have offered them the sort of choice described in Discipline with Dignity. A student who for any reason has not completed a task on (the teacher's) schedule is to be told, "You can do your assignment now or during recess" (Curwin and Mendler 1988, p. 15; also see Charney 1991, Collis and Dalton 1990). Remarkably, this is even commended to us as an illustration of letting students make decisions.

To begin with, notice that the options for the student have been gratuitously reduced to two—a practice that can sometimes be justified but ought not to be accepted without careful reflection. On closer examination, though, these sorts of examples do not present children with a real choice at all. Typically no child wants to miss recess. The teacher is really saying, "Finish your work now or I'm going to take away something you like"—or, in generic terms, "Do what I tell you or I'm going to punish you."

Wrapping this threat in the language of choice allows the teacher to camouflage a conventional use of coercion by pretending to offer the student a chance to decide—or, in the sanitized language preferred by one proponent of this technique, the teacher is "using choices … to elicit or motivate desired behaviors" (Bluestein 1988, p. 149). The fact that these behaviors are desired—indeed, required—by someone else means that the putative chooser doesn't really have much choice at all. "As soon as we say 'Either you do this for me or I'll do that to you,' the child will feel trapped and hostile" (Faber and Mazlish 1995, p. 90).

2. "You punished yourself." In a variation of this gambit that is a hallmark of Assertive Discipline, students are punished after disobeying the teacher's command, but the punishment is presented as something they asked for: "If they choose to behave in an inappropriate manner" as determined unilaterally by the teacher, "they will also choose to accept the negative consequences

of that choice" (Canter and Canter 1992, p. 169). Thus: "You have chosen to sit by yourself at the table" (p. 81); "you will choose to have your parents called" (p. 194); and so on.

Once again, the New Disciplines follow in lockstep. In Discipline with Dignity, we are encouraged to tell students who break the rules that they have "chosen to go home for the rest of the day" (Curwin and Mendler 1988, p. 15) or have "chosen five minutes in Siberia (time-out area)" (p. 107). In Cooperative Discipline, a child is likewise told that she has "chosen to go to [time-out in] Mr. Jordan's room" (Albert 1989, p. 77). And in a book called Teaching Children to Care, we find the same thing: "I see you are choosing to go to your time-out place" (Charney 1991, p. 114).

Again, the appeal of this tactic is no mystery: it seems to relieve the teacher of responsibility for what he is about to do to the child. (Apparently, students not only always choose their own behavior, but also choose the teacher's response! Teachers would seem to be exempt from the axiom that people are responsible for their own choices.)

Even in cases where we really can state unconditionally that a child has "chosen" to do something bad—notwithstanding the concerns about such sweeping statements raised in Chapter 2—the child certainly does not choose to be punished for it. The teacher does that to him. In short, this is a fundamentally dishonest, not to mention manipulative, attribution. To the injury of punishment is added the insult of a kind of mind game whereby reality is redefined and children are told, in effect, that they wanted to have something bad happen to them (see Crockenberg 1982, pp. 65–70).

"You've chosen a time out" is a lie: a truthful teacher would have to say, "I've chosen to isolate you."

3. "Choose … and Suffer." In yet another version of pseudo-choice, children are allowed or even encouraged to make certain decisions specifically so they will suffer from their own poor judgment. This technique falls under the rubric of what Dreikurs called natural (as distinct from logical) consequences, which he defined somewhat circularly as "the natural results of ill-advised acts" (Dreikurs and Grey 1968, p. 63).

Of course, there is a kernel of truth here: many times, we do learn from the unpleasant results that follow from poor choices. If I leave my books too close to the edge of the desk, they may fall over; if I stay up late, I'm probably going to be tired in the morning. However, letting a child experience the "natural consequences" of her action may not be particularly constructive, depending on her age, the nature of the action, and other factors. Many people like to point out, for example, that a child who constantly insults her peers will soon have few friends as a result. But to conclude that this will "teach" her to be a nicer person overlooks basic human psychology—specifically, the reciprocal relation between perceptions and behaviors, and the way they can spiral out of control. The fact that others steer clear of this child may simply cement her disagreeable image of them—or of herself.

Similarly, an aggressive child may eventually get his teeth knocked out by someone bigger than he is, but this will likely teach him the importance of making sure that he wins the next fight, not the futility (much less the immorality) of fighting. Lilian Katz (1984, p. 9) has observed that "the school of hard knocks, although powerful, is likely to provide the wrong lessons to children"— and the same could be said about many natural consequences.

In a program called Discipline with Love and Logic, children aren't merely allowed to live with the results of their actions; they are "forced to make … decisions" so that they will come to regret the bad ones (Cline and Fay 1990, p. 48). As a result, "children don't get angry at us; they get angry at themselves" (p. 78; also see Dreikurs et al. 1982, p. 118). The authors are quite clear about the intent: "We want our kids to hurt from the inside out" (Cline and Fay 1990, p. 91; emphasis in original). The sample dialogues offered in this manual suggest a smug satisfaction on the part of the adult who watches as children "learn" (read: suffer) from their own mistakes.

The salient questions here are these: What message do adults send when they deliberately allow something unpleasant to happen to a child even though they could have intervened? What conclusions does the child draw about how much the adult cares about him, or whether he is worth caring about, or how he should come to regard other people in general? Incredibly, the authors of Discipline with Love and Logic talk about the importance of empathy, even though precisely the opposite of empathic concern would seem to be communicated to a child by an adult following their prescription.

In conventional punishment, a child is at least left with a sense of self intact and the capacity to stand in opposition to the punisher. Not so with this insidious strategy, which tries to turn the child against herself. Any doubt about the lack of respect for children demonstrated by this approach is erased when the authors give us leave to ignore any objections that children may make to something we have done to them: "Once you encounter resistance, you'll know [the technique is] working" (p. 103).

A caring adult wants to help children learn to make responsible decisions about the things that matter to them—and to help them see the results of those decisions. That, however, is very different from what has become of the concept of choice in the New Discipline programs. Here, "consequences" are neither logical nor natural.

This chapter should not be taken to imply that there is nothing at all to recommend any of the New Discipline programs—or that they are interchangeable with each other, or just as coercive as Assertive Discipline. For example, there is no mistaking the latter for most of Positive Discipline in the Classroom (Nelsen et al. 1993), whose central concern is to let students participate in decision making through the vehicle of class meetings. The other programs, too, talk about phrasing requests respectfully, avoiding interventions that amount to public humiliations, and so on. Credit should be given for these and comparable features that are more humane than other approaches to classroom management.

But a careful reading of the New Disciplines compels the unhappy conclusion that, on balance, most of them are remarkably similar to the old-school approach in their methods—and, as we are about to see, their goals. These programs are merely packaged in such a way as to appeal to educators who are uncomfortable with the idea of using bribes and threats. The truth is what it has always been: a ruse is a ruse is a ruse.

Discussion Questions

1. How would you describe the term *logical consequences*?

2. Explain how *logical consequences* are different from punishment. How are they similar?

3. Why are consequences not perceived by children as a positive response to misbehavior?

4. What are the likely effects of using time out on children? What guidelines should be followed when choosing to apply time out to children?

5. What is the difference between *contrived* punishments and *naturally occurring* punishments?

6. Which are more commonly used in schools: contrived or naturally occurring punishments? Why?

7. Is punishment necessary? Explain.

8. What are some guidelines to follow for using punishment to ensure mutual respect between students and teachers?

9. How do strategies for encouraging students to internalize alter the use of punishment?

Kids Do Well If They Can

By Ross Greene

Kids with social, emotional, and behavioral challenges lack important thinking skills. Now there's an idea that can take some getting used to. Let's begin by considering your philosophy of kids: what kids are about, why they do what they do, what they're up to (if they're really up to anything).

Many adults have never given much thought to their philosophy of kids. But if you're trying to help kids with behavioral challenges, you're going to need one, because it's your philosophy of kids that's going to guide your beliefs and your actions in your interactions with them, especially when the going gets tough. The philosophy that serves as the foundation of what you're about to read is "kids do well if they can."

This philosophy may not sound earth-shattering, but when we consider the very popular alternative philosophy—"kids do well if they want to"—the significance becomes clear. These two disparate philosophies have dramatically different ramifications for our assumptions about kids and how to proceed when they do not meet our expectations.

When the "kids do well if they want to" philosophy is applied to a child who's not doing well, then we believe that the reason he's not doing well is because he doesn't want to. This very common assumption is usually wrong and causes adults to believe that their primary role in the life of a challenging kid (and the goal of intervention) is to make the kid want to do well. This is typically accomplished by motivating the kid, by giving him the incentive to do well, by rewarding him when he behaves in an adaptive fashion and punishing him when he behaves in a maladaptive fashion.

By contrast, the "kids do well if they can" philosophy carries the assumption that if a kid could do well, he would do well. If he's not doing well, he must be lacking the skills needed to respond to life's challenges in an adaptive way. What's the most important role an adult can play in the life of such a kid? First, assume he's already motivated, already knows right from wrong, and has already been punished enough. Then, figure out what thinking skills he's lacking so you know what thinking skills to teach.

Lagging Skills

If you know what thinking skills a kid is lacking, you'll be in a much better position to teach those skills. You'll also be in a better position to anticipate the situations in which challenging behavior is most likely to occur. If you don't know what skills a kid is lacking, they probably won't get taught, it will be much harder to anticipate his worst moments, the kid's challenges will linger (or get worse), and he will become increasingly frustrated, hopeless, and alienated, just as most of us would if we had a problem no one seemed able to understand and were being treated in a way that made the problem worse.

When is challenging behavior most likely to occur? When the demands being placed on a kid exceed his capacity to respond adaptively. Of course, that's when all of us exhibit maladaptive behavior. The problem for kids with behavioral challenges (and those around them) is that they're responding much more maladaptively than the rest of us, and much more often.

You see, there's a spectrum of things kids do when life's demands exceed their capacity to respond adaptively. Some cry, or sulk, or pout, or whine, or withdraw—that would be the milder end of the spectrum. As we move toward the more difficult end of the spectrum, we find screaming, swearing, spitting, hitting, kicking, destroying property, lying, and truancy. And as we move even further toward the extreme end of the spectrum, we find self-induced vomiting, self-injurious behavior, drinking or using drugs to excess, stabbing, and shooting. But all of these behaviors occur under the same conditions: when the demands being placed on a kid exceed that kid's capacity to respond adaptively. Why do some kids respond at the milder end of the spectrum while others are at the more severe end? Some kids have the skills to "hold it together" when pushed to their limits and some don't.

With this new perspective on challenging kids, much of what we say about them no longer makes sense. Take a look:

"He just wants attention."
We all want attention, so this explanation isn't very useful for helping us understand why a kid is struggling to do well. And if a kid is seeking attention in a maladaptive way, doesn't that suggest that he lacks the skills to seek attention in an adaptive way?

"He just wants his own way."
We all want our own way, so this explanation doesn't help us achieve an understanding of a kid's challenges. Adaptively getting one's own way requires skills often found lacking in challenging kids.

"He's manipulating us."
This is a very popular, and misguided, characterization of kids with behavioral challenges. Competent manipulation requires various skills—forethought, planning, impulse control, and organization, among others—typically found lacking in challenging kids. In other words, the kids who are most often described as being manipulative are those least capable of pulling it off.

"He's not motivated."
This is another very popular characterization that can be traced back to the "kids do well if they want to" mentality, and it can lead us straight to interventions aimed at giving a kid the incentive to do well. But why would any kid not want to do well? Why would he choose not to do well if he has the skills to do well? Isn't doing well always preferable?

"He's making bad choices."
Are you certain he has the skills and repertoire to consistently make good choices?

"His parents are incompetent disciplinarians."

This, too, is a popular way of thinking, but it fails to take into account the fact that most challenging kids have well-behaved siblings. Blaming parents doesn't help anyone at school deal effectively with the kid in the six hours a day, five days a week, nine months of the year that he's in the building.

"He has a bad attitude."

He probably didn't start out with one. "Bad attitudes" tend to be the by-product of countless years of being misunderstood and over-punished by adults who didn't recognize that a kid was lacking crucial thinking skills. But kids are resilient; they come around if we start doing the right thing.

"He has a mental illness."

While he may well meet diagnostic criteria for a psychiatric disorder and may even benefit from psychotropic medication, this description is a nonstarter. Fifty years ago, a psychiatrist named Thomas Szasz understood that "mentally ill" was a limiting (and potentially inaccurate and derisory) way to describe people with social, emotional, and behavioral challenges. He advocated for reconceptualizing these challenges as "problems in living," a more fitting and productive way of viewing things.

"His brother was the same way."

Ah, so it's the gene pool! Alas, we can't do anything about the gene pool, and it's likely that his brother was lacking some important thinking skills, too.

The following list is much more useful. It's the list of many skills frequently found lagging in challenging kids:

- Difficulty handling transitions, shifting from one mindset or task to another (shifting cognitive set).
- Difficulty mustering the energy to persist on tasks that are challenging, effortful, or tedious.
- Difficulty doing things in a logical sequence or prescribed order.
- Poor sense of time.
- Difficulty reflecting on multiple thoughts or ideas simultaneously.
- Difficulty maintaining focus for goal-directed problem solving.
- Difficulty considering the likely outcomes or consequences of actions (impulsive).
- Difficulty considering a range of solutions to a problem.
- Difficulty expressing concerns, needs, or thoughts in words.
- Difficulty understanding what is being said.
- Difficulty managing emotional response to frustration so as to think rationally (separation of affect).
- Chronic irritability and/or anxiety significantly impede capacity for problem solving.
- Difficulty seeing the "grays"; concrete, literal, black-and-white thinking.
- Difficulty deviating from rules, routine, original plan.
- Difficulty handling unpredictability, ambiguity, uncertainty, novelty.
- Difficulty shifting from original idea or solution; difficulty adapting to changes in plan or new rules; possibly perseverative or obsessive.
- Difficulty taking into account situational factors that would require adjusting one's plan of action.

- Inflexible, inaccurate interpretations; cognitive distortions or biases (e.g., "Everyone's out to get me," "Nobody likes me," "You always blame me," "It's not fair," "I'm stupid," "Things will never work out for me").
- Difficulty attending to and/or accurately interpreting social cues; poor perception of social nuances.
- Difficulty starting a conversation, entering groups, connecting with people; lacking other basic social skills.
- Difficulty seeking attention in appropriate ways.
- Difficulty appreciating how one's behavior is affecting other people; often surprised by others' responses to his or her behavior.
- Difficulty empathizing with others, appreciating another person's perspective or point of view.
- Difficulty appreciating how one is coming across or being perceived by others.

You may have noticed that this list contains no diagnoses. That's because diagnoses don't give us any information about the cognitive skills a kid may be lacking. All too often adults get caught up in the quest for the right diagnosis, assuming that a diagnosis will help them know what to do next. The reality is that diagnoses aren't especially useful for understanding kids with behavioral challenges or for helping adults know what to do next. Plus, kids don't generally exhibit challenging behavior in a vacuum. It usually takes two to tango: a kid who's lacking skills and an environment (teachers, parents, peers) that demands those skills. Diagnoses don't reflect that reality, they simply pathologize the child.

Let's focus on a few of the lagging skills on the list for the purpose of making clear the connection between lagging skills and how they can contribute to challenging behavior.

When you're faced with a problem or frustration, your primary task is to solve the problem that caused your frustration. To accomplish this task, these three skills will be absolutely essential. That's because problem solving requires a great deal of organized, planful thinking.

Let's ponder that for a moment. To solve a problem, you must first identify the problem you're trying to solve. Then you'll need to think of solutions to the problem. And then you'll need to anticipate the likely outcomes of those solutions so as to pick the best one. That's how people make decisions.

Many kids are so disorganized in their thinking—they have so much difficulty sorting through their thoughts—that they're unable to figure out what's frustrating them, in which case the process of problem solving comes to an abrupt halt, the problem doesn't get solved, and their frustration heightens (often setting in motion one of the behaviors on the spectrum). Many are so disorganized that even if they can manage to figure out what problem they're trying to solve, they can't think of more than one solution to the problem. Many are so impulsive that even if they can think of more than one solution, they've already done the first thing that popped into their heads. The bad news? Our first solution is often (not always, but often) our worst. Good solutions usually come to mind after we've inhibited our less optimal initial impulses and considered our better options in a more organized fashion. Many kids—often the disorganized, impulsive ones—are notorious for putting their "worst foot forward." In other words, there are many kids who are responding to life's challenges in a maladaptive fashion because they aren't very skilled at organizing their thoughts, thinking of alternative solutions, or anticipating likely outcomes.

Approaching problems in an organized, planful manner, considering a variety of solutions, and reflecting on their likely outcomes are crucial developmental skills. Most 2-year-olds don't yet possess these skills. Neither do a lot of challenging kids who—chronologically, at least—are a lot older.

Clearly, we have some skills to teach. But if the school discipline program emphasizes formal consequences, they're not going to get taught. Consequences only remind kids of what we don't want them to do and give them the incentive to do something more adaptive instead. But they already know what we don't want them to do, and they're already motivated to do something more adaptive instead. They need something else from us.

In Focus

Difficulty expressing concerns, needs, or thoughts in words.

Most of the thinking and communicating we do involves language, so it's no accident that many kids with language delays also have trouble handling the social, emotional, and behavioral demands that are placed upon them. For example, many kids have trouble finding the words to tell someone what's the matter or what they need. This can present a big problem; life's a lot easier when you have the linguistic wherewithal to let people know you "don't feel like talking," that "something's the matter," that you "need a minute to think," that you "don't know what to do," that

you "need a break," or that you "don't like that." The reminder "use your words" won't help at all if a kid doesn't have the words. It's the lack of words that often sets the stage for challenging behavior.

Some kids cry or become withdrawn when they lack the language skills to successfully manage interactions with classmates and teachers. Of course, that's the mild end of the spectrum. Other kids express their feelings or needs with "Screw you," "I hate you," "Shut up," "Leave me alone," and other more colorful expressions (now we're a little further down the spectrum). And still others vault right past these inappropriate verbal options and wind up expressing themselves physically (shoving, hitting, throwing things, destroying property, running out of the classroom).

A crucial developmental leap occurs when kids begin to use words to let the world know what's bugging them, what they need, and what they're thinking. The social, emotional, and behavioral challenges of many kids can be traced "back to a developmental lag in these and related domains. Regrettably, language-processing problems are frequently overlooked. Adults often don't think to assess language skills when they're trying to figure out why a challenging kid is challenging. And sometimes the testing instrumentation used in standard language assessments doesn't pick up on some of the finer-grained language issues that may be involved; in such cases, the test results may not only fail to pinpoint the kid's difficulties, but also erroneously conclude that the kid has no language difficulties at all.

Can kids be taught to articulate their concerns, needs, and thoughts more effectively? Absolutely. But not until adults understand that it's the lack of these skills that is setting the stage for challenging behavior.

Separation of affect refers to the ability to separate the emotions (affect) you're feeling in response to a problem or frustration from the thinking you must do to resolve the problem.

While emotions can be quite useful for mobilizing or energizing people to solve problems, thinking is how problems get solved. Kids skilled at separating affect tend to respond to problems or frustrations with more thought than emotion, and that's good. But kids who lack skill in this domain tend to respond to problems or frustrations with more emotion and less (or no) thought, and that's not good at all. Learning how to put your emotions "on the shelf" so as to be able to think rationally is an essential developmental skill, and one many challenging kids have failed to develop.

At the milder end of the spectrum, kids who are having difficulty separating thought from emotion may become highly anxious over, for example, an upcoming test, a new social situation, not understanding an assignment, or being embarrassed in front of their classmates. They may cry over a bad grade, at not being picked first for a team, or when they feel socially excluded. At the more extreme end of the spectrum, their emotions may burst through in such a powerful way that they scream, swear, throw something, hit somebody, or worse. These kids may actually feel themselves "heating up" but often aren't able to stem the emotional tide until later, when the emotions have subsided and rational thought has returned. Naturally, the heating-up process will be greatly intensified if adults or peers respond in a way that adds fuel to the fire.

Young kids tend to be fairly rigid, black-and-white, literal, inflexible thinkers. They're still making sense of the world, and it's easier to put two and two together if they don't have to worry about exceptions to the rule or alternative ways of looking at things. As kids develop, they learn that, in fact, most things in life are "gray," that there are exceptions to the rule and alternative ways of interpreting things. Sometimes we have a substitute teacher, a field trip needs to be rescheduled because of the weather, someone is sitting in our usual seat in the cafeteria, recess has to be indoors instead of outdoors.

Unfortunately, for some kids, "gray" thinking doesn't develop as readily. Though some of these kids are diagnosed with disorders such as nonverbal learning disability or Asperger's disorder, it's more useful to think of them as "black-and-white thinkers stuck in a gray world." Predictably, these kids are most likely to exhibit challenging behavior when the world places demands on them for gray thinking.

Many such kids are quite comfortable with factual information because it's black-and-white but grow uncomfortable when life demands problem solving because it's gray. These kids love details (black-and-white) but aren't so adept at handling ambiguity (gray) and often miss the "big picture" (gray). They love predictability (it's black-and-white) but don't do so well when things are unpredictable (gray). They love certainty (black-and-white) and routines (black-and-white) but don't handle uncertainty (gray) or changes in plan (gray) very well.

These black-and-white thinkers often present significant challenges to their teachers and classmates as they struggle to apply concrete rules and interpretations to a world where few such rules apply. Some sulk or become anxious when events don't conform to their original configuration or when they've interpreted an event in a distorted fashion. Some scream. Some swear. Or throw things. Of course, those are the things they do. All that tells you is where they are on the spectrum of challenging behaviors. Now you know why and when they're doing them. That's where the action's at.

Can black-and-white thinkers be helped to think more flexibly? To move from an original way of thinking and adapt to circumstances or perspectives they may not have taken into account? Most definitely … so long as adults recognize that it's hard to teach kids to be more flexible by being inflexible themselves.

There's a big difference between interpreting the lagging skills described above as "excuses" rather than as "explanations." When lagging skills are invoked as excuses, the door slams shut on the process of thinking about how to teach the kid the skills he lacks. Conversely, when lagging skills are invoked as explanations for a kid's behavior, the door to helping swings wide open.

Unsolved Problems

So far, you've read about a sampling of the lagging skills that can set the stage for challenging behavior, but there's another piece of information missing. We can learn a lot about a kid's social, emotional, and behavioral challenges, and identify potential avenues for intervention, by noting the situations in which challenging behavior is most likely to occur. A situational analysis can give you invaluable information about the circumstances or unsolved problems—sometimes called triggers or antecedents—that precipitate social, emotional, and behavioral challenges.

For example, if a kid is having some of his greatest difficulties during circle time, then circle time is a circumstance precipitating challenging behavior. If a kid is having difficulty getting along with other kids during recess, then getting along with other kids during recess is an unsolved problem precipitating challenging behavior. And if a kid is refusing to work when paired with a particular classmate, then working with that particular classmate is a circumstance or unsolved problem precipitating challenging behavior. A lot of adults nominate the word "no" as a trigger. But it's not specific enough. It's what the adult is saying "no" to—going to the bathroom (yet again), sharpening a pencil (yet again), excessive talking or teasing—that helps adults know the specific problem they need to solve (so they don't have to keep saying "no" so often). We know these problems haven't been solved yet because they're still setting the stage for maladaptive behavior.

New Lenses

There are many lenses through which challenging behavior in kids can be viewed. Here's the mantra that encapsulates the view of this author: Behind every challenging behavior is an unsolved problem or a lagging skill (or both).

Whether a kid is sulking, pouting, whining, withdrawing, refusing to talk, curling up in a fetal position, crying, spitting, screaming, swearing, running out of the classroom, kicking, hitting, destroying property, or worse, you won't know what to do about the challenging behavior until you've identified the lagging skills or unsolved problems that gave rise to it. Lagging skills are the why of challenging behavior. Unsolved problems are the who, what, when, and where.

Once you have a decent handle on a kid's lagging skills and unsolved problems, you've taken a major step in the right direction because the kid's challenging episodes are now highly predictable, which is good news if you're a teacher and have a class full of 25 other students. You don't have to wait until the kid is disrupting the class before you try to teach skills or solve problems; you can do it in advance because the disruption is predictable. A lot of adults find it hard to believe that a kid's challenging behaviors are highly predictable, believing instead that such behaviors are unpredictable and occur out of the blue. But that's not true, not if you know what skills the child is lacking and what his triggers are.

Illogical Consequences

Before moving on, let's consider why consequences may not be an effective way to teach skills or help kids solve problems. There are a variety of ways to address a kid's challenging behavior. One common option is to simply tell the kid you don't approve of his behavior and to suggest alternative behaviors. While this can be an effective approach for a lot of kids, it often isn't especially effective for the challenging ones because it doesn't teach any lagging skills or solve any problems.

What option invariably kicks in next? Those very powerful, ever-present, and inescapable natural consequences: praise, approval, embarrassment, being scolded, being liked or disliked, being invited to things (or not), and so forth. Challenging kids experience lots of natural consequences but are far more likely to experience the punishing variety than their less challenging counterparts. While natural consequences are inescapable, they don't teach lagging thinking skills or solve problems, so for many challenging kids they aren't especially effective at reducing difficult behavior.

If the first two options don't achieve the desired effect, adults usually turn to a third option and add more consequences, those of the imposed, "logical," "unnatural," or "artificial" variety. These include punishments, such as staying in from recess, time-out from reinforcement, detention, suspension, and expulsion; and rewards, such as special privileges. Of course, the kids who are on the receiving end of most imposed, logical consequences are the ones who haven't responded to natural consequences. But imposed, logical consequences don't teach lagging skills or help kids solve problems any better than natural consequences do. Indeed, when logical consequences are being liberally applied but are not effectively reducing a kid's challenging behavior, I think they're probably more accurately referred to as illogical consequences.

My view is that kids who haven't responded to natural consequences don't need more consequences, they need adults who are knowledgeable about how challenging kids come to be challenging, who can identify the lagging skills and unsolved problems that are setting the stage for maladaptive behavior, and who know how to teach those skills and help solve those problems. We've learned a lot about children's brains in the last 30 years. It's time for our actions to reflect our knowledge.

Discussion Questions

1. Describe the difference between the philosophies of "kids do well if they can" versus "kids do well if they want to."

2. Describe five lagging skills that you have seen students exhibit.

3. Why is diagnosing children's challenging behaviors not beneficial for teachers or children?

4. How do ineffective emotional responses prevent children from acting appropriately?

5. Describe how unpredictable circumstances often cause problems for children who have lagging skills.

6. Why does giving consequences often prevent children from improving their behaviors?

7. How can you help children develop solutions for their lagging skills?

Ground Zero

By Gregory Michie

My friend Mara was sitting in the reception area of a small Catholic school on Chicago's North Side, where she'd gone to inquire about registering her daughter for the 1999–2000 term. She wasn't sure she'd be able to afford the school's monthly tuition bills, but she'd decided to check things out anyway—ask a few questions, pick up some forms, maybe even begin the application process.

The principal, a pleasant, conservatively dressed woman of about fifty, welcomed Mara and then quickly ran through her sales pitch, emphasizing the school's small classes and exemplary level of parent involvement. She explained that Mara would be expected to put in her share of volunteer hours, then buzzed through basic information about student uniforms, tuition payment plans, and disciplinary procedures. "Oh, yes," she added, pulling a piece of paper from a file folder and handing it to Mara. "You'll also need to sign this."

Mara took the form and glanced at it. At the top of the page, in capital letters, it read "Zero Tolerance Agreement."

"All of our parents have to sign it," the principal said. "When you read it over, you'll see that it's a first-strike-you're-out situation. That means first offense—no discussion, no excuses."

Mara was taken aback by the conversation's sudden change in tone.

"We haven't had any complaints about the policy," continued the principal, perhaps noting the confusion on Mara's face. "The parents all think it's a good thing. With all the school shootings lately, just …" Her voice trailed off. "Well, we just don't want to take any chances."

Mara scanned the list of offenses that could result in a student's swift and automatic expulsion—weapon possession, drug use, gang activity, fighting. But all she could think about was that her daughter was only five years old.

I don't think I'd ever heard the phrase "zero tolerance" when I began teaching in the Chicago public schools in the fall of 1990. That was before Paducah, before Jonesboro, before Littleton. But even before school shootings became a regular item on front pages and nightly newscasts, the idea that schools were dealing with a frightening new breed of violent, amoral youth was beginning to take hold. Newspaper and television reports of rising crime rates played alongside stories of drive-by shootings, gang-related murders, and children killing children. During my first year in the classroom I remember listening to an older colleague's running commentary as she read a magazine article about youth violence. "These kids get worse every year," she said, shaking her head. "They'd just as soon shoot you as look at you."

It was in this climate of fear—some of it justifiable, some not—that zero tolerance policies began to be seen as a reasonable response to school safety concerns. Proponents argued that the measures would make educators' jobs easier by providing a clear framework for handling serious disciplinary cases. They said schools would be safer because students who caused problems would be removed and other students would be deterred from engaging in violent or criminal activity. Critics countered that zero tolerance policies would unfairly target students of color, who already often faced stiffer punishments than their white counterparts for similar offenses. But proponents insisted the policies would be fair— there would be no ambiguity. If kids messed up, they were out. Period.

It didn't take long for the idea to gain momentum, and soon it was appearing frequently in the speeches and policy statements of school board members, politicians, and teachers' union representatives across the country. Parent groups also jumped on the bandwagon, circulating petitions and doing grassroots organizing. To many, zero tolerance made perfect sense. After all, what teacher doesn't want his job to be a little less stressful? What parent doesn't want her child's school to be as safe as possible? What student doesn't want to receive the same treatment as her peers?

As a new teacher struggling to keep my head above water, I didn't pay much attention to these early rumblings. Not that I didn't think it was an important issue. I'd been as bombarded by media stories as the next person, and there were times—inside and outside the classroom—when I felt the paranoia creeping in. But I was more worried about getting LeShawn to come to school and getting Jason to pick up a book than about hypothetical situations involving weapons or drugs. I knew there was a real possibility that I might someday have to confront such a circumstance, but I guess I figured I'd cross that bridge if I came to it. I came to it about two months into my third year as a teacher.

The tardy bell had just rung at Seward Elementary, a mammoth 100-year-old building in a mostly Mexican-American neighborhood known as Back of the Yards. I was at my third-floor hall-duty post, a blur of young people blowing past me in both directions. I said hello to passing kids, a little preoccupied because I had nothing planned for my first-period class, which began in ten minutes, but otherwise feeling pretty good given that it was Monday morning. Then up walked Julio.

Lumbering, baby-faced, and—to use his understated self-description—"kinda chunky," Julio was an eighth grader who liked school a lot more than it liked him. He'd had little official academic success during his elementary career, but he showed up every day seemingly undeterred— cheerful, eager to learn what he could, ready to give it his best shot one more time. I didn't know him that well, but I sensed that he was a kid with a huge and generous heart.

"Hey, Michie," he said, reaching out one hand to shake mine, as he often did. He was carrying a dirt-smudged gym bag in the other.

"'Morning," I answered, grasping his pudgy palm.

He glanced over his shoulder, then looked down the hall in the other direction. It was almost empty. "I need a favor," he said.

"OK," I replied.

"It's a big one," he said, a hint of worry showing on his face. "A real big one."

"OK. What is it?"

"But you can't tell nobody," he said, grabbing his gym bag with both hands. "I mean, I don't wanna get in trouble. I don't wanna get kicked out."

As far as I knew, Julio had never been in trouble for anything, not even minor rule bending, so I couldn't imagine why he thought he was at risk of getting booted out of school. More puzzled than concerned, I motioned him into my classroom.

"I need you to hold my bag for me," he said in hushed tones. "Just till the end of the day."

"OK. You wanna tell me why?"

"Um, well, it's … uh," he stammered. "I brought something to school I wasn't supposed to bring."

I relaxed. I'd dealt with this one before: a kid brings some sort of technically-against-the-rules-but-really-not-such-a-big-deal piece of contraband to school, suddenly is fearful of being discovered, and wants me to stash it for the day. I wondered what Julio wanted me to hold for him. A tape with explicit lyrics? A pack of cigarettes? A hand-me-down copy of Playboy? A pager?

I asked to see what he had, and he partially unzipped the gym bag, pulling it open at one end. I peered inside and saw the unmistakable butt of a rifle.

I could hardly believe it. A gun? Contrary to popular belief, there wasn't a .22 in every desk and a knife in every backpack in Chicago public school classrooms. This was the first time I'd seen an actual weapon in school, and I had no idea how to handle the situation. I had no precedent to fall back on, no well of experience to draw from, nothing from my teacher education courses that seemed relevant. I knew that the Board of Education had a detailed "uniform disciplinary code" that spelled out five categories of student misconduct and a range of disciplinary options for each. I'd never used the code, but I'd looked at it enough times to know that weapon possession was a Group 5 offense, the most severe—a minimum of six to ten days' suspension and a maximum of arrest and expulsion. I remembered a clause buried somewhere in the document that mentioned mitigating circumstances, but I also remembered stories of kids getting suspended for possessing objects that fit the definition of a weapon far less neatly than a gun—nail files, box cutters, X-Acto knives.

All of this spun through my head in a matter of seconds, but it didn't help me figure out what to do. Relying on instinct—or maybe just stalling for time—I started asking questions.

Julio told me that it was a BB gun and that it wasn't loaded, though he had a box of BBs in the bag as well. He said he'd been visiting his uncle in the suburbs over the weekend and that he'd used his gym bag as a makeshift suitcase. His uncle liked to hunt, so Julio had taken along the BB gun, hoping the two might get in some target practice, though that didn't happen. He'd come home from his uncle's late Sunday night, woken up late for school, thrown on some clothes as fast as he could, and rushed out the door to beat the tardy bell. He pointed to his crazily cowlicked hair as evidence. It wasn't until he was inside the building that he'd remembered the gun.

I had no doubt that he was telling the truth. And it was obvious that he had no intention of using the gun, that he wasn't plotting any sort of attack, that bringing it to school was a complete accident. He wouldn't have told me about it otherwise.

So what did I do? I took the bag, locked it up in my closet, talked with Julio about the seriousness of the situation, and made him promise never to make such a mistake again. I returned the bag to him at the end of the day, watched him leave with it, and—until years later—never breathed a word of it to anyone. I had some further conversations with him about the dangers of guns and the risks involved with gun ownership, but other than that, nothing more ever came of the incident.

Julio graduated from eighth grade that June, scraping by with Ds in almost every subject, and went on to high school. I didn't think much more about the incident until several years later, when I read a story in *Teacher* magazine about an eleven-year-old student in Redwood City, California, who'd accidentally brought an unloaded BB gun to class. By this time Congress had passed the Gun-Free Schools Act—which mandated that any student caught with a firearm on campus be expelled—and school boards across the country had embraced zero tolerance as an all-purpose, get-tough, commonsense solution to school safety problems (the Chicago Public Schools adopted the policy in 1995). The boy in California was an honor student and had never been in trouble of any kind, but he was expelled from his elementary school under its zero tolerance policy for his entire sixth-grade year.

I flashed back to that morning with Julio and began wildly second-guessing myself. What if another kid had somehow gotten the gun out of my closet? What if on the way home Julio had decided to show off the gun and had accidentally shot someone? What if he'd been emboldened by my inaction and had shown up with a real gun later in the year? I knew I hadn't handled the situation perfectly. It was poor judgment not to tell any other adult at school what happened, and I could have been more thorough in my follow-up. But the more I thought about the situation and my response to it, the more I was sure I'd done the right thing. Maybe I should have worked out some sort of creative punishment—have Julio do a project on gun violence or arrange for a guest speaker on the topic—but what good would it have done to suspend him or arrest him or expel him for a year? It wouldn't have made our school a safer place, it wouldn't have sent any message to the other students that they didn't already know, and it sure wouldn't have helped Julio.

But in many other zero tolerance cases around the country, those factors didn't seem to enter the equation. Blind adherence to rules was winning out over doing what was in the best interest of children. Kids were being suspended or expelled for things like sharing a cough drop or a Midol capsule, bringing a steak knife to cut a piece of lunch-box chicken, or displaying a one-inch-long pocketknife during show-and-tell.

Even more troubling than the absurdity of the punishments in these instances was the willingness of adults in positions of authority to abdicate responsibility. Don't blame us, the administrators and school board members seemed to say. Our hands are tied; there's nothing we can do. It was an easy out. And that, I realized, had been part of the appeal of zero tolerance from the beginning: the promise of a simple solution to a tough and complex problem.

Maybe that was why I hadn't been completely turned off by zero tolerance proposals at first. Like most new teachers, I was still halfheartedly searching for magic pills—instructional methods that would work with every student, classroom-management techniques that would never fail. Deep down, I sensed that one-size-fits-all approaches were unrealistic, yet on the days—which were many—when I felt my classroom was like a torpedoed ship, I found myself looking for quick fixes. But the longer I taught, the clearer it became that one size didn't fit all. There was no one way to teach reading effectively, no single method of motivating students, no perfect way to bring history lessons to life. And as much as some educators might have wished it were otherwise, the same went for questions of discipline and school safety.

The week before Thanksgiving in 1996, Armando, a seventeen-year-old former student, came by my house to visit. He told me he'd been suspended from his South Side high school yet again, this time for cutting class. "Man, I'm sick and tired of that," he said. "I mean, they're just dropping kids like it's nothing. Sometimes my teacher takes a kid to get written up, and she'll come back and say to us, 'OK, who's next? I'll suspend you for five days right now!' If teachers want kids to do better, why do they suspend them? They should be keeping them in school, not kicking them out. The guy in the detention room, he tells us, 'If you're doing so bad in school, why do you even bother to come?' Sometimes you feel like they don't even want you there."

The zero tolerance policy the Chicago Public Schools adopted—which covers kindergarten through the 12th grade—had a dramatic impact in its first three years. According to Board of Education figures, student suspensions systemwide increased more than 51 percent (from 34,307 to 51,873) during this period and expulsions jumped from 21 in 1994–95 to 668 in 1997–98—an increase of over 3,000 percent. But as usual, the numbers tell only part of the story. While CPS's written zero tolerance policy targets violent and drug-related offenses, more and more students like Armando, who had no such marks on his record, found themselves kicked out for far less serious transgressions—excessive tardiness, skipping class, and failing to wear a student ID were a few of the most common. The uniform discipline code also allowed schools to suspend students for up to five days for repeated violations of catchall infractions such as "failing to abide by school rules" and "defying the authority of school personnel."

Critics of the Board of Education charged that schools were intentionally pushing students out in an effort to improve test scores. The central office denied the allegations, insisting that keeping students in school was a top priority. But while the board had initiated some legitimate efforts to curb the perennially high dropout rate, it had also turned up the heat on administrators to raise standardized test scores by any means necessary. Principals, fearing the threat of probation or school reconstitution, seemed to feel less of an incentive to hold on to kids who might be considered "problems." If those kids weren't in class, their low scores couldn't drag down the school's averages.

Once they were on the streets, it usually wasn't long before they got arrested for one petty offense or another, usually loitering. If schools had zero tolerance, some of the cops who worked in the community seemed to have even less. "All this neighborhood is," a white officer visiting my school once told me, "is one big gang." That sentiment isn't lost on the young people who live in the area. "The cops around here, they take advantage of their badge," says twenty-year-old Paco, who read books about Houdini and dreamed of becoming a magician back when he was in my sixth-grade classroom. "They push people around. They look at us and they think, 'You're a gangbanger, you ain't got no goals. You ain't gonna be nobody in life. You belong in jail.' So they try to lock us up for any kinda reason."

It was disheartening, to say the least, to watch so many of my students graduate from eighth grade and then get pushed out of school only to wind up on the streets or locked up. I knew most of these guys well enough to see that, although they'd made some poor choices, they still had plenty of potential. What they needed was another chance.

I was getting ready to leave for school one morning in February 1998 when I flipped on the radio to check the weather. I was only half listening to the news reports when the phrase "4900 block of South Paulina"—which isn't too far from

Seward—caught my attention. "Double murder last night … fourteen- and fifteen-year-old are dead … Teenager in custody … Police say it could be gang-related." Feeling my stomach tighten, I turned off the radio, grabbed my book bag, and headed out the door.

Soon after arriving at school, I found out that the twelve-year-old arrested for the murders was a seventh grader who was in my reading class. He'd been serving a week-long suspension from Seward for drawing gang signs in his notebook— the final straw in a series of run-ins he'd had with teachers and administrators at school over the previous several months. I'd visited the boy's house the previous afternoon, just hours before the shootings, to take him some assignments and a book to read. I found it hard to believe he'd committed the crime, but according to the police, witnesses said he got out of a car just after 6:30 p.m., walked up to the two other boys, and fired several shots at them point-blank. He tried to run, but a squad car caught up to him a block or so away. Once handcuffed and in the car, police said, he confessed to the killings.

For the next few days my classroom was crawling with reporters, and the story was front-page news in the Chicago Tribune and at the top of nightly newscasts. The coverage was often sensational-ized—a headline in the Salt Lake City Tribune read "Double Murder Halts Career of Chicago Gangster, 12." I could see zero tolerance supporters using the case as evidence of why such harsh measures were necessary. They could argue, "It's a good thing the accused student was suspended at the time of the shooting—just imagine what might have happened had he been in school that day."

But some people saw the shootings as evi-dence that inflexible disciplinary policies weren't working. One of them was Father Bruce Wellems, a priest at Holy Cross Church, which sits directly across the street from Seward. He saw the killings as a wake-up call, a clear sign that something

needed to be done, but he was looking for a better solution. "With something like zero tolerance, you're not dealing with the problem," he says. "You're not facing what the issues really are. It's like the Ten Commandments—'Thou shalt not, thou shalt not, thou shalt not.' OK, but what will you do? What's the other side of that?"

Born and raised in Albuquerque, Wellems had come to Chicago in the early 1980s to study for the priesthood. He'd landed at Holy Cross in 1991 with only a vague idea of what an inner-city ministry should be about and little commit-ment to the neighborhood's struggling youth. "I remember Tim McGovern, who was the park supervisor at the time, working with some of the gang kids, taking them on trips," Wellems says. "He'd always try to get me to come along, but I really didn't want to get into it. I was afraid. I kept trying to turn away from them, and Tim would keep turning me back again. One day we were at the park and I said, 'Tim, you know, these gang kids are really bad kids, they're really dangerous.' And I'll never forget what Tim told me. 'Bruce,' he said, 'these gang kids are your kids.' And he was right. They are our kids."

Wellems started working extensively with dropouts and gang members in the commu-nity, and he quickly discovered that most of them wanted one of two things—a decent job or the chance to continue their education. But finding schools that would accept the kids was hard, and keeping them enrolled was even harder—espe-cially after zero tolerance became the rule.

When Eddie, a fourteen-year-old who'd recently dropped out, was shot in a drive-by, he asked Wellems to help him get back into school. Wellems got him enrolled in a Catholic high school, and Eddie sailed through ninth grade until the final month, when a teacher caught him scribbling gang graffiti on a desk. In short order, he was expelled and given no credit for the course work he'd completed. Wellems tried to intervene, but the principal wouldn't budge. "We don't tolerate gang activity," the principal said. "That's our rule, and we follow our rules."

Fine, Wellems thought. If other schools don't want to help these kids, I'll start my own. He'd tossed around the idea of a community high school before but hadn't known how to get the right people behind it. When the city's attention turned to Back of the Yards in the wake of the two murders, he decided to try to use it to make something good come out of the tragedy. In late February, Chicago Public Schools' CEO Paul Vallas visited Seward, and Wellems tagged along on the tour, championing the idea of an alternative school at every opportunity. By the end of the morning, Vallas had made a verbal commitment.

Launching the high school became Wellems's mission. He decided to call it the Sister Irene Dugan Institute after a Religious of the Cenacle nun who'd worked with some of the neighborhood's gang members during the last year of her life. "Irene always used to tell me, 'Bruce, teach them to read,'" he says. "And that really made sense to me—the importance of learning to read. It does so many things. It raises their self-awareness, their awareness of what's going on around them, what they know, what they're able to know. And as they come to an appreciation of that, they calm down, they grow."

In the months that followed, Wellems formed a coalition of neighborhood educators, business leaders, community activists, and volunteers who worked together to map out details and build support. He visited alternative schools in Los Angeles to gather ideas about scheduling, curriculum, and encouraging parental involvement. Every Tuesday night he and a counselor, Sergio Grajeda, met with a group of 15 to 20 guys who were interested in signing up for the school—getting their input, keeping the momentum going.

As the weeks passed, Wellems cleared or kicked aside hurdle after hurdle, and by August 1998,

Dugan Institute was up and running. Housed in a small brick building on the back lot of Holy Cross that had once been used as overflow classroom space for Seward, the school opened with 19 students, many of whom had police records or were gang members. Several had been pushed out of other schools, often for minor offenses. "Society can say they won't tolerate this type of individual, and so can schools," Wellems says. "But what does that do? It makes the kid feel rejected. They're in a corner, and they give up. They're back out on the street affecting ten other kids in a negative way. How does a kid have room to screw up and grow when you have something like zero tolerance? How about having a kid atone for something? How is there any atonement if you just flat out reject a kid?"

The following June I watched as Dugan's first graduating class of six students walked across the front of Holy Cross's sanctuary to receive their diplomas. Four of them were the first in their families to graduate. The valedictorian, Federico Vega, was twenty-one years old, married with a baby boy, and working a full-time job in addition to his five hours of classes at Dugan. He'd been suspended from high school for fighting at the beginning of his senior year and had given up on returning until Dugan opened. "My life has changed a lot in this past year," he said in his commencement speech. "If I could turn back time I would change all of the negative choices I made in my life, and I would trade them with positive ones. But as you all know, that is impossible to do. I can't change the past, but I can change my future. I can learn from my mistakes and change my ways. I think all of us can."

So we find ourselves at a point where, in order to enroll her five-year-old for kindergarten, a mother must acknowledge the possibility—and the consequences—of her child bringing a pistol to school or attacking a classmate. I guess it shouldn't be surprising. During the ten years since I began teaching in Chicago, young people have become the enemy in America. In the media and in our imaginations, kids have become the scapegoats for our own worst misdeeds. But, examined more closely, this is clearly a distorted view—one that confuses cause for effect. If anything, the reverse is true. Urban children, particularly youth of color, are under attack. Whether through zero tolerance measures, or cuts in funding for arts programs, or antibilingual education crusades, or the exclusive use of biased standardized tests to evaluate student progress, city kids—particularly African Americans and Latinos—are suffering. The question we must ask ourselves is: How will we respond?

In his recent book about the mid-1990s Rwandan genocide and its aftermath, *We Wish to Inform You That Tomorrow We Will Be Killed with Our Families*, Philip Gourevitch tells of being stranded on a remote, muddy road in the mountains of central Rwanda one night when all of a sudden he hears a terrible scream—a woman's voice—off in the distance. The woman continues, in a kind of whooping sound, and soon other voices join in, seemingly mimicking her cry. The hollering rises to a peak and then subsides. About an hour later, Gourevitch sees a group of soldiers emerge from the hills with a prisoner in tow.

When Gourevitch asks one of the Rwandans he is traveling with what happened, the guide explains that the man in custody had been trying to rape the woman Gourevitch first heard scream. And the other voices? asks Gourevitch. The guide says the woman's call was a traditional signal of distress, and that it carried an obligation for anyone within earshot. "You hear it, you do it, too. And you come running," the man says. "This is how Rwandans live in the hills … I cry, you cry. You cry, I cry. We all come running … This is simple. This is normal. This is community."

Our challenges as educators are obviously far different from those of the people living in the

Rwandan hillsides. But, as youth workers like Father Bruce Wellems have shown, our responses can mirror theirs in terms of their compassion, their bravery, and their activism. "The ills of this society affect all of us, and it takes all of us to work together to do something about them," Wellems says. "We can try to blindfold ourselves to it or try to turn away from the kids who need our help, but they're not going away. We turn away because we're afraid to know them. But once you make the effort to get to know them, what you find is a lot life in these guys. I really believe some of our best leaders are going to come from these kids."

Discussion Questions

1. Describe the advantages and disadvantages of *zero tolerance*.

2. Do you believe that zero tolerance is always a necessary strategy for handling certain potentially dangerous situations? Explain.

3. Why is zero tolerance so commonly accepted as appropriate policy?

4. What events during the 1990s helped to mobilize the implementation of zero tolerance policies?

5. Why does zero tolerance mostly affect African American and Hispanic populations?

6. Describe zero tolerance cases you've heard about that demonstrate the absurdity on the part of those administering it.

7. How are students mistreated by zero tolerance policies?

8. What are the alternatives to zero tolerance policies?

Section Four

Managing Students with Special Needs

Introduction

Managing Students with Special Needs

By Dave F. Brown

Inclusion of students with special needs is mandated by law; thus, every general education teacher will have the responsibility of providing appropriate instructional and behavioral interventions to ensure that all students succeed within their classrooms. Students with high-incidence disabilities have been in general education classes for decades, and many strategies exist for identifying and meeting their behavioral needs. More recently identified special needs require new knowledge for how to ensure a cooperative classroom climate.

No teacher can afford to enter a general education classroom without the necessary knowledge and strategies to help students with special needs succeed. This section's authors offer articles on the following:

- behavioral traits of students with attention deficit hyperactivity disorder (ADHD) and attention deficit disorder (ADD);

- successful interventions for students with ADD and ADHD;
- cognitive traits of students with learning disabilities;
- intervention strategies for students with learning disabilities;
- behavioral characteristics of students with oppositional defiant disorder (ODD); and
- successful interventions for students with ODD.

Creating cooperative learning communities within a general education classroom means that teachers must have the additional tools of knowing how to identify and implement appropriate intervention strategies for students with special needs. The articles chosen for this section are intended to provide teachers with the basic components of meeting the needs of most students with high-incidence disabilities.

Teaching Tommy

A Second-Grader with Attention Deficit Hyperactivity Disorder

By Katherine Fachin

When Tommy walked into my second-grade classroom on the first day of school, I was happy to see a familiar face. I looked at him with sympathy and hope, wanting to make the year one of learning and of building self-esteem.

Tommy was coming to my class with a difficult year behind him. He had spent first grade in a highly structured classroom, and he had not conformed to its behavioral standards. The behavior modification used with him in that class had included the removal of rewards, and Tommy had experienced little success in keeping the rewards he earned. He was often in trouble, and everyone in the school knew his name. He was three-fourths of a year behind his peers in reading and writing. These experiences led Tommy to believe that he was stupid and bad. I was determined to replace his negative self-image with a positive one based on academic and social success.

Tommy and I already had a history before that first day of school, for I had tutored him once a week from May through July. Originally, Tommy had qualified for home tutoring because of a myringotomy and an adenoidectomy. In preparation for teaching Tommy at home, I talked to his first-grade teacher to find out about his capabilities and to see if she could recommend any materials, I was disappointed when I talked to her because she seemed so negative about him, yet she lacked any precise descriptions of his learning. I met Tommy with the impression that he had had a tough break—a little child facing a teacher who had no hope in him and who lacked the flexibility to meet his needs. Tommy's mother reaffirmed this impression when she described how the teacher wanted him tested and how she was afraid that they just wanted to drug her child so he would be easier to handle.

Tommy snacked on cupcakes and soda as we worked at the kitchen counter. The phone would ring, and siblings would be preparing to go to after-school activities. Tommy wiggled and slid about on the chair, and he would often take bathroom breaks. By remaining firm, I was able to get Tommy to read and write with me. We talked about his interests, and I got to know him. He had a very limited sight vocabulary and could not predict vowel sounds. He could identify most consonants but could not identify the correct vowels, nor was he familiar with how to spell common endings. Although Tommy did not like to read and write because it was such a struggle, he loved math. Using his fingers, he could calculate all first-grade-level addition and subtraction problems quickly and accurately. Tommy felt very confident of his mathematical abilities.

I became attached to this rough-and-tumble boy with the blue eyes and the big smile. He told me about his daredevil biking stunts and about jumping out of tree houses. Grass stains on his jeans, scrapes on his knees and elbows, and dirty hands were his hard-won war wounds. Tommy struck me as very inquisitive. He spoke of such experiments as creating a pocket of air under water with a bucket. I wondered how I could tap into his creativity in the classroom. Tommy was a very active boy who had trouble maintaining eye contact and concentration, but I attributed these characteristics to his personality, immaturity, diet, and environment. I couldn't understand why a teacher would be so negative about handling him in the classroom.

Over the course of the next school year, I found but why. But I also discovered the joys of teaching Tommy.

Second Grade

Because of my experience tutoring Tommy and my hands-on teaching style, Tommy was placed in my class for second grade. By the third day, I had contacted Dr. Mitchell, our school psychologist. Tommy was singing and making loud noises throughout lessons. He crawled on the floor during transitions and sometimes even during class. As he laughed and shoved his way through the class to line up, he injured other children. He was playful and destructive at the same time. Instead of picking up the blocks when it was time to clean up, he would scatter them wildly with flailing arms and a big grin. Just when a bucket was filled with blocks, Tommy would dump it.

Throughout that first month I used "time out" with Tommy and had him write about his behavior—to no avail. Positive reinforcement, coupled with ignoring Tommy as a negative consequence, also did not increase Tommy's on-task behavior. Indeed, the research shows that these methods are commonly insufficient for children with Attention Deficit Hyperactivity Disorder (ADHD). I think that ignoring Tommy not only didn't work to improve his behavior but was actually harmful to him. When I made it clear that I was ignoring him, he would feel unloved and bad about himself. On one occasion Tommy curled up in fetal position behind the computer. I had to be careful to let him know that I loved him and believed that he was a good and smart boy. When he needed to be reprimanded, I used a firm monotone voice to correct him succinctly. Still, I felt I had to find a way to help Tommy achieve more success in school.

Token Economy

At the suggestion of Dr. Mitchell, I instituted a token economy system of rewards for Tommy. Tangible rewards coupled with positive verbal reinforcement have been shown to be much more effectual than praise alone.[2] From the very beginning, though, Dr. Mitchell made it clear that I needed to document Tommy's behavior. In late September I explained the program to Tommy and then later to his mother over the telephone. He could earn play money in $5 bills for raising his hand, keeping his hands to himself, and being a model student. I would not take away any money that he earned. We would count it up at the end of the day and chart it. At the end of the week, Tommy could use the money to purchase time on the computer, time to play with the math manipulatives, or time for drawing in his journal.

As soon as the system was in effect, Dr. Mitchell observed Tommy in the classroom and charted his behavior at one-minute intervals for 30 minutes. Tommy was out of his seat 76.6% of the observed time, he rolled on the rug 16.6% of the time, and he spoke out of turn 63.3% of the time. Moreover, he exhibited aggressive behavior toward property or individuals 26.6% of the time. For example, he crushed some science material on a shelf, and he also tried to throw an object. Only 3.3% of the time were Tommy's eyes on the teacher while he listened and followed directions. For 86.6% of the time Tommy exhibited excessive or incidental movement, and he was off-task 93.3% of the observed time.

Dr. Mitchell called a meeting that included Tommy's father, Dr. Mitchell, the acting principal, and me. I offered specific examples of Tommy's impulsivity, distractibility, and motoric overflow. His father was upset when he heard about Tommy's behavior and acknowledged that he had wanted Tommy tested last year. He even supported the idea of the token economy and said he would have Tommy use his classroom money to purchase television time, dessert, and video-game time at home. In the coming months Tommy's father very consistently reinforced the token economy at home and signed the papers for Tommy to be tested.

When we began the token economy in September, Tommy averaged $18 a day for the remainder of that month. During October, he averaged $27 a day, with $10 as the lowest amount and $65 as the highest. For November Tommy averaged S31 a day, with a range from $5 to $110. During December Tommy averaged $51 a day, with a range from $15 to $105. With his parents' support for the system at home and Tommy's own interest in the token economy, I was pleased with the improvement.

Although Tommy was somewhat less disruptive, he would still step on other children as we sat on the rug, make intermittent loud noises, call out to other children, fall out of his chair on purpose, and get up from his desk during lessons. When we used blocks for mathematics, he would play with them and knock them off his desk unless I remained right beside him. If he raised his hand and I didn't call on him immediately, he would get angry and within a minute would be off task. His pencil and notebook could be found anywhere in the room but inside his desk. The situation was most difficult during whole-class times and transitions.

On the other hand, Tommy wanted very much to please me, and he would write me apologies and notes about how he loved me. After the fact, he felt bad about hurting other children and disrupting the class, so I tried to show him affection at every good opportunity.

Despite these difficult times, Tommy also showed his potential to succeed in school. Three days a week for 45 minutes, my instructional support teacher, Mrs. DeVito, worked with Tommy in a small reading group while I worked with two other groups. The fit between Mrs. DeVito's teaching style and Tommy's needs was perfect. Mrs. DeVito enthusiastically and dramatically offered her students positive reinforcement, and Tommy would glow from her praise. She also used a fast-paced, question-and-answer format for lessons that would not allow Tommy to lose focus. He looked forward to his time with Mrs. DeVito and showed great progress in reading. His sight vocabulary and word-attack skills were improving steadily.

ADHD as a Motivational Disorder

This disparity between Tommy's highly distractible and impulsive behavior during whole-class activities and his focused and appropriate behavior in the small reading group was very disconcerting for me. Throughout the year I analyzed and reanalyzed my teaching. I too am a lively and interactive teacher who uses a variety of visual and tactile methods. I made modifications for Tommy so that he could take breaks, vary his tasks more frequently, and stand up while working. I reorganized the classroom so that he was surrounded by calmer children and was seated directly in front of me as I taught. Why couldn't I achieve the same attending behavior as Mrs. DeVito could?

Russell Barkley explains this discrepancy in behavior by characterizing ADHD as a motivational disorder.[3] A child with ADHD can attend well in a highly motivating situation, such as while watching a favorite television program or playing a video game. When the situation is less intrinsically motivating or when there is delayed rather than immediate feedback, the child will display the characteristics of ADHD. This is why the token economy was somewhat successful during whole-class times when Tommy would not be called on as frequently as in a small group.

After seven months, Tommy continued to exhibit frequently every one of the 14 characteristics that the American Psychiatric Association lists as diagnostic criteria for ADHD. (For a list of these characteristics and a brief description of how they can be used in diagnosis, see Anna M. Thompson, "Attention Deficit Hyperactivity Disorder: A Parent's Perspective," page 433, this *Kappan*.)

Interventions

At the classification meeting in December, I found out that Tommy was classified as perceptually impaired because of the discrepancy between his general cognitive ability and his specific achievement in reading and language arts. Although a neurologist had diagnosed Tommy as exhibiting ADHD, this condition was not included in his individualized education program (IEP) in January because the psychologist explained that there was no separate classification in education for ADHD. In January 1995 an IEP was written that allowed Tommy three half-hour sessions in the resource room for language arts and provided an in-class aide each day from 1:30 p.m. to 2:30 p.m.

Resource room. The resource room teacher, Miss Steven, focused on Tommy's spelling. She created an individualized list for him using words from the Dolch list as well as words that exhibited a regular spelling pattern. She scrambled the letters in the words for him to correct, asked him to write his homework sentences in the resource room, and let him write words with colored glue on cards. Using the glue was very motivating for Tommy. When it dried, Miss Steven instructed him to trace over it with his finger. The success of this use of colored glue is consistent with research that suggests that ADHD students "selectively attend to novelty such as color, changes in size, and movement."[4] Tommy went from getting at least 50% wrong on every spelling test to getting all but one word correct. His journal writing also reflected this change.

In-class aide. Tommy was assigned an aide, Mrs. Hellwell, in the last week of February. I gave Mrs. Hellwell a list of appropriate behaviors, inappropriate behaviors, and interventions. She reinforced Tommy's appropriate behavior and provided one-on-one tutoring in the classroom. When he was highly disruptive, she also provided alternative activities. At the end of the day, Mrs. Hellwell monitored Tommy as he counted and charted his earned money. This was a tremendous help to me because it was simply exhausting to manage Tommy and the token economy all day while trying to teach and pay attention to the needs of the rest of the class.

To help with transitions, particularly the transition from lunch recess to afternoon classroom activities, I employed relaxation techniques.[5] I walked the children in from the school yard and asked them to sit at their desks. One row at a time, I called them to lie or sit on the rug. (This usually helped keep Tommy from stepping on anyone.) Then I turned out the lights and talked the children through a breathing exercise; cued them to tense, hold, and relax their muscles; and used guided imagery of peaceful places and activities. Sometimes I encouraged them to think of themselves doing something challenging and achieving success.

At first Tommy wouldn't hold still for these techniques, so I began to sit knee to knee in front of him on the floor as I led the class. After some experience with relaxation, he gradually became able to participate without my sitting with him. As I led the class from a chair, I could see him following my cues for breathing in and out and witnessed his body growing still. Tommy also displayed some enthusiasm for the practices. One day, after I asked the children to try thinking of their own images of succeeding, Tommy told us about how he imagined himself winning a karate match he was nervous about that evening. My long-range goal was to be able to suggest to Tommy that he use the techniques on his own during the day to relax himself. As we walked down the hall, I would say to him, "Tommy, do you notice how you are making loud noises or knocking into the walls? Try breathing like we do after lunch. Can you breathe in a color? Sometimes he used my suggestions independently, and sometimes I had to take the time to help him use the techniques before we continued walking.

Peer tutoring. At the beginning of the year, the other children in the class thought Tommy was funny and enjoyed his daring and his flouting of classroom rules. Then they became jealous of the extra attention he got from me and tried to imitate his behavior or to win my attention in other ways. Eventually, though, they began to grow angry with him for hurting them or for not waiting his turn or for disrupting class. I felt I had to find a role for the other children in the class.

All through the year I had talked to the whole class about how I was responding to Tommy and had discussed how everyone should act and why. One day, Tommy pulled a chair out from under another child, causing her to hit her head hard as she fell. He started in horror as she cried. A couple of days later, I talked about how we sometimes think of our conscience as a devil on one shoulder and an angel on the other. Tommy called out, "I think my devil killed my angel," and " I'm evil." I asked, "How did you feel when Susan hit her head? A bad person would not feel sad. You have an angel. It just talks to you too late. We need to teach your angel to give you advice before you do something." I had never seen such a look of relief and peace on Tommy's face. I could have cried.

Then I was able to enlist the help of the other students. Each day, a different student, alternating boys and girls, would be a peer tutor and help Tommy's angel "talk." I got an empty desk to put next to Tommy's for his peer tutor. I coached the peer tutor to remind him of proper classroom behavior in a nice way, to set a good example, and to accompany him when he used his money for rewards. Attitudes toward Tommy improved as the other students saw themselves as his helpers and saw Tommy as not a bad kid. Of course, not every match worked, and the boys especially found it difficult not to incite Tommy's off-task behavior and then to goof off with him.

Modifying the behavior modification. After using the token economy for five months, I felt as if Tommy was hitting a plateau. His behavior in whole-class situations was still unacceptable. I decided to buy a digital timer to help him set goals. I would set the timer for five minutes, and he could earn $5 only if he raised his hand before speaking and generally acted appropriately for the full five minutes. I discovered that he tried very hard but could make five minutes only about 60% of the time. He never made it to six minutes.

It was February, and Tommy was getting into a lot of trouble on the bus and during recess. He often found himself in the principal's office. His mother was being called every day. I had tried so hard, and yet his year in my class was turning out just like the previous year. The art and physical education teachers came to me out of frustration about his behavior, and we talked about assertive discipline and about ways to manage Tommy. In a letter to Dr. Mitchell, they expressed their concerns about how Tommy was detracting from the learning experiences of the other students in the class.

Changing placement. What else could we try? Dr. Mitchell said that our last resort would be to explore different placement options for Tommy next year. A regular classroom might be inappropriate. Since our district did not have a special education classroom, that would mean an out-of-district placement. Based on my feelings of loyalty to Tommy and his parents, I asked that I be the one to discuss this with his parents.

I called Tommy's father at the beginning of March and described the situation. I told him that we needed to explore other school placement options if Tommy's behavior did not change. During our telephone conversation I also mentioned that perhaps he and his wife might reconsider taking Tommy to his pediatrician and trying medication. We met two weeks later at parent/teacher conferences to discuss the situation in more depth. I came to the meeting with a prepared presentation detailing Tommy's behavior, the interventions that had been tried, an analysis of his progress, and the options for the future. Tommy's father informed me at that time that they would be taking Tommy to the pediatrician to try medication. They had already reached a decision before our meeting.

Medication. Tommy was on Ritalin for the last month of school. For five days he would take a dose of five milligrams before school, and it would wear off around noon. The first day he was on the medication, he earned the most money he had ever earned in a day, $110. He behaved appropriately for 15-minute intervals. He never lost his sense of humor or energy or bubbliness.

The difference was remarkable. I would see him begin to call out and then stop himself to raise his hand. He would set the timer and look at it to monitor himself. All his behaviors seemed to indicate that he was more receptive to reinforcers. The entire class responded to Tommy with spontaneous encouragement and praise, though they didn't know he was taking medication. On the first day, one beaming student told me, "This is such a good day!" Tommy was riding so high from the morning that his general sense of feeling good about himself helped him make it through the afternoon. Although he would lose his pencil constantly in the afternoon and rush from one thing to another, he tried successfully to follow classroom rules.

Even on the medication, though, the daily variation in Tommy's behavior remained. Some days he was simply more active than others. For example, on the third morning after he began taking medication, Tommy was still shaking his leg and foot the whole time he was leading the pledge.

Every day I talked to his father after school on the phone to inform him of Tommy's reaction to the medication. His father was so relieved to hear of Tommy's success. He said that he would contact the pediatrician about an afternoon dose.

Tommy continued until the end of the school year with both a morning and an afternoon dose of Ritalin. There were days when I questioned whether or not he was given the dose before he came to school, but I didn't voice these concerns. We also had some difficulty establishing exactly when the second dose should be administered, and I had difficulty remembering to send him to the nurse's office before he exhibited severe off-task behavior.

I do not mean to argue for the use of medication to address the needs of all ADHD students. I see medication as a last resort and one that should be used in combination with a comprehensive behavioral and academic program. I offered Tommy an activities-based curriculum to tap into his energy and creativity. I taught abstract ideas concretely and contextually. I consistently used and adapted behavior modification techniques and tried other techniques like relaxation exercises. I let Tommy know that I thought he was a great kid and a talented person, too. I had the class support Tommy as peer tutors and as members of project teams, literature study groups, and cooperative learning groups. The district provided instructional and noninstructional support. But Tommy needed something more to enable him to benefit from these interventions. Tommy's ADHD was severe, and the medication helped him achieve success in the classroom.

From my experience with Tommy and his family, I have come to believe even more strongly that it is vital to gain the trust of parents. Their faith in our efforts and concern for their child must be the basis for communication and teamwork between home and school. I also realize how painful it can be for parents to accept that their child might need extra help and even medication. By fielding my colleagues' complaints about Tommy's behavior, I got a small taste of what parents must feel when they are told by friends, family members, and doctors that they don't know how to discipline their children. More painful than the frustration of trying to deal with the condition of ADHD itself is enduring the criticism and condemnation that come from others. I think that this holds true for the student, the parents, and the teacher.

Notes

1. Lee A. Rosen et al., "The Importance of Prudent Negative Consequences for Maintaining the Appropriate Behavior of Hyperactive Students," *Journal of Abnormal Child Psychology, vol. 12,* 1984, pp. 581–604.
2. Linda J. Pfiffner, Lee A. Rosen, and Susan G. O'Leary, "The Efficacy of an All-Positive Approach to Classroom Management," *Journal of Applied Behavior Analysis, vol. 18,* 1985, pp. 257–61.
3. Russell A. Barkley, *Attention Deficit Hyperactivity Disorder: A Handbook for Diagnosis and Treatment* (New York: Guilford Press, 1990).
4. Sydney S. Zentall, "Research on the Educational Implications of Attention Deficit Hyperactivity Disorder" *Exceptional Children, vol. 60,* 1993, p. 143.
5. Sandra F. Rief, *How to Reach and Teach ADD/ADHD Children* (New York: Center for Applied Research in Education, 1993).

Discussion Questions

1. What do you know about children with attention deficit hyperactivity disorder (ADHD)?

2. What are Tommy's personal eating habits like? Does diet have any effect on children with ADHD behaviors? What are the physical/cognitive factors that affect and cause ADHD?

3. What are the general intelligence levels of children with ADHD or ADD? How are ADD and ADHD different from one another?

4. What are some instruments that are used to determine if a child might exhibit ADHD traits?

5. Would token economies likely be successful with most children with ADHD? What are some

valid rewards for a token economy? Can token economy be used with only one or two students in a class?

6. Make a list of all of the interventions that Ms. Fachin used with Tommy.

7. Which of these interventions would you be willing to use? Which would you never consider?

8. How can teachers, parents/caregivers, and medical professionals ensure that medication is successful for children who take it for ADD or ADHD?

Students with Attention Deficit Hyperactivity Disorder

by Mark Boynton and Christine Boynton

Students who display characteristics of attention deficit hyperactivity disorder (ADHD) or have been diagnosed with this disorder present many challenges to their own learning and to school staffs. MacKenzie (1996) states that ADHD affects 3 to 5 percent of the school-age population and crosses all socioeconomic, racial, and cultural groups, affecting more boys than girls. Barkley (1990) says that 3 to 9 percent of the general population meets the criteria for ADHD. Due to this high incidence level, it is extremely important that educators are knowledgeable concerning the disorder and are familiar with approaches that are successful in dealing with these students..

MacKenzie (1996) says that attention deficit disorder (ADD) and ADHD are both described as ADHD in the literature, although ADD doesn't include the hyperactivity symptoms. The behavioral and neurological features of ADHD include problems in attention span, increased activity level, and decreased impulse control. Symptoms include distractibility; difficulty listening and staying on task and focused; difficulty following directions; a tendency to jump among tasks;

difficulty keeping track of assignments and materials; and a tendency to be easily frustrated and overwhelmed. Without intervention, students with ADHD can get caught in a cycle of frustration and falling behind, and their behaviors can have a negative impact on their achievement and success in school.

Zametkin and colleagues (1993) state that ADHD is genetic, the result of problems with activity in certain areas of the brain that control impulsivity, arousal, and sensitivity to rewards and punishments. MacKenzie (1996) says that the good news is that the disorder is treatable and that early diagnosis and treatment are the most beneficial to students. Assessment for ADHD involves a battery of medical, psychological, behavioral, and academic tests conducted by a variety of educational and medical professionals. It includes using instruments such as behavioral rating scales, observations, history information, and educational records. The school team does an assessment following a 504 or individualized education plan (IEP) process. The medical assessment is needed to rule out any medical issues that may be contributing to the diagnosis. The treatments are also collaborative, involving a team that combines medical management, classroom accommodations, counseling, and behavior modification by the appropriate professionals (MacKenzie, 1996). In this chapter, we will focus on the classroom and educational strategies.

Behavior management techniques are often not different than those used with other students. It is just that more are needed with students with ADHD. Consequences must be imposed more frequently, and it is more important to have parallel management systems between home and school (MacKenzie, 1996). It is essential to remember to avoid punitive measures and permissive approaches; these result in power struggles that are ineffective, waste time, and damage the relationship between teacher and student.

Another point to remember is that because even some students who aren't labeled as ADHD also exhibit many of the ADHD characteristics, these strategies can help with other students as well (Levin & Shanken-Kaye, 1996). Following are strategies for the education and management of students with ADHD.

Teaching and Management Strategies for Students with ADHD

Selectively Ignore Misbehaviors

It is important for teachers of students with ADHD to "select their battles." If you do not distinguish between behaviors that are significant enough to warrant interventions and those that can be ignored, you may find yourself constantly disciplining the student with ADHD for minor inappropriate behaviors that are often beyond the student's control. If a behavior is not significantly impacting the classroom environment or the student's learning, you might consider ignoring the behavior. This is where meeting with the

school's team—its multidisciplinary team (MDT), individualized education plan team, or case study team—is important so that the individuals with training and experience in dealing with these situations can come together and support both student and teacher in determining which approaches to take and which specific behaviors to deal with.

As an example, let's look at Josh, a 3rd grade student who has been diagnosed with ADHD. He has a number of ADHD behaviors, including rocking in his chair, fidgeting, and calling out without raising his hand. The MDT working with Josh's teacher has identified that the major behavior that is disruptive to the classroom is calling out without raising his hand. They work with the teacher to develop a plan to focus on that behavior, giving Josh positive points each time he raises his hand rather than calling out for the teacher's attention.

Redirect with Prearranged Signals and Nonverbal Gestures

Some students with ADHD respond well to nonverbal gestures and reminders. Shrigley (1985) says there is a hierarchy that should be used with all students in dealing with disruptive behaviors, moving from nonverbal intervention to verbal intervention to the implementation of more direct consequences. In addition, Shrigley remarks that nonverbal and verbal interventions are shown to effectively manage 75 percent of classroom disruptions.

MacKenzie (1996) also notes that using a secret signal to get a student's attention or using consistent signals, like saying, "Eyes on me," is effective. In using special nonverbal signals with a student with ADHD, privately meet with the student to remind him that certain signals will be used to redirect his behaviors. This approach can prevent the need to call negative attention to the student. For example, a red card placed on his desk can remind him to raise his hand before answering a question.

Avoid Classroom "Down Time"

Students with ADHD often struggle with breaks in the day when they have nothing to do. An effective strategy is to keep them task-oriented and active at all times. For example, as students enter the classroom in the morning, they should have an assignment to work on immediately, such as a daily assignment shown on the overhead projector.

Provide an Alternative Activity

If you are in tune with the behaviors of the student with ADHD and you notice she is becoming especially restless, you can avoid further problems by giving her a task to do to divert her energy. An example would be to have her erase the chalkboard or take a message to the office. Often this break is just enough to calm the student down and help her to get back to work.

Display Desired Behaviors on Charts and Graphs

Students with ADHD often respond well to charts and graphs that display behaviors that have been targeted as goals (Rief, 1998). These charts and graphs not only serve as reminders to the student of the desired behaviors, but also act as incentives for attainment of the goal.

For example, a chart could be made for tracking when the student works quietly at her desk during independent seat work. Or a chart could be used to check each time the student raises her hand rather than shouting out a response or request. The teacher, another student, or the ADHD student herself can be responsible for making the

checks. It is important to chart desired behaviors that are within the student's ability level.

Teach Step-by-Step Behavioral Expectations

Many students with ADHD struggle when faced with a series of behavioral steps and expectations, when they transition from one activity to another or when given multistep directions. Make instructions clear, and give them one at a time. Giving directions verbally and in writing will also foster success for the student (MacKenzie, 1996).

Examples of transitions that may be difficult include getting ready for P.E., changing from one subject to the next, or preparing to go to lunch. A strategy that is often successful is to preteach expectations to the student with ADHD before each of these transitions. Sometimes, using another student to work with the student with ADHD is also helpful. Also, prepare the ADHD student by giving him warnings before transitions.

Schedule Breaks and Activities

Many students with ADHD become restless and disruptive after being seated and working on academics for a significant time period. It is advisable to schedule breaks during long academic periods (MacKenzie, 1996).

Also, scheduling P.E. classes, library time,, computer sessions, or group discussions between periods of academic study are ways to add movement and variety to break up long sessions of concentration for the student with ADHD, as well as for the rest of the class.

Select a "Buddy" to Help

This has been mentioned in a couple of earlier examples, but it is often helpful to assign a responsible student to be a friend who can quietly help the student with ADHD in certain areas. Examples of ways other students can help include keeping track of appropriate behaviors being charted and modeling how to follow step-by-step directions (MacKenzie, 1996).

Establish a Nonstimulating and Quiet Location

Often students with ADHD benefit from having an opportunity to go to an area of the classroom or building where they will not be distracted by classroom stimuli (Rief, 1998). A study carrel in the back or a corner of the room or a time-out location in the office can be helpful. It is important that these areas are introduced and implemented as helpful strategies for the student rather than as a punishment or consequence for inappropriate behaviors.

Ask the Student to Repeat Directions

Many students with ADHD struggle with directions they are to follow when preparing for an activity, assignment, or transition. Quietly asking them to repeat the directions to the teacher, to a buddy student, or to the class as a way to check for understanding helps students with ADHD remember each step (Rief, 1998).

Allow the Student to Hold Something During Teacher-Led Instruction

Some students with ADHD find themselves better able to focus and stay on task when they are allowed to hold something in their hands, such as a small squeeze ball, during teacher-led discussions (Rief, 1998). If this strategy is put into practice, it is important that it be used with a student who will not take advantage of it. Also, a diplomatic explanation to the rest of the class regarding the exception to the rule of "no objects on the desk" is warranted.

Set Clearly Defined and Marked Classroom Boundaries

Some students with ADHD have a difficult time staying in one location and not going to areas of the room that are off limits. These students will also sometimes get into other students' space. Placing tape around the student's desk to delineate acceptable boundaries can help her remember to stay in a certain area (Rief, 1998). However, consider the age and the issue of embarrassment when using this strategy, keeping the student's parents informed about the rationale for this strategy is also a good idea.

Encourage Participation in Extracurricular Activities

Many students with ADHD not only enjoy but excel in athletics and other extracurricular activities, such as art, music, and crafts. Extracurricular activities not only provide a great deal of enjoyment for students with ADHD; they also often help them to develop self-esteem. It is important for teachers to assist and encourage students with ADHD to become involved in activities they are interested in and in which they have special skills. Reminding students of registration deadlines, talking to coaches about their skills, and giving them positive reinforcement for their involvement in these activities are strategies to use (Levin & Shanken-Kaye, 1996).

Adjust Homework Expectations

Most students with ADHD struggle with homework. Homework can also create severe challenges and frustration for the student's parents as they attempt to help their child. Teachers should remember that homework that might take an average student 20 minutes to complete often takes the student with ADHD three to four times as long. It is advisable to assign homework that is at the student's ability level and the appropriate length (MacKenzie, 1996). Also, make certain that homework assignments are reviews of material rather than new learning. A good strategy is to have a buddy student that the student with ADHD can check with on the phone regarding homework assignments.

Use Auditory and Visual Cues to Help Focus Attention and Emphasize Critical Points

When you are conducting teacher-directed instruction, it often helps to use additional cues in order to aid students with ADHD in focusing on critical concepts. Writing with colored chalk, varying your voice level, emphasizing critical points with a laser pointer, and using illustrations often help students with ADHD grasp and remember critical concepts (Rief, 1998).

Consider Letting Students Use Headphones

Allowing students with ADHD to block out noise distractions and auditory stimuli by letting them wear noise-stopping headphones in the classroom is often desirable (Rief, 1998). Appropriate times to use this strategy are during tests and independent seat work activities.

Teach Appropriate "Help Needed" Strategies

Whereas most students become frustrated during independent seat work when they need help or are confused, the concern is more significant for students with ADHD. You should take the time to teach these students acceptable ways to indicate they need help. Using a "help needed" flag on the corner of the desk or displaying an index card with "help" written on it are ways of signaling that

a student needs your attention. When a help signal is displayed, you should make every effort to provide the needed assistance as quickly as possible.

Select Assignments at the Correct Level of Difficulty

Students with ADHD often become frustrated and upset when their academic assignments are at a level that is much higher than their ability levels. While this can be a problem for all students, the likelihood of its happening with ADHD students is higher because they typically struggle with work that the average student can handle. Classroom teachers should participate in forming the student's IEP, meet with the special education teacher, and examine tests and achievement patterns closely when monitoring the student's academic performance. They should also not hesitate to modify assignments to meet the student's needs (MacKenzie, 1996).

Place the Student's Desk in a Nondistracting Location

The location of the desk of a student with ADHD can have a critical impact on his academic and behavioral performance. MacKenzie (1996) suggests placing the student's desk near the teacher's desk, with his back to other students. Remember that students with ADHD can easily be distracted when they sit next to windows, mobiles, and artistic displays. They should be in low-traffic areas, such as away from the door, the drinking fountain, and the pencil sharpener. It is desirable to place the desk next to students who are calm and have a history of sitting quietly during teacher-led discussions and independent seat work.

Assign Jobs

Assigning classroom jobs whenever possible to students with ADHD will help build their self-esteem, improve the teacher-student relationship, and diffuse high levels of energy (MacKenzie, 1996). Examples of appropriate jobs include collecting student work, taking messages to the office, taking down students' chairs, and passing out papers. A key time to do this in order to head off further problems is when the student is beginning to become disruptive.

Use Stretch Times

With all students, but especially with students with ADHD, it's a good idea to have stretch breaks embedded within or between long periods of academic study, such as extended discussion periods or long tests.

Use Findings from Time Studies

Time studies indicate that short-term memory peaks at 9:00 a.m. and long-term memory peaks at 3:00 p.m (Armstrong, 1999). You should use this knowledge in planning your daily schedule. Plan to give pop quizzes, lectures, and drills in the morning and focus on motor activities, projects, music, P.E., and art activities in the afternoon.

Build on Incidental Learning Capabilities

Studies indicate that students with ADHD often learn incidental facts that they aren't taught (Armstrong, 1999). For example, they may know how many dots are on the wall or the number of cars in the parking lot. Take advantage of this skill by posting spelling words on the wall before tests or putting math facts on bulletin boards.

Discussion Questions

1. Describe five interventions teachers can make that prevent misbehaviors from occurring for students with ADHD or ADD.

2. Which of the strategies suggested by the authors help with organizational skills?

3. Which suggestions prevent students from receiving too many stimuli?

4. What are some strategies for helping students with ADHD or ADD meet with success in completing and turning in homework?

5. Under what circumstances should teachers meet with parents/caregivers to rewrite a child's individualized educational program/plan?

6. What is the role of teachers in determining if a child needs medication to assist him or her in performing successfully at school, either behaviorally or academically?

Numbers and Letters, Stand Still!

By Christopher Lee and Rosemary Jackson

Up and Over
Up and Over
And in-between,
The Letters,
Words,
Paragraphs
Wash Over Me.
Like a thunderstorm
In Georgia on a summer afternoon Full of
Sound and Fury
I am drenched and overwhelmed
I search the puddles (now muddy)
I sift and sort and wash clean the concepts.
I then send these thoughts to You.
I struggle to be understood by you
Do you understand? I am now Clear as Mud.
                                   —Carolyn Phillips

There is a specific feeling I have about letters, words, and numbers. Perhaps the description that best fits my feelings would be "chaotic emptiness." The chaotic part is that the symbols swirl around in my head, never sticking in one place long enough for my mind to lock onto them; the emptiness part is that they have no meaning or soul. For years I was fascinated about why my mother would stay up late at night and read, not to mention her ability to get lost within her books. It seemed to me that everywhere I turned, people were entranced with the written word—a government conspiracy, I was sure. The bus stations, airports, supermarkets, libraries, streets … everywhere I looked was the written word. It just didn't make sense to me why—or better yet, how—anyone could fall in love with written language. I hated it! It invaded my life in every area and caused me to develop an intense dislike of school from the beginning. My strongest feelings of chaotic emptiness are attached to years of homework rituals.

I rub my eyes as I flip open my fifth grade social studies book. I hate this book! It looks and feels like a tree sandwich, sliced thick on the outside and extra thin on the inside. I have many times felt sorry for the trees that were sacrificed for all the social studies books that have been wasted on me, always shadowing me. I can't seem to lose this sandwich. It's in my locker, on my back, at my desk … and here at the dining room table. What a terrible thing to do to a tree! Trees are meant for climbing to the sky, building forts, carving initials, swinging through the air, and, most importantly, hiding from parents. I guess I don't get it. Why would anyone want to slice and dice a perfectly good tree for a book? I'm sure this is the same book that I had last year, and even the year before. It's got to be a trick—a con game. The pile of letters inside the cover has not changed. The only difference year after year is the shiny new cover that displays the "picture of the year," a picture that lets me know that this book is a social studies book rather than one of its counterparts—history, math, English—or one of those other heavy sandwiches that follow me year after year.

A familiar presence enters the room, hovering, speaking not a word. Our eyes meet … a nightly ritual: mom and son, battling it out over homework. However my mom and I have an understanding. By this time in my school career, we have fought every fight and tested each other's limits; she has become a master at finding my hiding places, even the ones in the trees. I glance at the top of the page. Placing my palm on the page, I rub it hard. Up and down, up and down. I imagine how cool it would be to be able to read with the palm of my hand … to have all of those menacing letters absorb into my bloodstream to be carried to my brain for dissection and understanding. If only this were a real possibility rather than a fantasy. Instead, I must use my eyeballs to read this text. I must have the weakest eyeballs on this planet! They tire easily and leave me stranded, most often at the beginning of the page. My eyeballs are unlike my legs. You see, I'm the fastest guy in the fifth grade. I can run and run without ever getting tired. I am a champion runner, but a loser when it comes to reading. My legs understand what needs to be done in order to win a race. But my eyeballs get lost trying to perceive the random shotgun blast of letters, numbers, and symbols that come at me off the page.

Closing my eyes to rest, I reopen them to search for the one thing in books that makes sense to me: pictures. Where are they? This page has none. What will I do? Pictures are my guides, leading me through a fantasy world that the letters and words lock me out of. Taking a moment, I flip through the next few pages, hoping to suck out the meaning of this chapter. Pictures of Indians and Pilgrims are scattered across the pages. I look closely at them all, assessing each one, hoping that they will show me the story that is apparently spelled out in ink. But it's another lost cause, another race my eyeballs will lose.

Intuitively, Mom sits down beside me. Without any questions, she begins to read aloud to me, somehow able to make sense of all those ink blobs in front of us. Nine-thirty comes. As I crawl into bed, I take a deep breath and fall into my own pity pit, which is close to overflowing. I am stupid, stupid, stupid! Staring out my window, I lock my eyes on the moon, wishing that my teachers could make those letters and numbers stand still. If they were really good teachers, they would be able to fix my brain.

As an adult thinking back to the time in my life when I was a little kid struggling to understand why I could not read, I realize how naive my beliefs were about myself as well as about my teachers. I was a ten-year-old boy blaming myself and my teachers for my lack of ability to recognize words and comprehend their meaning. I needed the letters and words to stand still on the page. The letters held no meaning for me because I could not attach sounds to most of them. The words undulated on the page like amoebae. Sentences represented a marathon during which I had to constantly stop and start at each individual letter, getting more confused and anxious the farther I read.

I don't remember ever being officially labeled as an "anxious" child. You know, the type of child who tapped his pencil constantly on the desk or broke into hives when a stranger would enter the room. However, as I have grown older I have reexamined the amount of stress and anxiety that I was dealing with as a child growing up with a hidden disability. Everyone has experienced anxiety-causing situations. As a student athlete, I was always under pressure to beat the guy next to me or to make a specific cut-off time. This pressure at times caused me to be anxious. However, in looking back to my childhood, I now know that same feeling I felt on the starting block was with me every day in the classroom. My controlled anxiety was deep within me and never left. It ran as an undercurrent all the time. It traveled with me wherever I went. I obviously had control of my anxiety, but what I realize now is that it fed off me for years without my dealing with it. Reading was one of the major players in my anxiety. Like plaque eating away at teeth and gums, anxiety slowly ate away at what little self-confidence I had at the time. Even though my anxiety did not show on the outside, it would flare up when I was presented with any sort of reading material: books, menus, cards, tests, signs, magazines, comic books, or whatever. The anxiety came from a feeling of failure for not being able to read or comprehend what was placed before me. As my eyes would scan the secret code, letter by letter, I would strain to decipher things. Depending on the day and my state of mind, my reading ability would fluctuate. In fact, it was a mystery to my teachers why I was able to read relatively well one day and not at all the next. I felt that I read better when I was in a good state of mind. This would happen on a few occasions when the forces of the planets were properly aligned, my friends weren't teasing me, my mom wasn't mad with me and I had placed well in a swimming competition. On those days, I was able to figure out (decode) more words

than usual, which led to comprehending my reading material a little better.

Decoding

A learning disability that specifically affects reading and spelling is often referred to as dyslexia, a term with which I am all too familiar. Teachers cannot help me or other students with dyslexia break the reading code by using the same techniques they use with other students because we don't perceive the same code as everyone else. Phonics rules and word-attack skills are based on the premise that sounds consistently go with certain letters and that letters are placed in words in certain patterns. I perceive letters, words, and symbols differently than everyone else. My brain is a factory that produces its own secret codes. This factory in my head processes the written word in a chaotic fashion, working in a manner that does not correspond to other student factories. At times I feel that the employees running my factory are from a variety of different countries, each trying to help me perceive the written word in his or her own language.

I have spent many hours trying to understand my reading process. I know that the first stumbling block I encounter is my lack of ability to connect sounds and symbols. This is not caused by poor auditory or visual acuity; my eyesight is fine and my hearing is strong. However, somewhere in my brain I am not able to make the link between certain letters and their sounds. For instance, I confuse four out of the five vowels, meaning that when I see an O, I might say the sound for I or E. Quite often when I see a U, I say the sound for O. The sounds and symbols for E, I, O, and U are interchangeable in my mind. They always have been and probably always will be. At any point in time, my brain may confuse letter sounds and symbols; however, one letter I can always count on misperceiving is R, which my brain does not seem to process at all. This is evident in my speech; any word with an "r" comes out somewhat distorted so that a boy from the South often sounds as if he has a Northern drawl.

The more letters are put together, the more difficult they are to read. People have tried to teach me the rules of phonics, along with vowels and blends and digraphs, and I can be successful at times in applying those rules and reproducing sound combinations. However, when I try to apply what I have learned to attack a word, I am usually unsuccessful, because the individual vowel sounds and combinations change their sounds and forms when they all get together, in most cases making it a guessing game. It's like a crowded party where all the sounds and faces run together. For example, the word church should be easy to sound out according to the sounds and rules of phonics. However, the middle two letters—ur—elude me because of my brain's inability to maintain the connection between the U and its sound, the R and its sound, and the entirely new sound created by the U and R together. It's much like walking along the shore and looking back to discover that your footprints are vanishing before your eyes. The part of my brain that recognizes groups of letters or words decodes the letters much like the game, "Musical Chairs." The letters seem to fall into the chairs in a different order every time I look at them. For example, it is often difficult for me to recognize my own name. Sometimes the s and the i switch places, so that my name comes out as Chrsitopher. At other times when I read my name, certain letters are missing, especially ones in the middle, so that my name might read as Chrtopher or Christher or Chrtpher. Christmas is a terribly confusing time of year for me because the word Christmas is so similar to Christopher. When I was younger, I found it almost impossible to distinguish between the two. Looking around and seeing my name everywhere, I knew Christmas had to be a very special holiday.

The second part of reading, after one learns to decode the sounds and symbols, is attaching meaning to those words, or comprehension. As one might imagine, it is difficult to comprehend the meaning of words when you can't decode the words themselves. I have been told that one of the keys to comprehension is the ability to predict what is going to happen. Teachers ask questions to help students figure out what they are about to read. The ability to predict appears to be one of my strengths. If I can decode just a few words in a sentence, I can make an educated prediction about what the sentence means. Then I can add the key words from all the sentences together with my intuition and prediction skills to make a pretty good guess about the meaning of a paragraph.

If I could go back and talk to my teachers, I would tell them that making me read aloud did not help my reading ability at all. Having me read aloud focused only on my decoding abilities, which were essentially nonexistent. When allowed to read silently, I developed my own survival skills. In fifth grade, I was a gambler in training. I gambled on the combination of a few key words to give meaning to an entire paragraph, and I counted on luck to help me know when to answer questions in class or keep quiet. I was able to gather some important facts, which I use every day of my life; however, there are big chunks of information that are missing. I know this now because when I go to retrieve information I was supposed to have learned—from history, science, math, and so on—the information is not there. Key words sometimes float to the surface; however, I never seem to be able to recall "the big picture."

Using the Table of Contents at the beginning of a book is a way to get "the big picture," and I regularly use that strategy now. However, when I was in school, I never understood the true intention of what the Table of Contents was supposed to do. I made no linkage from the Table of Contents to the rest of the book. To take this a step further, I also didn't understand why the chapters were in the order they were. Every book was a maze of words. I never saw a beginning or ending or understood where I was going in the big scheme of things. It would have been nice to have had an aerial view of the maze I was in. Then the path would have been clearer. Teachers should not assume that what is obvious to them and most other students is obvious to the student with learning disabilities. I did not truly get the importance of the Table of Contents until it was described to me as a kitchen table with dinner courses laid out in a sequential manner. As a child, I must have taken the word table literally, not understanding the difference between a table of items and a table at which you eat. I believe I got confused at an early age about why the word table was being used in this context. Because I did not understand the difference, I rarely used the Table of Contents in any setting. I now understand that there is a certain order in which the information needs to be presented to me. I understand this because I can visualize the content as the different entrees on a table. Chapter One is the appetizer. Chapter Two is the salad. This is only one example of many concepts I have misunderstood through the years. To this day, I have great difficulty recognizing that words can look the same and sound the same but have two completely different meanings.

I wish my teachers could have spent a day in my head. Teachers have such a love of books that I think they might overuse the written word as a teaching tool. I have trouble remembering any teacher who deviated from the textbook when teaching. I was afraid of that book. I needed to be introduced to that book. We needed to shake hands. One of the largest mistakes most of my teachers made was to assume that I was on the same page in the book as everyone else. I am not talking about the actual page number, but "place," in the sense that I was going into the lesson with the same knowledge base as everyone else in the class. It would have been helpful if my teachers had started their lessons in a manner so creative that it would have intrigued all the students, while at the same time establishing a foundation for students like me. For example, in dealing with history, instead of a teacher having students start by opening the history book to a certain page to begin a lesson, it would have been helpful for my teachers to introduce the chapter in a creative manner that reviewed the time period and laid the foundation for what was to come. One of the most effective ways I got information into my brain with any given subject was to have a good introduction to the material before jumping into it. Just as a runner needs to warm up before starting a run, a student with learning disabilities also needs a warm-up time to prepare for the journey ahead. When developing individual lesson plans, I think it would be helpful for teachers to begin with an "attention-getter" that is designed to draw students' attention to the lesson, to establish the relevance of the lesson to their lives, and to lay the foundation for the information to come.

It wasn't until my public speech class in college that I understood the important contributions that Dr. Martin Luther King made to our history. The class was studying his famous "I Have a Dream" speech. I realized quickly that my classmates had much more of a foundation on this important figure than I did. I felt alone in the class. I was frustrated with why I did not know more about Dr. King. How did I miss this important lesson, which I now know is a vital part of history and is addressed throughout the education curriculum? My college professor, as most teachers would, assumed that all of us in the class were "on the same page." He had no idea that after class, I had to go back and fill in the holes in my Swiss cheese brain before I could start the class assignment. While everyone else was able to immediately begin to analyze the speech, I had to go back and figure out who Martin Luther King was. It amazes me, and saddens me for personal reasons, as to why I got so little out of my academic years while my friends and colleagues were enriched with so much. Sometimes I long to have those years back, and I find myself in the evening staring at the moon wishing that my brain was not made of Swiss cheese.

Comprehension

I wish my teachers had focused on helping me with comprehension instead of decoding. I always felt like I never got past first base in reading. There I stood, watching the game go on around me. Year after year, the books would fly by me. I would see these books as they slid past first base, but I was never able to grab on to them and follow them around the bases. At first base, I could hold the book and look at the pictures and guess what the book was about. At second base, it was my responsibility to make sense of (decode) the squiggles on the pages and try to turn them into words. If I accomplished that successfully, I could then go to third base, where I would get an understanding of what I was reading. The goal of any baseball player (reader) is to make it all the way around the bases to reach home plate—to "own" the book.

I could never get past first base. Because of the way my brain processes information, I could not make sense of the squiggles. This put a barrier between me and third base. I now know that I can get to Base Three, where comprehension takes place, without ever having to touch Base Two. I can take a short cut. If I can run from Base One to Base Three, I have a second chance of catching the book before it passes me by. My goal in the Game of Reading is to comprehend what is in front of me, no matter what method I have to use.

For years, my teachers worked hard on teaching me how to decode. I learned from them that reading was figuring out the words. It wasn't until my English 102 class during my sophomore year in college that I reached third base and started to understand what reading was all about. The teacher's name was Amelia Davis-Horne, and she was effective because she made the words come alive. She gave life to the pages in front of me. In that class, it didn't matter that the words did not stand still. What mattered was that, for the first time, the words made sense. Although there were pages of reading requirements, the class was never about reading; it was about meaning—transporting ourselves from the classroom right into the story.

That English 102 class was the start of the development of my own comprehension action plan. Ms. Davis-Horne taught me the basics. She made first base a great place to be. Her introductions to the stories brought instant interest, even to subjects that had previously held little interest for me. The story could be about bird watching—when I was nineteen, I could not imagine anything more boring—and she would be able to make it interesting. This teacher would be able to transport me into the mind of a bird watcher. She did this by setting the stage. She used whatever props she needed in order to entice us. If that meant bringing in a bird, she brought in a bird. She was a master at developing scenery. Her podium became a stage that would change story by story. She used videos when we were to read anything about historic events. Intertwined throughout the stories, she would often play music. The music was never really connected to the plot of the stories but was used to create a mood. If it was a sad story, we might hear some mournful music from Chopin, while Beethoven played for us to drive home a powerful point. Role playing was another one of her favorite teaching strategies. She turned students into actors who would become characters in a scene. Even the most complex material would come clear to me. For the first time, I was able to talk intelligently about these stories. Because she immersed my mind totally in the story, I wanted to get involved—which is the key to teaching children to read.

If teachers focus on comprehension, students are going to want to read. To develop my own reading comprehension action plan, I have analyzed what helps me comprehend best. I have also traveled across the country and listened to children who are like me. There are basic things that I hear that work for other students struggling to understand the written word, and from those children as well as from adults like me who still struggle to read, I would like to pass along the following suggestions to teachers.

Don't Assume the Obvious

Children are always asking questions: What are we having for dinner? When are we going to Six Flags? How many days till Christmas? Having answers to these questions is essential for children to organize their day-to-day lives and helps them to anticipate and prepare for what is to come. Children naturally want to know what to expect. Use this same philosophy to start off every lesson. For instance, start by going to the Table of Contents and training your students to do this. This will help orient the students to where they are in the book, remind them of what they have already studied, and show them where they are going. Most students with learning disabilities have the ability to understand the structure of their day. They should be able to comprehend the gist of what they are studying, even if they can't comprehend the words in every passage. Don't assume that what is obvious to you and most other students is also obvious to the student with

learning disabilities. The Table of Contents is, in fact, made up of words!

Alive and Kicking: Make New Vocabulary Words Come Alive

Always introduce new vocabulary words in an interesting manner, and then directly link them to where they are placed in the book. It is important to remember that you are responsible for making the words come alive. Don't assume that your students will automatically recognize the word when they meet it in the passage. Help them out by giving them colored transparent tape to lay over the new words in their books or some other medium that will help pull out the words from the passage. This will help make the connection and give life to the passage.

Picture Reading

It would have been helpful for me to have a visual outline of the stories and books that teachers wanted me to read as a child. One of the most effective ways for me to comprehend "the big picture" of anything I read is to use a graphic organizer. Although I have difficulty decoding symbols, my brain recognizes visual diagrams and pictures with ease. These pictures are processed as a unified whole, a complete thought, whereas letters, words, and numbers are fragmented into puzzle pieces in my brain. For example, when I see a picture of a cake, it stays with me. I recognize it immediately and attach meaning to it. When I see the word cake—c/a/k/e—I often fail to recognize it, because the letters are like pieces of a recipe that have been torn apart and thrown at me. They offer little meaning, and they are clouded with negative feelings. Graphic organizers use pictures and diagrams to illustrate concepts and organize text into a sequence that is easy for me to store and retrieve.

I started using graphic organizers when I was in college, although I had no idea that was what they were called. I was allowed to substitute a series of selected courses in place of my foreign language requirements. Ironically, the selected courses were all literature courses offered by the English department. (A lot of good that did! The printed word, even written in English, is, at times, foreign to me.) Having taken a total of six literature courses, it was as if I had minored in a foreign language. However, it was through these courses that I perfected my use of graphic organizers to comprehend large amounts of complex reading material. In one year, I had to read the Iliad, the Odyssey, Virgil's Aenead, and Dante's The Inferno. It was the first time I had truly "tasted" literature and was exposed to the feeling of what knowledge was all about. I finally understood why my mother stayed up night after night reading book after book. Through these adventures, a new world opened. Even though I rarely spoke in class discussions of these assignments, my mind was bursting with activity. I started visualizing myself on the journeys taken by the heroes of these stories. With Rosemary Jackson, I developed my own reading style. At first nothing would stick, whether I had Rosemary read the stories aloud to me or whether I was listening to them on tape or attempting to read them myself. It took another step to achieve comprehension and retention. It all started with a doodle that Rosemary drew in an effort to explain a piece of the story to me. However, it ended with the pencil in my hand, diagramming the story in pictures as she read to me. One of my better doodles was Odysseus's confrontation with the Cyclops, which I'm sure haunted Rosemary's nightmares that evening. I spared no red ink on the gory details and passed the discussion test a few weeks later with red ink in hand. The graphic organizer was a perfect fit for me. It allowed me a way of getting the information out of the book and into my mind.

I think there are two types of students who might use graphic organizers for reading. Some students will pick up the technique naturally, while other students may need to be taken through the steps of how to use this technique effectively. Teachers can use graphic organizers with the entire class by diagramming the reading material with words and pictures while simultaneously talking through the process.

There are books available with preconceived graphic organizers especially designed for specific types of reading material, such as biographies, sequential events, comparison and contrast, and so forth. There is also software available that allows you to create your own computer-generated organizer. For some students, this process comes naturally, and the best thing is to give these students a pad of paper and turn them loose to create their own organizers. Some helpful tips for using graphic organizers to help improve reading comprehension in students with learning disabilities include the following:

- Show examples of the various looks an organizer can have so students will understand that there is no "right" or "wrong" way to complete them.
- Make sure your students are on the right track as they progress through the reading material. Don't allow them to complete the organizer incorrectly; communicate with them throughout the process.
- Let your students be natural with the designs they come up with: boxes, circles, pictures—they should be encouraged to use whatever works.
- Be particularly careful with timelines and other sequenced information; check often to be sure that students correctly sequence

a series of events. It should not matter whether the sequence goes from top to bottom, bottom to top, right to left, left to right, or even diagonally across the page as long as the events are placed in the correct sequence from the starting point.

- Have students try out different mediums for creating their graphic organizers, such as lined paper, blank paper, colored paper, manipulative objects, colored pencils, crayons, markers, computers, and so on. Often, the farther away one gets from traditional paper and pencil, the more memorable and meaningful the final product will be.

Primal Teaching: Tap into Your Students' Emotions

One reading comprehension strategy that has always worked for me is my teachers' abilities to tap into my emotions. This strategy is easier said than done. As a student, I always carried around deep frustration, anxiety, and anger. The most effective teachers were the ones who were able to use my emotions to tie me into the context of whatever we were reading. There are several core characteristics that many students with learning, disabilities share: a basic lack of self-worth, the feeling that everyone is watching you, and a feeling that you're going to get caught at "faking it." Teachers can draw on these emotions to make their students feel passionate about reading. Books that I remember from my high school years are books that made an emotional impact on me. For some reason, my connection with the book overrode my disability. A good example of this is from high school, when I sat through the class-reading of a difficult book: A Tale of Two Cities. I was able to relate personally to the characters in the book, particularly Madam DeFarge. At that time in my life, I was very angry and really

involved in manipulating myself through the education system. I identified with the character of Madam DeFarge because she was strong and was not going to let anyone beat her. I know that my English teacher at that time had no idea that she had tapped into a unique strategy that worked for me, but, to this day, the few books I do remember are the ones that I am in some way emotionally connected to. Most of my areas of difficulty are tied to the part of my brain that's in charge of language; therefore, comprehension strategies that work the best come when that part of my brain is bypassed and the most primal part, the emotional part, is stimulated.

Books on Tape: Have Students Listen to Good Reading

Students with dyslexia have difficulty decoding symbols, in part, because the symbols don't "stick" to the page. One of the most effective reading strategies I have ever used is one that combines visual and auditory input. Books on tape have given me a new perspective on life. Through the use of this medium I have been able to go places that I was not capable of going before. It started as a survival skill. Due to the large amount of required reading I had in college, I was unable to keep up with the work. Something had to be done, so we began to order my textbooks on tape. For the first time that I could remember, I actually began to keep up with and understand my reading assignments. From talking with teachers and students, I am aware that people know about books on tape but typically view them as an accommodation rather than a reading-improvement strategy, and thus, de-emphasize the use of taped texts. This assumption is a mistake. I strongly believe that books on tape should be implemented on a daily basis with students who have difficulty with reading for three major reasons: (1) The combination of audio and visual cues combines two modalities for better comprehension, (2) following the text while listening helps your eyes learn to track the words more smoothly, and (3) the process builds better word recognition.

Multisensory learning is one of the best techniques for working with students who have processing deficits. Using books on tape while following along in a text involves both sight and hearing. I often follow the line of words with my finger or a ruler, adding a third modality. Hearing, seeing, and touching the words at the same time immediately heightens the clarity. I can almost feel the different parts of my brain being stimulated. I began using books on tape with a clunky, bright yellow, four-track tape recorder especially designed for people who are blind or visually impaired, but I have now upgraded to a sporty Walkman model. This allows me to add a fourth modality—movement, which is how I've always learned best. By reading, listening, feeling, and moving, my brain decodes the words much more efficiently, which increases my comprehension tremendously.

To my surprise, another benefit that arose from using books on tape was the development of the muscles in my eyes. No longer do I read with the same stopping and starting motion that plagued me for years. From years of hearing and following smooth reading, my eyes now transition smoothly from letter to letter and word to word.

Finally, I now recognize more words when reading on my own. It is hard for me to quantify the number of words I now recognize compared to those I knew before I started using books on tape; however, my confidence about smaller words, such as there, was, has, and so forth, has increased. Seeing, hearing, and touching the words over and over has improved my ability to decode on my own.

I now use books on tape throughout every part of my life, whether in school, in work, or in the social realm. Without this tool, it would be very difficult for me to access the information from magazines and books that is available to everyone around me. I wish that books on tape had been available to me as a child. As an adult, it is an invaluable tool.

Colored Transparencies

Another mechanism that I have found very effective for myself and others who have difficulty decoding letters, symbols, and words is the use of colored transparency sheets. The easiest way for me to explain why this technique works is that it helps pull the reading material out from the page, giving it a type of three-dimensional effect. The scientific explanation is that colors can sometimes slow the letters and words from reaching the brain just enough to give the dyslexic brain a little more time to process the information. I have found it very helpful to use colored transparency overlays when I am reading a book or any other document from which I need to draw important details. I have experimented with several types of colors and have found that blue, gray, yellow, and green are the most effective for me. I have found that the red is ineffective, and, in fact, tends to make decoding more difficult. When I use this technique, it really does feel like the information I am trying to decode is slowed down by the colors, allowing my brain to process the information more efficiently. Cutting the transparency sheet into a small rectangular marker and placing it on the page to use as a guide is also helpful. I have seen some students tape the strips onto hand-made cardboard rulers so that when the ruler is placed over the sentence to be read, the transparency highlights the words.

Colored transparencies do not work for everyone, and, depending on the reading disability, may or may not be effective. I would suggest trying several colors before choosing one. There are two good sources of transparencies. Office or school supply stores will usually carry the page-length transparency sheets. A second source is your local high school or community theater, which uses transparency strips, called gel paper, for stage lighting. In fact, drama departments will sometimes have sample books from which they order. These sample books contain over two hundred colors of ready-made strips that make wonderful markers.

Magnifying Aids

Even though I have good eyesight, an effective way for my brain to get information from a page of squiggles is by using magnifying aids. There are several types of magnifying aids on the market. Most are developed for senior citizens or people with visual impairments. One of the most effective is the magnifying page, which is like a sheet of paper that is transparent to the eye and has the effect of a magnifying glass. Placing the magnifying sheet over a paragraph helps enlarge the print and makes it easier to read the text. If this strategy is helpful, there are other magnifying devices that use light and distance to help the reader. It is important to remember that learning disabilities are perceptual disabilities and not connected to physical problems with the eyes; however, some aides designed for individuals with visual impairments can be helpful in aiding the brain to perceive. Of course, enlarging print is a popular accommodation; however, a low-cost magnifying sheet is portable, unobtrusive, and available to almost any reading situation. To locate these magnifying aides, contact an independent-living vendor for a catalog (see the Appendix).

Highlighters and Highlighting Tape

I use highlighters to help me decipher words that look similar and need emphasis. For instance, due to the way my brain processes symbols, I cannot distinguish between similar words. When reading a passage, I have trouble distinguishing between has and was, been and done, there and they, and numerous other pairs of words. Numbers are just as difficult. Nines and sixes, threes and eights, and twos and fives consistently elude me. Using colored highlighters or colored highlighter tape, I mark the similar words in different colors so that I know they are different words when I reach them. I use this strategy when I am reading something important, in which the details have to be clear.

In addition to highlighting similar words, I have at times made myself a definition chart to use while reading. For instance, when I took biology in college, many of the words started with the prefix phy- and looked similar. I had difficulty with not only decoding the words, but also remembering their meanings. Rosemary would often write the words and definitions at the top of the page and then select colors to highlight each one so that when I encountered that word in the passage, I could refer to the chart. Eventually, I would connect the color to the word and definition and use the chart less and less.

Although this is a great study technique, the public schools usually frown upon letting students highlight books or write in their margins. Students with learning disabilities may need to purchase their textbooks so they can use the strategies they need to use; however, the recent invention of highlighter tape is a removable alternative to permanent highlighter pens. Students can use the tape as study aids just as they would use highlighter pens. The tape is also handy for teachers who may want to preview chapters and highlight the important information before students take them home to read. This helps students learn how to use highlighters to pull out only the most important information.

Conclusion

If I had only known as a child what I now know about reading, my life would have been a little easier. As an adult with a reading disability, I have learned how to use effective strategies and technology that I have discovered on my own. I now know the joy of literature. Whether I read a book or listen to it on tape, my life is enriched by the written word. I've also learned that there is no magic pill to correct my reading disability. It follows me around, never leaving my side, whether I am faced with reading a menu, a birthday card, or a road sign. To be effective, strategies must be able to follow me through these different environments. The most effective strategies are the ones that are portable and nonintrusive. It is my experience that when these strategies become a habit in my day-to-day life, I read more effectively and efficiently. Reading becomes a habit rather than a struggle. I have made reading a part of my life. Just as I get up every morning to go to work, I also read the newspaper on the Internet with my screen reader.

The philosophy in most school systems is that children are failures if they cannot read on their expected grade levels. When this happens, teachers, parents, and students panic. At that point, they frequently pull back to what has worked for everyone else instead of thinking "outside the box" and experimenting with things that might work for that individual student. I have my own individualized reading plan. I know how I read best: I like to read standing up, not sitting down; the lights cannot be too bright or dim; absolutely no fluorescent lights art allowed; I use color whenever I can—black and white bores me; if the environment is too noisy, I use earplugs; if it's too quiet, I make my own noise; sometimes I walk backwards when I read—for some reason, this relieves anxiety; I read best in the morning and worst at night; I always ask for help when I can—life is too short to be stuck on a word; my favorite strategy is to have someone read for me. About 30 percent of the time, I read off a computer, using screen-reading software; about 20 percent of the time, I listen to tapes; and the additional 50 percent of my reading is on my own, using a variety of self-selected strategies. This last 50 percent is the hardest and is not by choice.

As a child, I lay in bed and cried because I could not read like everyone else. As an adult, I no longer cry for myself but for all the other children who may never learn to love the written word as I have. To them, their books will always be tree sandwiches, and their hiding places will be harder to find.

So, I urge the teachers and parents who are reading this book not to let your children go to bed staring sadly at the moon because they can't make the words stand still, when the important thing is to make the words come alive.

Discussion Questions

1. Describe the anxiety that Christopher experienced as a child trying to read.

2. What were the effects of frustration with reading on Christopher's self-esteem and confidence as a learner?

3. Describe how Christopher's brain worked during the process of reading.

4. What are some traditional instructional reading processes that don't work for students with learning disabilities such as Christopher's?

5. Describe the value and importance of pre-reading activities for students with learning disabilities. Describe beneficial pre-reading activities for students with learning disabilities.

6. How can teachers make stories "come alive" for students with learning disabilities?

7. Explain the value and importance of visual aids in reading activities (e.g., graphic organizers).

8. What does emotion have to do with learning?

9. Describe some auditory aids that would help students with learning disabilities.

Students with Oppositional Defiant Disorder

by Mark Boynton and Christine Boynton

Students who have been diagnosed with oppositional defiant disorder (ODD) can pose extreme challenges to teachers and other building staff. Throughout the years, these students have been given various labels, such as explosive personality disorder, behavior disorder, adaptive behavior disorder, and antisocial disorder (Hall & Hall, 2003). Some of the common behavior patterns these students display in and out of the classroom include frequent aggression, temper tantrums, failure to respect others' property, defiance, refusal to comply with instructions, violent behaviors, and repeated displays of resentment.

It is important for staff members to be careful with the term ODD, as there is sometimes a tendency to refer to a student as having ODD if he or she exhibits some aggressive or destructive behaviors. Staff members must remember that for a student to be diagnosed as having ODD, that student must have had an official assessment that involves a team of professionals (Hall & Hall, 2003).

In this chapter, you will learn some characteristics and factors related to ODD, strategies that should be avoided when working with students with ODD, and techniques that can help the students improve and better control their behaviors.

ODD Factors

There are several factors that can increase the likelihood or severity of ODD. These include family stress, poor parenting skills, genetic factors, and watching numerous acts of violence and crime on television (Staub, 1996). Hall and Hall (2003) list temperament, parental stress, and parents with marginal disciplining and nurturing skills as the three main factors that put children at risk for ODD. According to the Halls, some children are hard to parent due to inherent temperament—they throw tantrums and can become inconsolable at a young age. Parents with poor parenting skills reinforce noncompliance by withdrawing requests when their children become defiant. Parental stress can be triggered either by external forces (single parenting, poor parenting skills) or internal ones (depression or some other mood disorder). If all three of the Halls' factors are present, it is almost inevitable that a child will develop ODD. Once this happens, the child's response to failure is often one of aggression; the pattern is set for a future of failure unless the child is dealt with in ways that decrease the negative behaviors and increase the positive ones.

Misconceptions Regarding ODD

There are a number of myths and misconceptions regarding ODD and how to deal with it. Following is a review of some of these misconceptions and the realities concerning them (Hall & Hall, 2003).

Ignoring the behavior of a student with ODD will extinguish the behavior. Reality: The behavior of students with ODD is driven by impulses, so ignoring the behavior will not have any effect. Also, students with ODD don't even notice that they're being ignored, so they are immune to that response.

Harsh punishments improve the behavior of students with ODD. Reality: Punishments mean little to the student with ODD and do little to change the impulse-driven behavior of the student.

Students with ODD will modify their behaviors in order to attain long-term rewards and goals. Reality: The student with ODD may work for short-term rewards, but long-term rewards are often unattainable for them due to their impulsive behavior. They are victims of their own emotions. This interferes with long-term goals set to earn rewards.

Idle time helps students with ODD improve their behavior. Reality: These students are better behaved when they can be active and task-oriented.

Surprises and sudden changes inspire and motivate students with ODD. Reality: Students with ODD need structure, order, and consistency in their lives.

Threats of severe punishment will intimidate students with ODD. Reality: Threats of punishment only create more defiance in these students.

Stimulating and exciting classrooms inspire students with ODD. Reality: Students with ODD often struggle with overstimulation and clutter.

Praise is a powerful motivator for students with ODD. Reality: Students with ODD often perceive praise as manipulation and control and may react negatively to it.

Strategies for Working with Students with ODD

As difficult as students with ODD are to have in the classroom, there are in fact specific strategies that have been identified as being successful in working with them to improve their behavior and help them be successful in school (Hall & Hall, 2003). As you consider these approaches, however, remember the earlier cautions that one size does not fit all and that some strategies work better than others with specific students.

Redirect the Student's Behavior

When correcting a student with ODD, attempt to redirect her behavior rather than order her to stop what she's doing. For example, rather than saying "Sit down now!" when she is out of her seat, ask her to look at the schedule and find out what she should be doing at that moment.

Ask Questions That Provide Acceptable Alternatives

When attempting to encourage a student with ODD to change a certain behavior, ask questions that provide alternative acceptable behaviors. For example, instead of saying, "Johnny, work on your math now," say, "Johnny, would you rather work on your math or your social studies right now?" Any option you offer must be acceptable to you in order to be included in the question.

Help with Time Management

Students with ODD often become frustrated and rebel when they run out of time for completing academic assignments. Therefore, it is helpful to provide them with prompts regarding deadlines and how much time they have left. Examples include putting deadlines on the blackboard, having a class assignment schedule, or using quiet verbal reminders with the student.

Avoid Surprises

Students with ODD often react angrily and rebel when faced with unexpected and sudden changes. The reaction becomes more severe when the change results in the delay of a special event that they have been looking forward to. Unexpected events and sudden changes are part of life and not totally within your control. However, whenever possible, give the student a warning about a change that is about to occur to help her better deal with and prepare for the change. An example is that early in the day, you state to the class, "Yesterday I told you that we were going to have our free time today at one o'clock, but the principal just announced that we are having an emergency assembly at that time, so we'll reschedule our free time for immediately after the assembly."

Watch for Initial Signs That the Student Is Becoming Upset

Usually there are indications that a student with ODD is becoming upset or irritated. Watching for these signs and proactively touching base with the student can sometimes head off a disruption. For example, when a student starts to get upset, you might ask, "Billy, how are you doing? Would you like to be alone for a while in the quiet corner?"

Build Relationships

Often students with ODD have few, if any, positive adult relationships. Welcoming the student each morning, showing a personal interest in her as an individual, caring for her needs, and communicating that you like her are powerful ways to build a relationship that can result in a willingness to please in the student.

Adjust the Academic Schedule

Like all students, those with ODD have certain subjects they enjoy working on more than others and some subjects that easily trigger outbursts. When it is obvious that the student is having a difficult day, you should consider allowing him to work on a subject he enjoys and is successful with. Although this is not suggested as something to do on a regular basis, this approach often helps the student to get through the day without a serious disruption when indications are strong that trouble is brewing.

Meet the Ability Level of the Student

Many students with ODD struggle with academic challenges that their peers can handle with ease. When students with ODD are given assignments that are beyond their ability levels, there is an increased chance that they will become frustrated and disruptive. It is critical not only to understand the academic ability level of your students but also to adjust their assignments accordingly. Work with the special program teachers in diagnosing the students' ability levels and in prescribing appropriate assignments for them.

Have Preset Procedures for Classroom Removal

With most students with ODD, it is inevitable that there will be a time when you need to remove them from the classroom because of an outburst. It is important that every staff member who works with the student participate in a process to determine what behaviors will warrant removal from the classroom and how the process will be followed. The teacher should review the removal plan with the student so that she is clear about which behaviors will result in her being removed from the class and how that will occur. Parents should be involved in making the plan and should be in agreement regarding their part in supporting the plan. Hall & Hall (2003) suggest including the student with ODD in the development of the plan so that she won't feel that once again the adults are in control. In such a situation, the student can help identify at what point she needs to go to a place for a cooling-off period and where that place should be. When, however, it gets to the point that the student has become a danger to others or to property, there needs to be a plan in place that has been communicated to all involved and that will be implemented quickly. Figure 17.1 is an example of a removal plan for a student.

Another group of students that can be difficult to deal with are those who exhibit behaviors consistent with the diagnosis of attention deficit hyperactivity disorder. We will review strategies for working with these students in the next chapter.

REMOVAL PLAN

Student: _____

Date: _____

When the student displays behaviors that endanger others or endanger property, the following steps should be followed:

1. Teacher calls the office.

2. Office contacts the following trained staff members: _____ .

3. These staff members immediately go to Room _____ and escort the student to the office.

4. Parents are called. Name and phone number: _____ .

5. Teacher documents the incident.

Figure 17.1 Removal Plan

Discussion Questions

1. Describe some of the typical behaviors of students with oppositional defiant disorder (ODD).

2. What are the known causes of oppositional defiant disorder (ODD)?

3. Describe some common mistakes that teachers make in responding to students with ODD.

4. Describe some behavioral interventions for students with ODD.

5. Describe some academic interventions for students with ODD.

6. Describe some strategies for building relationships with students with ODD.

7. Describe appropriate ways of including other professionals and parents/caregivers in helping with students who exhibit ODD symptoms.

Section Five

Culturally Responsive Management: A New Paradigm

Introduction

Culturally Responsive Management: A New Paradigm

By Dave F. Brown

Public schools continue to be the primary location for successfully educating immigrant children. Research on culturally responsive instruction is prolific, and the information available is critical to ensuring the success of immigrant students. The strategies required for succeeding with these students are critical skills that must be adopted by a primarily European American teaching force who enters the teaching profession.

For White teachers to succeed in classrooms with ethnically diverse students, they must adopt different philosophies, new perspectives, progressive ideas, and practical research-based strategies that meet the needs of a population of students whose lives are nothing like theirs. The authors provide articles on the following topics in this section:

- effects of student populations on teachers' attitudes toward students and chosen instructional processes;

- language differences and strategies for addressing different discourse patterns;
- strategies for meeting the needs of students who code-switch;
- classroom-management strategies for teaching children from diverse ethnic and low socioeconomic backgrounds; and
- identifying oppositional identity and implementing strategies to fight it.

Engaging ethnically diverse students in learning requires a unique perspective that cannot be obtained through childhood experiences that most teachers received as learners in traditionally all-White schools. A necessity exists for all teachers to comprehend the philosophy of cultural responsiveness due to the many diverse learners in all states. The future success of many immigrant and African American children depend on teachers comprehending and adopting culturally responsive instructional and classroom-management practices.

Language Considerations in Instructional Processes

by Dave F. Brown

[T]he achievement of students is increased when teachers modify their instruction to make it more congruent with the cultures and communication styles of culturally diverse students.

Howard (2001, 183)

Culturally Responsive Instructional Communication

Communicating effectively through nonverbal, oral, or writing processes is a powerful way to achieve outcomes. Nonverbal actions are more meaningful and powerful than oral communications. Every action by teachers from how discussions are held to how much individual assistance is provided is an opportunity to either encourage or frustrate students. As you go through a day of teaching, reflect on how all of your social behaviors, especially nonverbal cues, might affect students' perceptions of their ability to grow and succeed academically. Think about how you respond to students' mispronounced words, different dialects, syntax mistakes among second language learners, and classroom discussion patterns. How do you provide feedback to students to validate their cultural norms? How accepting are you of those speaking patterns that differ from what you expect? The importance of communicating with students from diverse backgrounds is made clear by Saravia-Shore's and Garcia's (1995) finding: "The aspects of culture that influence classroom life most powerfully are those that affect the social organization of learning and the social expectations concerning communication" (57).

You will likely discover more about your verbal and nonverbal communication styles by videotaping a few lessons. Notice your actions and student reactions to your behaviors when you review the tape. You may discover that some students are not reacting well to your nonverbal or verbal behaviors. Review the tape with a colleague of a different culture to help you evaluate your discourse styles.

Two middle school teachers, one European American, Karen, and the other African American, Jennifer, conducted a study in which they took turns observing one another teach (Obidah and Manheim Teel 2001). They each naturally had preconceived notions about how students should communicate in school. Karen perceived her African American students' communication characteristics as a demonstration of

1. an aggressive communication style
2. unfamiliar expressions
3. the need to save face in front of peers
4. a demand for respect from peers and the teacher
5. vocal and honest expressions of dissatisfaction with the class
6. a tendency to test her as a person of authority.

The communication styles of Karen's African American students didn't match how she, as a white middle-class person, believed students should respond to each other or an adult figure. Because of her ignorance of African American cultural communication patterns, Karen often engaged in power struggles with students. At other times, her negative reactions to their verbal behaviors discouraged students from participating at all. Jennifer identified these culturally biased teaching behaviors and was able to help Karen understand more about African American discourse patterns. Fortunately, Karen was professional enough to listen with patience and accept the advice from Jennifer about how she could alter her communication style and accept students' discourse patterns to become a better teacher.

Teachers often discourage student learning because many don't realize that discourse styles and preferences and the social rules associated with communication are all influenced by a person's culture. Geneva Gay (2000) described the relationship between culture, communication, and teaching: "Culture provides the tools to pursue the search for meaning and to convey our understanding to others. Consequently, communication cannot exist without culture, culture cannot be known without communication, and teaching and learning cannot occur without communication or culture" (77). Teachers judge their students' growth, understanding, and potential based on how they communicate with each other. The high percentage of culturally diverse students in urban schools naturally creates a challenge to effective communication exchanges between students and their primarily white Anglo female teachers. If you expect to communicate effectively with your students, you will need to comprehend their preferred discourse styles, and if your students are from several different ethnicities and cultures, you'll have much to learn from each student.

Saravia-Shore and Garcia (1995) provided research support for the fact "[T]hat students learn more when their classrooms are compatible with their own cultural and linguistic experience" (57). They added,

When the norms of interaction and communication in a classroom are very different from those to which the student has been accustomed, students experience confusion and anxiety, cannot attend to learning, and may not know how to appropriately seek the teacher's attention, get the floor, or participate in discussions. By acknowledging students' cultural norms and expectations concerning communication and social interaction, teachers can appropriately guide student participation in instructional activities. (57)

Now, urban teachers must know what specific norms their students expect and how they can accommodate those communication needs.

Accepting Nonstandard English Discourse Patterns

Approximately sixty to seventy percent of African Americans often speak in a different dialect than standard English, referred to as Black English Venacular (BEV) (Wiley 1996). Other nonstandard forms of English exist in the United States including Hawaiian Creole English and Appalachian English, but less students are speaking those dialects than BEV (Ruddell 1999).

I have worked with in-service teachers who want to know if students should be corrected and asked to use standard English every time they use BEV. The answer is "No!" Correcting students has the effect of frustrating them. Howard (2001) explained, "Teachers should recognize that any attempts to invalidate or denigrate the use of nonstandard English might have detrimental effects on the academic prospects for African American students" (200). Ruddell (1999) provided an important philosophy and instructional statement about BEV: "Standard English should not be viewed as a replacement for children's nonstandard dialects but as an alternative dialect that can be used in school and work when appropriate and necessary" (292). Permitting students to use BEV to engage in discussions, exchange ideas with classmates, respond to teachers' questions, and speak to you privately or publicly are appropriate because, in listening nonjudgmentally, you recognize and honor a child's cultural personality.

If you're like most teachers, holding your tongue may be challenging at first. You will need to get used to it. When you demonstrate respect for African American children and adolescents in this manner, you have a much greater opportunity for establishing positive relationships. As Delpit (1995) stated, "To suggest that this [BEV] form is wrong or even worse, ignorant, is to suggest that something is wrong with the student and his or her family" (53). Constant correction of language differences leads to the development of severe negative feelings toward teachers. Furthermore, no evidence exists that permitting the use of BEV negatively affects academic achievement (Dwyer 1991).

Providing advice on the appropriate time and place to use standard English should become part of specific lessons that demonstrate to students the oral and writing rules of standard English in context with meaningful learning experiences. Delpit (1995) described how one white teacher had her students teach her rules that govern creating rap songs. Following their teaching, she compared their rules to some of the rules expected in speaking and writing standard English. In this exchange, the teacher recognized students' language while sharing the knowledge that they needed to successfully maneuver through different cultural and economic communities.

Appropriate Instructional Activities

Although you don't have to speak BEV to your students, in a few studies, academic achievement improved in classrooms where teachers frequently spoke BEV and permitted its use as acceptable discourse (Howard 1998; Williams 1997; Lee 1993). Gay (2000) described some of the communication styles of African American students' culture that contributed to their academic success:

- dramatic presentation styles
- conversational and active participatory discourse
- gestures and body movements
- rapidly paced rhythmic speech
- metaphorical imagery (87).

Adrienne, from a Los Angeles high school, uses conversational instructional processes with her African American students: "I use activities such as book talks, literature circles, plays, and courtroom trials." Jackie, who taught in New York City and now in Philadelphia, discusses the kinds of strategies that are successful with her primarily African American students: "I place a great deal of emphasis on theatre and art activities. For example, having students act out Charlottes Web (White 1952) and then write a play much like it. I'll have students design a stage set and do all the painting of props. I have huge success also with videotaping their reenactments of books."

Lee (1993) discovered that high school students made gains in their literary analysis skills when they were permitted to use *signifying* or *sounding* in classroom discussions. *Signifying* involves using insults, insinuation, and exaggeration during class discussions to insult each other (Gay 2000). This strategy may not match your views of proper protocol for classroom discussions, yet its use improved student engagement and understanding of text. Students who use *sounding* during class discussions may brag in a demonstrative manner, using exaggerated phrases and a loud voice as if arguing with others rather than merely sharing information.

The participatory interaction style referred to as *call-response* is related to signifying. During call-response, students may provide encouragement, give compliments, or loudly disagree *while* teachers are speaking (Gay 2000). For some European Americans, these behaviors may seem rude; yet they are a part of expected discourse patterns in some African American communities. Effective teachers accept frequent indirect comments during class discussions and recitations as long as students aren't emotionally hurt. Accepting these types of discourse may be more challenging for female teachers whose perspectives on appropriate communication styles may be less assertive than that of males. Tannen (1990) and Sadker and Sadker (1994)

explained how it is common for many women to use much less aggressive conversational practices than males. Many women may also prefer to avoid conflictual communication situations. Accepting a more varied discussion pattern than the traditional turn taking, raising hands, and an "Only one person talks at a time" policy, means renegotiating both cultural perspectives and gender roles for many women teachers. Each of these seemingly different discourse characteristics meet the learning needs of many African, Hispanic, and Asian American, and Native Hawaiian students in the sense that they provide more active student involvement in the learning process.

Communicating with Second Language Learners

It seems that many Americans share the egocentric view that if someone enters our borders they should be able to speak English well, especially if they plan to stay for any length of time. That response shows the limited experiences of many Americans who have been isolated from other countries by geographic boundaries, thus requiring no need to learn of or share in the culture and language of other peoples. Some Americans who have visited other countries are more understanding of the challenges and processes of effectively communicating in another language. Perhaps when they return to the United States they are more sympathetic of SLL students.

Please recognize that achieving enough English-speaking proficiency to succeed academically can take from four to seven years, depending on the backgrounds of second language learners who enter school (Collier 1989). California's recent educational policy to limit bilingual instruction to one year suggests that some legislators and residents think one year of English instruction is sufficient for students to succeed in school without further assistance (Ohanian 1999).

Helping SLL students succeed academically begins with establishing a comfortable and stress-free learning environment, particularly for adolescents who face the fear of making mistakes and being embarrassed by peers. The classroom rule of insuring that no students will be ridiculed must be explicitly stated and enforced to encourage SLL students to practice their English. If English isn't spoken at home, school must be the environment where students are able to practice and experiment with the language with classmates and teachers.

Becoming Acquainted with Second Language Learners

An integral aspect of a teacher's role for creating an optimal learning environment for SLL students is demonstrating a respect for and value of their familial cultural heritage. Teachers must validate the cultural backgrounds of students rather than deny that differences exist, especially because the larger society often denigrates the cultures and languages of diverse populations. As mentioned earlier, understand that students are clearly cognizant of your feelings and attitudes about them by the way you act individually with each one and in large group situations.

Effective educators of SLL learners do as much personal research as possible to understand the social, linguistic, and other cultural characteristics of their students. Your role in helping immigrant students is to acquaint yourself with how different their languages are, that is, to attempt to understand the rules for the structure of their language. You need to determine, for instance, syntax patterns (the order of words for speaking and writing), challenges they experience in pronouncing certain English sounds, and discourse styles; that is, is the language more orally based than written?

Consider for instance, the differences in vowel pronunciations between Spanish and English; subject–verb agreement challenges for some Asian SLL students; syntax differences between the Hmong language and English; and, the fact that many sounds in English do not even exist in other languages (Cary 2000). An awareness of these language differences will help you assist students in English-language development. Added aspects of cultural awareness include understanding a child's perspectives and expectations about learning and being in America. Attitudes affect students' interests, effort, and motivation to learn English.

Your research also should provide information on a student's native country: geography, historical information, and current political status. Knowing more about your students' backgrounds will assist you in creating a friendly place to learn—an environment where students are comfortable taking risks. Knowing all of this information is necessary if you expect students to begin to engage in classroom conversation freely and comfortably. You'll know if you have connected with your SLL students by their eventual oral involvement in class discussions. Despite their need to listen for extended periods to learn language, they also need to engage in genuine conversations to extend their growth. Your encouragement is a needed component, and the more you know about their native lands and culture the better chance you have of drawing them into conversations. Ramirez (1985) discovered in his research that the more positive the attitude toward the culture of the people that spoke the new language, the higher language proficiency was among those learning it.

Accepting Code Switching

Deciding how to engage SLL students should be based on the research on how a second language is learned. First, realize that students do not completely ignore or cease to speak their native language once they begin second-language acquisition. Many of their utterances involve *code switching*, that is, using words from both languages simultaneously while speaking. This is typical and does not prevent SLL students from understanding or learning standard English conventions (Padilla and Liebman 1975). For older students, code switching may involve their own construction of mixed language with its own specific language rules, as in the use of Spanglish or Calo—combinations of Spanish and English (Garcia 1999).

The implication for teachers is to accept and understand those utterances without providing unnecessary negative responses to code switching. As with students who use BEV during class discussions, teachers should not correct the mistakes made by SLL students as they speak and code switch, but instead, provide modeling later through their own use of standard English. As Garcia (1999) indicated, "It [code switching] is not to be taken as evidence of a language disability or confusion" (184). The development of second language parallels original development of language by native speakers (Dulay and Burt 1974). If you know children between the ages of two and four, listen to how they develop language, and you will ultimately understand how language develops for anyone learning a new language. It is truly amazing how patient adults are with toddlers learning the language compared to the attitudes they have about second language learners. You can understand how constant correction of SLL students can discourage speaking and development in the language.

Understand that language and cognition are closely linked; therefore, it is imperative that SLL students maneuver through their learning of English with many opportunities to speak in both languages without undue pressure to pronounce every word correctly or use the appropriate word. Preventing code switching negates the child's opportunities to use the brain efficiently in learning a new language (Garcia 1999). Gary (2000) explained the advantage of a teacher ignoring the mistakes of her SLL students: "Giving students permission to get language wrong went a long way in helping them to get it right" (59).

Bringing Text to Life

A common challenge for second language learners is making sense of miles of confusing text material. Because one goal of American educators is to encourage students to read, interpret, and react to decontextualized text, many urban teachers falsely believe that pushing abstractly written texts at SLL students and having them memorize aspects of language growth is appropriate. Many students do not succeed at learning English or interpreting text through decontextualized teaching or books. SLL students need reality—real materials, videos, pictures, reenactments, plays, presentations, and demonstrations to connect principles while learning language. They need to use all the senses while they are learning to fully comprehend the principles being taught. Researchers refer to this type of experiential teaching as contextualized language instruction; in other words, content is connected to reality—real events, objects, and authentic discussions (Duquette 1991).

Discussion Discourse Patterns

The type of discussions that occur in traditional American classrooms are not typically discussions at all—they are actually recitations. *Recitations* are like the game Jeopardy: the teacher asks a question; a student responds (usually the first one with a hand up); the teacher responds with a "That's right!" or "No, not exactly," or "That's not it, anyone else have an answer?" Then, another question is asked and the pattern is maintained. This pattern—teacher question, student response, teacher response, then another teacher question—might continue for an entire period. In an hour's time, perhaps students spoke for ten percent of class time. There is no discussion when teachers speak this much! Students are denied opportunities to speak to each other or to respond for long enough periods of time to actually learn language. The pace of the class is too fast for many students, particularly SLL students. As a result, students are not likely to engage in the recitation if they have limited English proficiency.

A recitation discourse pattern does not correspond to the cultural, oral interaction patterns of many SLL students. Recitations are primarily teacher directed with little, if any, student engagement. Naturally, families (including African, Hispanic, and Native Americans) use more conversational discourse at home than the question-answer format commonly used in many American classrooms. The discourse practice of raising hands to gain permission and taking turns to speak is not culturally congruent with these families either. The result among students placed in recitation-learning formats is typically silence due to reluctance to participate. These passive language-learning activities are unproductive for SLL students.

SLL students need opportunities to speak to each other and to the teacher as equal-status participants in a genuine discussion format in which the teacher acts merely as any other student in the class who wants to occasionally add something to class discussions. Class discussion topics should be genuine issues that address the interests and tap the background knowledge of students in the class. In support of greater student-to-student discourse during class discussions, Boggs (1972) reported a "[R]eluctance of Native Hawaiian children to respond to direct questioning" strategies used by teachers (cited in Garcia 1999, 189). The

Hawaiian students became more verbally engaged when teachers permitted discussions among students with multiple speakers to support one another.

Altering the format alone will not correct the problems of many traditional American instructional practices for SLL students. Many teachers, for instance, ask short, known-answer questions of students that require minimal thought and even less verbal interaction between and among students and teachers. These types of questions further discourage the development of language acquisition for SLL students because they aren't allowed much time to respond either. Children and adolescents need time—time to think in their language and respond in English, or time to respond with more elaboration, which can increase English acquisition. Language acquisition is a complex process. Designing instruction so that students have extensive time to engage in both large and small group discussions increases the probability of greater gains in language knowledge (Garcia 1999).

Culturally responsive instructional discourse patterns for some learners should also permit and encourage spontaneous verbal interruptions and additions in a discussion rather than one person speaking at a time after being recognized by the teacher. Native Hawaiian students respond in discussions with a strategy referred to as "*talk-story* or *co-narration* which involves several students working collaboratively, or talking together, to create an idea, tell a story, or complete a learning task" (Gay 2000, 92). Talk-story is similar to the interactive conversational styles of African Americans referred to as call-response, explained earlier (Gay 2000). Teachers must demonstrate acceptance of these multiple conversations to recognize students' cultural discourse patterns while encouraging the development of their language acquisition.

Research indicates that Chinese American students prefer independent help while learning with a focus on teacher-directed instruction (Garcia 1999). You'll certainly be challenged when you have an equal number of Chinese American and Chicano students in your classroom because each group has a different preferred discourse pattern.

Realize that every suggested strategy in this chapter is based on the experiences of many successful teachers and a supportive research base. However, research studies provide generalizations in many instances that naturally do not apply to every student from that cultural background. Many urban classrooms do, however, contain wide variations of students from a diverse set of cultural heritages. Responding appropriately to the learning needs of your students requires as much individualization as generalization. Providing for the needs of all students requires adapting instructional strategies for each child or adolescent in some way.

Specific Instructional Strategies for Second Language Learners

The single most effective and appropriate assistance for SLL students is for learning to occur in their native language *and* English (Cary 2000). *Bilingual education* provides students with opportunities to learn in both languages daily. If you want to have a significant educational impact on your classroom of primarily Spanish-speaking students, for instance, then learn Spanish and speak both languages when the situation calls for it during the day. Learning at least some of students' native languages will have a positive impact on many features of culturally responsive teaching.

Because you may not be well versed in Spanish, Hmong, Chinese, or Russian yet, knowledge of how to incorporate components of Specially Designed

Academic Instruction in English (SDAIE) will go a long way in helping your SLL students. SDAIE is often referred to as *sheltered instruction*. Sheltered instruction involves many active instructional processes to help make the abstract content in textbooks and other instructional materials clear for SLL students. Gary (2000) described some of these meaningful learning activities:

- organization of students learning into "small collaborative workgroups"
- peer assistance for most learning activities
- extensive use of objects, drawings, maps, graphs
- videos to build background knowledge
- teacher modeling of how to do activities
- storyboarding
- kinesthetic activities
- role playing and dramatic presentations
- art activities to extend concept development
- pairing of SLL students with native English speakers during learning activities (55–56, 84).

An example of using sheltered instruction is described by Pete, a Philadelphia high school teacher. He relies on socialization processes to teach his students: "I get them up and moving around and interacting with each other. I allow students the freedom to talk to each other and exchange ideas during class. When you're learning language, you have to allow students to speak it! I also use videotaping as they orally present their written autobiographies. We did a unit on fables, and the students wrote them and illustrated them. Then we invited kindergarten students in as judges, and my students had to perform their fables in front of the kindergarten students as they graded the fable presentations. We videotaped all of those also." Pete obviously found a way to create genuine language activities for his SLL students that matched their instructional level while challenging them at the same time.

Ruddell (1999) provided the following philosophy for using sheltered instruction: "The key purpose of SDAIE is to make information accessible to students through careful planning and scaffolding, while at the same time avoiding oversimplification of the curriculum" (299). To that end, Ruddell provided the following four goals for SLL students engaged in sheltered instruction:

- learn to communicate in English
- learn content-area material
- advance in higher-level thinking skills
- master literacy skills (299).

Be realistic about your influence in a single year on the growth of SLL students' English proficiency. Use instructional processes that match their developmental levels and language ability skills.

Garcia (1999) provided an additional list of instructional ideas that can assist you in teaching SLL students:

- increase wait time following your questions and after their responses to promote elaboration and more processing time
- simplify your language—don't speak louder, rephrase comments or questions instead
- don't force students to speak
- pair SLL students with proficient English speakers
- adapt instructional materials to make them more comprehensible
- build on students' prior knowledge
- support the student's home language and culture (adapted from 315).

Responding to Questions and Writing

Classroom learning activities in many American classrooms are often dominated by a focus on oral discussions, or reading and writing processes. You know how the game is traditionally played: the teacher initially provides an orderly explanation of what you need to know to complete an assignment or provides detailed information on a specific content area. These are typically teacher-centered activities in which students are asked to passively consume information. Gay (2000) described this traditional practice as *topic-centered* instruction. In Gay's description of topic-centered teaching, when educators speak they, "[F]ocus on one issue at a time, arrange facts and ideas in logical, linear order; and make explicit relationships between facts and ideas" (96). This is indeed a linear approach to teaching that mirrors deductive learning. You have seen and experienced this structured approach to learning. Au (1993) contended that African, Native, and Hispanic Americans as well as Native Hawaiians prefer *topic-associative* speaking and writing over topic-centered. Gay described the topic-associative style of speaking and writing as [E]pisodic, anecdotal, thematic, and integrative" (96). Also called *topic-chaining,* this style of speaking is much less structured than topic-centered instruction, with speakers weaving stories into comments and text while disregarding a linear delivery. This type of speaking or writing may sound to others like the speaker is completely disorganised.

If teachers take the initiative to deliver instruction in a topic-associative manner, such as using story telling to explain principles, then lessons may have more meaning for African, Hispanic, and Native American learners. Accepting the fact that students respond orally to teacher questions using topic-chaining discourse will also assist in reacting appropriately and with support of students' speech patterns.

Another noticeable communication characteristic of some African and Hispanic American students is their more highly charged emotional state while engaged in discussions. Teachers must learn to accept that some African and Hispanic Americans may act emotionally in their support for issues and that these emotions may be unleashed during class discussions, even on teachers, as a way for students to communicate their support. Discussions for many African American students may be more like debates (Kochman 1981).

Topic-associative writing may also be a challenge for teachers to accept. Because many African American students write using topic-associative style, it may appear to you that they are writing in a manner to merely fill the page with words unrelated to one another and that their response is quite indirect. Upon closer scrutiny, you will realize that their paragraphs are connected to one another in a more fluid manner than topic-centered writing. Topic-chaining writing appears as narrative with storytelling evident in the text (Kochman 1985). Again, your evaluation of and feedback to students' writing must demonstrate specifically how you support their progress. The focus should initially be on story line, characterization, or descriptive processes. Mini-lessons may be used later to demonstrate the differences between discourse writing patterns among cultures and how writing may be altered or structured for different purposes.

Appropriate Questioning Strategies

Other traditionally Eurocentric instructional patterns are in direct conflict with the cultural communication and learning needs of many urban students. The types of questioning strategies employed by teachers may easily discourage students through their simplistic expectations for responding. For instance, Delpit (1995) spoke of the ineffective practice of asking students questions that have known answers. You know the kind: "Please raise your hand and tell me what the main character's occupation is in this story?" or "Which number in the problem is the dividend?" Please realize, if the answer can be found in the book, no critical or creative thinking is required, no problem solving is needed, no introspection is encouraged, and you need to find more appropriate strategies for designing questions. These traditional questioning strategies do nothing to engage students in genuine learning! It appears European American students are the only ones who have the patience to listen and respond to these types of questions.

Heath (1983) described how the practice of asking more complex questions matched the discussion styles of African American students' home situations. African American students were more likely to become engaged in discussions when they were required to make connections between text and their lives or use problem-solving strategies to answer questions. Lee (1993) explained that African American students demonstrated more complex understanding of literature when discussions "[W]ere more student-initiated" rather than teacher directed, "As well as consistently focused on difficult, inferential questions" (cited in Gay 2000, 89). The back-to-the-basics curricular focus, intense phonetic approaches to teaching reading, or use of known-question-answer recitation formats appear to be ineffective in engaging African American learners despite a call for these kinds of pedagogy every time someone takes an interest in urban students' test scores (Kohn 2000).

Responding to the needs of students whose family and cultural backgrounds differ from yours is a continuous learning process. You have to learn to accept and understand how students communicate differently to help them develop. Sure, you're done with your undergraduate days at college, but your education on how to reach the lives of many urban students is just beginning. May you be open minded enough to grow as a professional educator as you accept and build on these strategies for helping urban students.

References

Au, K. H. 1993. *Literacy Instruction in Multicidtural Settings.* New York: Harcourt Brace.

Boggs, S. T. 1972. "The Meaning of Questions and Narratives to Hawaiian Children." In *Functions of Language in the Classroom,* edited by C. Cazden, V. John, and D. Hymes. New York: Teachers College Press. 299–330.

Cary, S. 2000. *Working with Second Language Learners: Answers to Teachers' Top Ten Questions.* Portsmouth, NH: Heinemann.

Collier, V. P. 1989. "How Long: A Synthesis of Research on Academic Achievement in a Second Language." *TESOL Quarterly 23,* no. 3: 509–531.

Delpit, L. 1995. *Other People's Children: Cultural Conflict in the Classroom.* New York: New Press.

Dulay, H., and M. Burt. 1974. *Natural Sequence in Child Second-Language Acquisition.* Toronto: Ontario Institute for Studies in Education.

Duquette, g. 1991. "Cultural Processing and Minority Language Children with Needs and Special Needs." In *Language, Culture, and Cognition,* edited by G. Duquette and L Malve. Philadelphia: Multilingual Matters. 200–213.

Dwyer, C. 1991. "Language, Culture, and Writing." *Working Paper No. 13.* Berkeley, University of California: Center for the Study of Writing.

Garcia, E. 1999. *Student Cultural Diversity: Understanding and Meeting the Challenge. 2nd. ed.* Boston: Houghton Mifflin.

Gay, G. 2000. *Culturally Responsive Teaching: Theory, Research, and Practice.* New York: Teachers College Press.

Heath, S. B. 1983. *Ways with Words.* Cambridge: Cambridge University Press.

Howard, T. C. 1998. *Pedagogical Practices and Ideological Constructions of Effective Teachers of African American Students.* Ph.D. diss., University of Washington, Seattle.

——2001. "Powerful Pedagogy for African American Students: A Case Study of Four Teachers." *Urban Education 36,* no. 2: 179–201.

Kochman, T. 1981. *Black and White Styles in Conflict.* Chicago: University of Chicago Press.

——. 1985. "Black American Speech Events and a Language Program for the Classroom." In *Functions of Language in the Classroom,* edited by C. B. Cazden, V. P John, and D. Hymes. Prospect Heights, IL: Waveland. 211–261.

Kohn, A. 2000. *The Case Against Standardized Testing: Raising the Scores, Ruining the Schools.* Portsmouth, NH: Heinemann.

Lee, C. 1993. "Signifying as a Scaffold to Literary Interpretation: The Pedagogical Implications of a Form of African American Discourse." *National Council of Teachers of English Research Report No. 26.* Urbana, IL: National Council of Teachers of English.

Obidah, J. E., and K. Manheim Teel. 2001. *Because of the Kids: Facing Racial and Cultural Differences in Schools.* New York: Teachers College Press.

Ohanian, S. 1999. *One Size Fits Few: The Folly of Educational Standards.* Portsmouth, NH: Heinemann.

Padilla, A. M., and E. Liebman. 1975. "Language Acquisition in the Bilingual Child." *The Bilingual Review/LaRevista Bilingue* 2: 34–55.

Ramirez, A. 1985. *Bilingualism Through Schooling.* Albany, NY: State University of New York Press.

Ruddell, R. B. 1999. *Teaching Children to Read and Write: Becoming an Influential Teacher.* 2nd ed. Needliam Heights, MA: Allyn & Bacon.

Sadker, M., and D. Sadker. 1994. *Failing at Fairness: How Our Schools Cheat Girls.* New York: Touchstone.

Saravia-Shore, M., and E. Garcia. 1995. "Diverse Teaching Strategies for Diverse Learners." *In Educating Everybody's Children: Diverse Teaching*

Strategies for Diverse Learners, edited by R. W. Coles. Alexandria, VA: Association for Supervision and Curriculum Development. 47–74.

Tannen, D. 1990. *You Just Don't Understand: Women and Men in Conversation.* New York: Morrow.

White, E. B. 1952. *Charlotte's Web.* New York: Harper.

Wiley, M. S. 1996. "Environmental Education in the School Culture: A Systemic Approach." *Clearing House* 94: 25–27.

Williams, R. L. 1997. "The Ebonics Controversy." *Journal of Black Psychology 23,* no. 3: 208–214.

Discussion Questions

1. How do language differences among diverse ethnicities affect the ability to successfully communicate nonverbally with others?

2. What are some traditional teacher communication processes that might be misunderstood by ethnically diverse students?

3. Which student communication styles might be threatening to teachers?

4. What are some language patterns/characteristics that emanate from ethnically diverse students that differ from standard English?

5. How can teachers accept Black English Vernacular (BEV) without discouraging students, yet help students to comprehend the differences between BEV and standard English?

6. How can teachers of African American and Hispanic American students accept sounding, signifying, and call-response in their classrooms in a productive manner?

7. How does the acceptance of code-switching positively affect ethnically diverse students' attitudes and academic performance?

8. Describe how teachers can alter traditional classroom discourse patterns to positively influence ethnically diverse students' attitudes.

9. Describe several culturally responsive instructional processes that encourage greater academic success for ethnically diverse students.

10. How can teachers merge topic-chaining and topic-associative speaking and writing with topic-centered writing to ensure students' success on writing tests?

11. How do traditional questioning strategies prevent many diverse students from participating?

Becoming Adept at Code-Switching

By Rebecca S. Wheeler

It was September, and Joni was concerned. Her 2nd grade student Tamisha could neither read nor write; she was already a grade behind. What had happened? Joni sought out Melinda, Tamisha's 1st grade teacher. Melinda's answer stopped her in her tracks. "Tamisha? Why, you can't do anything with that child. Haven't you heard how she talks?" Joni pursued, "What did you do with her last year?" "Oh, I put her in the corner with a coloring book." Incredulous, Joni asked, "All year?" "Yes," the teacher replied.

Although extreme, Melinda's appraisal of Tamisha's performance and potential as a learner is not isolated. In standardized assessments of language acquisition, teachers routinely underrate the language knowledge and the reading and writing performance of African American students (Cazden, 2001; Ferguson, 1998; Godley; Sweetland, Wheeler, Minnici, & Carpenter, 2006; Scott & Smitherman, 1985). A typical reading readiness task asks the student to read five sentences (*The mouse runs. The cat runs. The dog runs. The man runs. Run, mouse, run!*). As Jamal reads, *Da mouse run. Da cat run. Da dog run. Da man run. Run, mouse, run,* his teacher notes 8/15 errors, placing him far below the frustration level of 3/15; She assesses Jamal as a struggling reader and puts him in a low reading group or refers him to special education.

Through a traditional language arts lens, Tamisha's 1st grade teacher saw "broken English" and a broken child. Through the same lens, Jamal's teacher heard mistakes in Standard English and diagnosed a reading deficit. These teachers' lack of linguistic background in the dialects their students speak helps explain why African American students perform below their white peers on every measure of academic achievement, from persistent over-representation in special education and remedial basic skills classes, to under-representation in honors classes, to lagging SAT scores, to low high school graduation rates (Ogbu, 2003).

Across the United States, teacher education and professional development programs fail to equip teachers to respond adequately to the needs of many African American learners. We know that today's world "demands a new way of looking at teaching that is grounded in an understanding of the role of culture and language in learning" (Villegas & Lucas, 2007, p. 29). Unfortunately, many teachers lack the linguistic training required to build on the language skills that African American students from dialectally diverse backgrounds bring to school. To fill this need, elementary educator Rachel Swords and I have developed a program for teaching Standard English to African American students in urban classrooms (Wheeler & Swords, 2006). One linguistic insight and three strategies provide a framework for responding to these students' grammar needs.

One Linguistic Insight

When African American students write *I have two sister and two brother; My Dad jeep is out of gas, or My mom deserve a good job,* teachers traditionally diagnose "poor English" and conclude that the students are making errors with plurality, possession, or verb agreement. In response, teachers correct the students' writing and show them the "right" grammar.

Research has amply demonstrated that such traditional correction methods fail to teach students the Standard English writing skills they need

(Adger, Wolfram, & Christian, 2007). Further, research has found strong connections among teachers' negative attitudes about stigmatized dialects, lower teacher expectations for students who speak these dialects, and lower academic achievement (Godley et al., 2006; Nieto, 2000).

An insight from linguistics offers a way out of this labyrinth: Students using vernacular language are not making errors, but instead are speaking or writing correctly following the language patterns of their community (Adger et al, 2007; Green, 2002; Sweetland, 2006; Wheeler & Swords, 2006). With this insight, teachers can transform classroom practice and student learning in dialectally diverse schools.

Three Strategies

Equipped with the insight that students are following the grammar patterns of their communities, here is how a teacher can lead students through a critical-thinking process to help them understand and apply the rules of Standard English grammar.

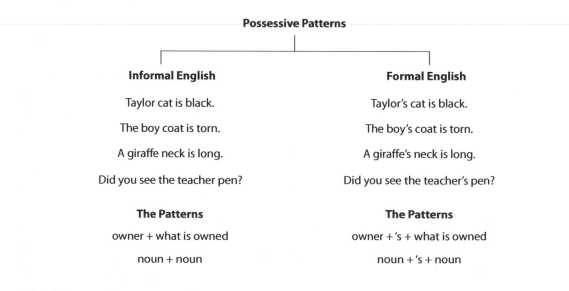

Possessive Patterns

Informal English	**Formal English**
Taylor cat is black.	Taylor's cat is black.
The boy coat is torn.	The boy's coat is torn.
A giraffe neck is long.	A giraffe's neck is long.
Did you see the teacher pen?	Did you see the teacher's pen?
The Patterns	**The Patterns**
owner + what is owned	owner + 's + what is owned
noun + noun	noun + 's + noun

Scientific Inquiry

As the teacher grades a set of papers, she may notice the same "error" cropping up repeatedly in her students' writing. My work in schools during the past decade has revealed more than 30 informal English grammar patterns that appear in students' writing. Among these, the following patterns consistently emerge (see also Adger et al., 2007; Fogel & Ehri, 2000):

- Subject-verb agreement (*Mama walk the dog every day.*)
- Showing past time (*Mama walk the dog yesterday or I seen the movie.*)
- Possessive. (*My sister friend came over.*)
- Showing plurality (*It safe 24 hour to rotate.*)
- "A" versus "an" (*a elephant, an rabbit*)

A linguistically informed teacher understands that these usages are not error, but rather grammar patterns from the community dialect transferred into student writing (Wheeler, 2005). Seeing these usages as data, the teacher assembles a set of sentences drawn from student writing, all showing the same grammar pattern, and builds a code-switchinig cart (see fig. 1). She provides the Formal English equivalent of each sentence in the right-hand column. She then leads students through the following steps:

- *Examine sentences.* The teacher reads the Informal English sentences aloud.
- *Seek patterns.* Then she leads the students to discover the grammar pattern these sentences follow. She might say, "Taylor cat is black. Let's see how this sentence shows ownership. Who does the cat belong to?" When students answer that the cat belongs to Taylor, the teacher asks, "How do you know?" Students answer that it says Taylor cat, or that the word Taylor sits next to the word cat.

- *Define the pattern.* Now the teacher helps students define the pattern by repeating their response, putting it in context: "Oh, Taylor is next to cat. So you're saying that the owner, Taylor, is right next to what is owned, cat. Maybe this is the pattern for possessives in Informal English: *owner + what is owned?*" The class has thus formulated a hypothesis for how Informal English shows possession.
- *Test the hypothesis.* After the teacher reads the next sentence aloud, she asks the students to determine whether the pattern holds true. After reading *The boy coat is torn,* the teacher might ask, "Who is the owner?" The students respond that the boy is the owner. "What does he own?" The students say that he owns the coat. The teacher then summarizes what the students have discovered: "So the boy is the owner and the coat is what he owns. That follows our pattern of owner + what is owned." It is important to test each sentence in this manner.
- *Write Informal English pattern.* Finally, the teacher writes the pattern, *owner + what is owned,* under the last informal sentence (Wheeler & Swords, 2006).

Comparison and Contrast

Next, the teacher applies a teaching strategy that has been established as highly effective—comparison and contrast (Marzano, Pickering, & Pollock, 2001). Using *contrastive analysis,* the teacher builds on students' existing grammar knowledge. She leads students in contrasting the grammatical patterns of Informal English with the grammatical patterns of Formal English written on the right-hand side of the code-switching chart. This process builds an explicit, conscious understanding of the differences between the two language forms. The teacher leads students to explore what changed between the Informal English sentence *Taylor cat is black* and the Formal English sentence *Taylor's cat is black.* Through detailed comparison and contrast, students discover that the pattern for Formal English possessive is *owner + 's + what is owned.*

Code-Switching as Metacogitition

After using scientific inquiry and contrastive analysis to identify the grammar patterns of Informal and Formal English, the teacher leads students in putting their knowledge to work. The class uses *metacognition,* which is knowledge about one's own thinking processes. Students learn to actively code-switch—to assess the needs of the setting (the time, place, audience, and communicative purpose) and intentionally choose the appropriate language style for that setting. When the teacher asks, "In your school writing, which one of these patterns do you think you need to use: *Owner + what is owned* or *owner + 's + what is owned?*" students readily choose the Standard English pattern.

Because code-switching requires that students think about their own language in both formal and informal forms, it builds cognitive flexibility, a skill that plays a significant role in successful literacy learning (Cartwright, in press). Teaching students to consciously reflect on the different dialects they use and to choose the appropriate language form for a particular situation provides them with metacognitive strategies and the cognitive flexibility to apply those strategies in daily practice. With friends and family in the community, the child will choose the language of the community, which is often Informal English. In school discussions, on standardized tests, in analytic essays, and in the world of work, the student learns to choose the expected formal language. In this way, we add another linguistic code, Standard English, to the student's language toolbox.

A Successful Literacy Tool

Research and test results have demonstrated that these techniques are highly successful in fostering the use of Standard English and boosting overall student writing performance among urban African American students at many different grade levels (Fogel & Ehri, 2000; Sweetland, 2006; Taylor, 1991). Using traditional techniques as a teacher at an urban elementary school on the Virginia peninsula, Rachel Swords saw the usual 30-point gap in test scores between her African American and white 3rd grade students. In 2002, her first year of implementing code-switching strategies, she closed the achievement gap in her classroom; on standardized state assessments, African American-students did as well as white students in English and history and outperformed white students in math and science. These results have held constant in each subsequent year. In 2006, in a class that began below grade level, 100 percent of Sword's African American students passed Virginia's year-end state tests (Wheeler & Swords, 2006).

Transforming Student Learning

Fortunately, Joni knew that Tamisha was not making grammatical mistakes. Tamisha did know grammar—the grammar of her community. Now the task was to build on her existing knowledge to leverage new knowledge of Standard English. When Joni tutored her after school, Tamisha leapfrogged ahead in reading and writing. Despite having started a year behind, she was reading and writing on grade level by June. How did she achieve such progress? Her teacher possessed the insights and strategies to foster Standard English mastery among dialectally diverse students. Even more important, Joni knew that her student did not suffer a language deficit. She was able to see Tamisha for the bright, capable child she was.

Joni has laid down the red pen and adopted a far more effective approach, teaching students to reflect on their language using the skills of scientific inquiry, contrastive analysis, and code- switching. We have the tools to positively transform the teaching and learning of language arts in dialectally diverse classrooms. Isn't it time we did?

References

Adger, C. T., Wolfram, W. & Christian, D. (Eds.)., (2007). *Dialects in schools and communities.* Mahwah, NJ: Erlbaum.

Cartwright, K. B, (in press). *Literacy processes: Cognitive flexibility in learning and teaching.* New York: Guilford Press.

Cazden, C. B. (2001). *Classroom discourse: The language of teaching and learning (2nd ed.).* Portsmouth, NH: Heinemann.

Ferguson, R. E (1998). Teachers' perceptions and expectations and the black-white test score gap. In G. Jencks & M. Phillips (Eds.), *The black-white test score gap* (pp. 273–317); Washington, DC: Brookings Institution.

Fogel, H., & Ehri, L. (2000). Teaching elementary students who speak Black English vernacular to write in Standard English: Effects of dialect transformation practice. *Contemporary Educational Psychology, 25,* 212–35.

Godley, A., Sweetland, J., Wheeler, S., Minnici, A., & Carpenter, B. (2006). Preparing teachers for dialectally diverse classrooms. *Educational Researcher; 35(8),* 30–37.

Green, L. (2002). *African American English: A linguistic introduction.* Cambridge, UK: Cambridge University Press.

Marzano, R., Pickering, D., & Pollock, J. (2001). *Classroom instruction that works: Research-based strategies for increasing student achievement.* Alexandria, VA: ASCD.

Nieto, S. (2000). *Affirming diversity: The sociopolitical context of multicultural education (3rd ed.).* White Plains, NY; Longman.

Ogbu, J. (2003). *Black American students in an affluent suburb: A study of academic disengagement.* Mahwah, NJ: Erlbaum.

Scott, J. C., & Smitherman, G. (1985). Language attitudes and self-fulfilling prophecies in the elementary school. In S. Greenbaum (Ed.), *The English language today* (pp. 302–314). Oxford, UK: Pergamon.

Sweetland, J. (2006). *Teaching writing in the African American classroom: A sociolinguistic approach.* Unpublished doctoral dissertation, Stanford University.

Taylor, H. U. (1991). *Standard English, Black English, and bidialectalism: A controversy.* New York: Lang.

Villegas, A. M., & Lucas, T. (2007). The culturally responsive teacher. *Educational Leadership, 64(6),* 28–33,

Wheeler, R. (2005). Code-switch to teach Standard English. *English Journal, 94(5),* 108–112.

Wheeler, R., & Swords, R. (2006). *Code-switching: Teaching Standard English in urban classrooms.* Urbana, IL: National Council of Teachers of English.

Discussion Questions

1. Describe what code-switching is; use a few sentences to demonstrate the kind of code-switching frequently necessary for African American children who primarily speak Black English Vernacular (BEV).

2. What are some code-switching situations that college students experience in their lives in specific contexts outside of a university classroom? Describe how immigrants often need to code-switch to speak a different language.

3. Why does traditional marking of incorrect grammar on students' papers or in their speech not encourage change among African American students who speak BEV?

4. What are some typical BEV grammatical mistakes—either in oral or written language?

5. Describe how to conduct a code-switching lesson so that students are not made to feel shame about their home or native language.

6. At what grade level do diverse speakers no longer need code-switching instruction?

7. What are the connections between a family's home language and mutual respect between teachers and students at school?

Urban Teachers' Use of Culturally Responsive Management Strategies

By Dave F. Brown

I didn't think I could make it through the year. It was so many things—including a new culture. I wondered what I was doing there; I wondered if I was making a difference; and, I wondered if this was good for me.[1]

These are the words of Jackie, an urban teacher, as she described her first year of teaching in Harlem in New York City. Jackie now has 15 years of urban teaching experience and is much more confident than she was that first year when the principal who hired her proclaimed during the interview, "Honey, we don't need missionaries in this school, we need teachers!" That sentiment is a powerful message clearly evoking teachers' responsibilities for impacting the academic growth and development of their students. Effective urban teachers play the role of "conductors" or "coaches" who assume responsibility for their students' academic development rather than playing the role of "custodians" who spend the day merely watching over students (Ladson-Billings, 1994, p. 23). They explicitly establish a cooperative, businesslike learning environment in which reasonable expectations for academic performance are clearly stated, and they provide the necessary tools for students to meet these expectations.

Establishing and maintaining reasonable learning expectations and conditions are often challenging propositions in urban classrooms. Several reasons exist for the challenges of managing urban classrooms. First, as Crosby (1999) suggested, "The new wave of immigrants of the past 25 years from Hispanic countries, from the Middle East, and from Asian countries has washed over the urban schools like a tidal wave bringing with it additional challenges, this time cultural and linguistic" (p. 104). Classroom management in urban schools is more difficult than in rural or suburban schools because gaining students' cooperation while ensuring their learning involves addressing students' cultural, ethnic, social, identity development, language, and safety needs, as well as their academic growth. This is a considerable responsibility if not an impossibility. Second, although many of these personal growth issues should be handled at home, the responsibilities fall on teachers when the resources and time are not forthcoming from urban youths' caretakers. Finally, the challenges for teachers are increased due to their inadequate knowledge of the strategies needed to connect to diverse students. As Crosby indicated, a high percentage of urban teachers will be and are inexperienced middle-class White European Americans:

> The teacher turnover rate in urban schools is much higher than in the suburban schools … The result is that urban schools, especially those in the inner cities, are often staffed largely by newly hired or uncertified teachers. These teachers, who were trained to teach students from middle-class families and who often come from middle-class families themselves, now find themselves engulfed by minority students, immigrants, and other students from low-income families—students whose values and experiences are very different from their own. (p. 302)

Urban educators must be prepared to address the many differences that exist between their cultural and ethnic beliefs and those of their students if they are to engage urban children and adolescents in genuine learning.

Interviewing Urban Teachers

As a professor of a classroom management course, I was curious about how effective urban teachers developed a classroom management system that encouraged cooperation, addressed diverse students' ethnic, cultural, and social needs, and led to genuine learning. My curiosity led to the implementation of a qualitative study with 13 urban teachers from seven U.S. cities. All of the teachers were selected through identification by fellow colleagues or acquaintances, and all of the teachers were

volunteered to be interviewed. The interviewees were from the following grade levels and cities:

- two middle school and two high school teachers from Philadelphia
- one primary teacher from New York City
- two teachers from Chicago, one primary and one high school
- two teachers from Los Angeles, one primary and one high school
- two intermediate teachers from San Francisco
- one middle school teacher from Minneapolis
- one high school teacher from Wichita

Nine of these teachers are European American, one is native Sri Lankan, one is African American, and two have Hispanic backgrounds. The teachers' experience ranges from 2 to 33 years with an average of 16 years as educators. Their students come from a wide variety of ethnic and cultural backgrounds. Some of these teachers have refugee students and most have second language learners in their classrooms. All teach in economically impoverished communities.

I reviewed the literature on culturally responsive pedagogy prior to initiating the interviews (Brown, 2002; Delpit, 1995; Gay, 2000; Howard, 1999; Ladson-Billings, 1994; Wlodkowski & Ginsberg, 1995). Several factors within teachers' control affect their ability to make meaningful connections with ethnically and culturally diverse students, thus positively influencing their academic growth. Effective urban teaching involves implementing culturally responsive communication processes and instructional strategies, developing respectful student/teacher relationships, and recognizing, honoring, and responding to the many cultural and language differences that exist among students. Examination of teachers' responses to the extensive interview questions revealed the use of several management strategies that reflect the literature on culturally responsive teaching. Three primary themes that emerged from the interviews are described here.

Caring for Students

"You're there to teach kids—not subjects! We often forget this point." This response from Jeff, a high school English teacher in Wichita, Kansas, demonstrates a critical aspect of his philosophy of teaching—caring for students. Jeff confirmed this philosophy in describing how he initiated and cultivated out-of-class conversations with his students to get to know them personally: "I try to get to know as many kids as possible on a personal level. So when I see them in the hall, I can ask about their families. I try to see them in other settings outside of school." This is one strategy that reflects the importance of caring for students and thinking about their needs, which can be used for planning and delivering instruction—similar to the coaching role Ladson-Billings (1994) described. All of the 13 teachers interviewed described actions that demonstrated genuine care for students.

Several researchers who have studied urban teaching and the characteristics of urban children and adolescents recognize care and psychological safety as critical components of urban classrooms. The personalized care children and adolescents need is sometimes missing from urban students' homes. Dryfoos (1998) noted that at-risk urban adolescents, "lack nurturance, attention, supervision, understanding, and caring," and may have inadequate communication processes with adults in their homes (p. 37). Students' need for care must be met at school if teachers expect students to focus on academic tasks during the day. Ladson-Billings (1994) described the classrooms of effective teachers of African American students:

"Psychological safety is a hallmark of each of these classrooms … The students feel comfortable and supported" (p. 73). Gordon (1999) added, "The best urban teachers show warmth and affection to their students and give priority to the development of their relationships with students as an avenue to student growth" (p. 305).

Brown (1999) interviewed African American urban middle school students who reported a desire to develop more meaningful personal relationships with teachers than the typical student-to-teacher roles. Howard (2001), through his interviews with urban African American elementary students, discovered that students preferred, "teachers who displayed caring bonds and attitudes toward them, and teachers who establish community- and family-type classroom environments" (p. 131).

Several interviewees' remarks demonstrated how they cared for their students. Pete is a Philadelphia high school ESL teacher who describes the importance of caring for students: "It doesn't matter what good content you have, or what good curriculum you have, or what exciting lessons you have; if you don't care about students and they know that, you don't have a chance to get to them." Several of Pete's students are refugees who experience the added stress of attempting to adapt to a hostile community and school environment in Philadelphia while living with the psychological scars of surviving a war in their native lands. Pete explains how he develops a classroom community: "I like to create a friendliness and kind of security and belonging that has been my focus above the academic stuff. The academic stuff is there, but that can't happen unless students feel safe, valued, and secure." Pete creates this safe place by spending the first few weeks of the school year engaging students in social games and establishing school- to-home relationships to build trust between the school and students' families.

Adrienne, a Los Angeles high school English teacher whose students are primarily African American, indicated, "I do a lot of hugs—I use body language. I rarely raise my voice. I treat them with respect. I'm friendly, but not their friend."

The importance these urban teachers placed on developing caring relationships demonstrates their willingness to respond in a manner that represents a cultural responsiveness to their students. From these teachers' views, the development of trusting and respectful relationships with their students was critical to successful urban teaching.

Being Assertive and Acting with Authority

I think my strong personality comes through to my students, which says, "You're here to learn, and this is what you're going to do." If students don't seem to understand that, then I contact their parents right away and let them know I went to school here when I was a child. I'm not asking them [students] to fly out windows. I don't ask them to do anything I wouldn't ask my own children to do.

These comments are from Anita, a Philadelphia middle school teacher, who has taught in this school for the past 25 years. Anita identifies students' academic strengths and weaknesses, then demands the kind of effort she knows students can deliver. She acts with assertiveness, recognizing that many of her primarily African American students need this kind of guidance and support. Eleven of the thirteen urban teachers I interviewed described how the assertive behaviors they used were critical in establishing the authority they needed to maintain a business-like learning atmosphere.

The literature on culturally responsive teaching supports teachers adopting an assertive stance with urban students. Weiner (1999) explained that teachers in urban schools need to develop a moral authority to be successful:

Urban teachers' primary source of control is their moral authority, which rests on the perception of students and parents that the teacher is knowledgeable about the subject matter, competent in pedagogy, and committed to helping all students succeed, in school and life. (p. 77)

Delpit's views (1995) support Weiner's beliefs in her description of the expectations of many African American students:

Black people often view issues of power and authority differently than people from mainstream middle-class backgrounds. Many people of color expect authority to be earned by personal efforts and exhibited by personal characteristics. In other words, "The authoritative person gets to be a teacher because she is authoritative." Some members of middle-class cultures, by contrast, expect one to achieve authority by the acquisition of an authoritative role. That is, "The teacher is the authority because she is the teacher." (p. 35)

Urban teachers must explicitly demonstrate assertiveness and establish authority through their verbal exchanges with students. Delpit (1995) noted that urban children expect more direct verbal commands than most suburban or rural students. She explained that urban students may ignore commands that are phrased and expressed like questions rather than as direct commands. Wilson and Corbett (2001) added that urban teachers should have expectations that are clearly stated, should accept no excuses from students, and should immediately deal with inappropriate behaviors.

The urban teachers I interviewed indicated a use of an assertive demeanor and acted with authority in the classroom. For instance, Polly, a Chicago teacher in a specialized high school for adolescents who have failed academically in their neighborhood schools, describes her management style as,

> Tough love—I use it with students and teachers. I tell students, "I'm here to help you. I'm not going to let you slide! You're not going to get away with acting the wrong way or not doing the work." We use very structured routines here. Students know what to expect down to every little detail.

Colette, from a Philadelphia high school, provides this advice for urban teachers:

> I think somebody that really wants to be an urban teacher has to have heart; but they have to have chutzpah, too. You can't come in here all soft-voiced and meek and mild. They're going to eat you up and spit you out. And those kids can sense whether you're afraid of them or not. I said in a joking manner, while I was wearing a Burger King crown one day, "I'm the queen in here!"

These urban teachers demonstrate assertiveness through establishing and making clear a set of academic expectations for students; enforcing rules, policies, and behavioral expectations; and contacting care givers as a strategy for garnering support for their efforts. Their assertive style of communicating with students also demonstrates their confidence in asking for and receiving students' cooperation.

Communicating Effectively with Students

Congruent communication between students and teachers is critical to the success of urban teachers in responding to students' cultural and ethnic needs. Urban educators must be aware of specific verbal and nonverbal communication styles that affect students' ability and motivation to engage in learning activities. Listening is one of the most powerful means of establishing effective communication patterns with students. Colette, from Philadelphia, frequently has students visit her room during their study halls and lunch periods to chat with her. She explains the interactions:

> I'll listen to them. A kid told me, "I can tell you anything." I don't have any children and these teenage males want to talk to me about personal stuff. Why are they telling me? Don't they have anyone at home to talk to? I think it's just another indicator that they feel comfortable. I think they know I care about them.

Differences in communication styles can affect the quality of relationships between teachers and African, Hispanic, and Native American students. Gay (2000) noted that some African Americans prefer a social interaction style referred to as "call response," in which students may speak out loud while the teacher is speaking as a response to her/his comments. These remarks are meant as acknowledgments of agreement or perhaps concerns about teachers' comments rather than as rude disruptions or demonstrations of disrespect. Gay explained,

> African Americans "gain the floor" or get participatory entry into conversations through personal assertiveness, the strength of the impulse to be involved, and the persuasive power of the point they wish to make, rather than waiting for an "authority" to grant permission. (p. 91)

Obidah and Manheim Teel (2001) explained that when educators react negatively to call response behaviors it may accentuate strained relationships between students and teachers. Adrienne describes how she responds to the oral discourse of her African American high school students from Los Angeles: "Conversation is their primary priority. It's so unconscious. They are from very verbal environments. I find that they can handle side discussions and engage in the main discussion at the same time. They're not talking to be disruptive." Recognizing this communication characteristic can help urban teachers develop instructional activities that build on these verbal interactions instead of being disrupted by them.

Recognizing other communication patterns among diverse learners is important for providing meaningful learning activities. Some nationalities of Asian American students, for example, may avoid correcting fellow students' verbal mistakes, or avoid responding in a competitive manner in class discussions or recitations. Gay (2000) explained that these students may be influenced by "traditional values and socialization that emphasize collectivism, saving face, maintaining harmony, filial piety, interdependence, modesty in self-preservation, and restraint in taking oppositional points of view" (p. 105). It is clear that the competitive instructional processes that often dominate American classrooms may be unsettling for many immigrants.

Second language learners who are recent immigrants tend to be relatively quiet during class as they attempt to learn English through listening to other conversations rather than by speaking themselves (Cary, 2000). This lack of response may be troubling for some teachers; however, an acceptance of this behavior combined with the use of student collaborative learning experiences may better fit the needs of urban students.

Several of the teachers I interviewed mentioned that immigrant students needed opportunities for socialization within instructional activities to promote and encourage the development of their English. Teachers of second language learners were particularly conscious of students' needs for student-to-student verbal interaction. For example, Lisa, a Los Angeles primary grades teacher, uses class time to permit her immigrant Mexican American students to settle disputes with their friends:

> They're always into arguments with each other. I use conversation to get them to think about their behavior and to learn to negotiate—even with me on certain issues. I expect them to talk. That's how they learn the language.

Pete, who teaches high school ESL students, describes an activity he implemented:

> When you're learning language, you have to allow students to speak it. This year we did a unit on fables, and the students wrote and illustrated them. Then we invited kindergarten students in as judges, and my students performed their fables in front of them.

Developing a mutually respectful relationship with students requires considerable knowledge of their communication styles—both verbal and nonverbal. Recognizing the differences, responding as a listener, and designing instructional activities that reflect students' needs are critical to a productive classroom learning environment.

Conclusion

Managing students in a way that creates a smoothly operating learning environment involves a series of highly fluid and dynamic teacher actions. The 13 teachers I interviewed demonstrate an awareness of several management principles required to create cooperative and academically productive classrooms in urban schools. The development of a comfortable learning environment for urban teachers often overpowers the use of effective curricular and instructional strategies in influencing students' growth. Wilson and Corbett (2001) identified the value of attending to these concerns: "Classroom environment differences had little to do with gradations of individuals' acquisition of knowledge or with nuances in the content covered; instead, environmental characteristics determined whether the majority of students learned anything at all" (p. 42).

In writing of culturally responsive teaching, educational theorists have provided educators with specific strategies for addressing the learning profiles and academic needs of diverse students (Brown, 2002; Cary, 2000; Delpit, 1995; Gay, 2000; Howard, 2001; Ladson-Billings, 1994; Weiner, 1999). Urban student bodies reflect great variations in culture, ethnicity, social and emotional health, and scioeconomic conditions. Attempting to meet urban students' needs requires that teachers develop awareness of and explicitly respond to their ethnic, cultural, social, emotional, and cognitive characteristics.

These 13 urban teachers create caring classroom communities by showing a genuine interest in each student. They gain student cooperation by being assertive through the use of explicitly stated expectations for appropriate student behavior and academic growth. And these teachers demonstrate mutual respect for students through the use of content communication processes. These three principles are effective classroom management techniques that provide urban students with opporities for academic success.

References

Brown, D.F. (1999). The value of advisory sessions: Perceptions of young adolescents at an urban middle school. *Research in Middle Level Quarterly, 22(4)*, 41–57.

Brown, D.F. (2002). *Becoming a successful urban teacher.* Portsmouth, NH: Heinemann.

Cary, S. (2000). *Working with second language learners: Answers to teachers' top ten questions.* Portsmouth, NH: Heinemann.

Crosby, E.A. (1999). *Urban schools forced to fail. Phi Delta Kappan, 87(4)*, 298–303.

Delpit, L. (1995). *Other people's children: Cultural conflict in the classroom.* New York: The New Press.

Dryfoos, J. (1998). *Safe passage: Making it through adolescence in a risky society.* New York: Oxford University Press.

Gay, G. (2000). *Culturally responsive teaching: Theory, research, and practice.* New York: Teachers College Press.

Gordon, G.L. (1999). Teacher talent and urban schools. *Phi Delta Kappan, 81 (4)*, 304–307.

Howard, G.R. (1999). *We can't teach what we don't know: White teachers, multiracial schools.* New York: Teachers College Press.

Howard, T.C. (2001). Telling their side of the story: African American students' perceptions of culturally relevant teaching. *The Urban Review, 33(2)*, 131–149.

Ladson-Billings, G. (1994). *The dreamkeepers: Successful teachers of African American children.* San Francisco: Jossey-Bass.

Obidah, I.E., & Manheim Teel, K. (2001). *Because of the kids: Facing racial and cultural differences in schools.* New York: Teachers College Press.

Weiner, L. (1999). *Urban teaching: The essentials.* New York: Teachers College Press.

Wilson, B.L., & Corbett, H.D. (2001). *Listening to urban kids: School reform and the teachers they want.* Albany, NY: SUNY Press.

Wlodkowski, R.J., & Ginsberg, M.B. (1995). *Diversity and motivation: Culturally responsive teaching.* San Francisco: Jossey-Bass.

Discussion Questions

1. Are there any types of classroom management behaviors that should be different in an urban classroom from those in a suburban class? If so, what might be different?

2. Why do many novice teachers struggle with classroom management in urban classrooms?

3. How do teachers demonstrate care to students in an urban classroom? Is it any different from the way teachers demonstrate care in suburban classes?

4. What does teacher assertiveness look like in classrooms? Why is it so necessary to act assertively in urban classes?

5. What aspect of communication is the most critical to gaining students' cooperation? How can teachers encourage effective communication with their students?

6. Why is fear of students a recipe for failure in urban classrooms?

7. How can teachers avoid power struggles with urban students and instead encourage cooperation?

Section Six

Ensuring Students' Daily Success

Introduction

Ensuring Students' Daily Success

By Dave F. Brown

Effective classroom management is dependent upon their making a multitude of decisions that affect teachers' ability to connect with, understand, and respond to their students' social, emotional, physical, and cognitive needs. Once successful, cooperative relationships have been established, teachers can focus on instructional decisions that also affect their ability to keep students engaged in meaningful learning. Meaningful learning means teachers provide the interventions necessary to ensure that each student reaches some academic success daily.

Students' opportunities for success are dependent on teachers protecting them, both physically and psychologically. Authors in the last section of the book offer articles on

- bullying prevention and student protection;
- strategies for differentiating instruction for the diverse learners;

- understanding the differences between *standards* and *expectations*; and
- developing appropriate and realistic expectations for every student.

The primary purpose of effective classroom management is ultimately students' academic success. Students expect teachers to provide a safe classroom environment where they can develop and enjoy relationships they form with classmates and engage in meaningful learning experiences. Students expect teachers to act with assertiveness in quelling disturbances and maintain a classroom of mutual respect. Every child and adolescent is entitled to participate in learning experiences that meet their social, emotional, physical, and cognitive needs. Teachers are responsible for providing that atmosphere. May these articles provide the research-based knowledge necessary for your success as a professional educator.

How We Treat One Another in School

By Donna M. San Antonio and Elizabeth A. Salzfass

When rising middle school students are asked to name their biggest worry about going to a new school, they most often answer, "That I will not have any friends" or "That people will make fun of me" (San Antonio, 2004). The prospect of being friendless or getting teased looms large for many students at this age and can profoundly affect their sense of affiliation with school. Students tell us with heartbreaking regularity of the pain and anger they feel when their peers do not see them, include them, or care about them. At the extreme, some students not only are treated with indifference but also become targets of bullying.

Devastating Effects

Olweus (1993) defines bullying as verbal, physical, or psychological abuse or teasing accompanied by real or perceived imbalance of power. Bullying most often focuses on qualities that students (and the broader society) perceive to be different from the established norm, such as expected gender specific behavior for boys and girls, dress and physical appearance, and manner of speaking. Bullying is connected to diversity, and reducing bullying means taking steps to make the community and the school safe for diversity of all kinds.

Research indicates that bullying—with its accompanying fear, loss of self-efficacy, anger, and hurt—negatively affects the school environment and can greatly diminish students' ability to engage actively in learning (Hoover & Oliver, 1996). Being bullied has been linked with high rates of school absence (Fried & Fried, 1996); dropping out of school (Weinhold & Weinhold, 1998); and low self-esteem, anxiety, and depression (Banks, 1997). A U.S. Department of Education study (1998) found that students who had experienced sustained threats and verbal and physical peer aggression carried out two-thirds of school shootings.

Some researchers and practitioners believe that the impact of bullying is as devastating and life changing as that of other forms of trauma, such as physical abuse. The effects of bullying may linger long into the victims' adulthood (Kaltiala-Heino, Rimpelae, Rantanen, & Rimpelae, 2000). Recent research has documented increased levels of depression and anxiety in adults who had been bullied in their youth (Gladstone, Parker, & Malhi, 2006).

Because of the documented harmful effects of bullying—as well as other forms of social isolation—on school climate and student achievement, educators are taking this problem seriously. Many schools have explored the benefits of implementing school wide programs to promote social and emotional learning, prevent bullying, and nurture positive peer relationships.

A survey of middle school students that we recently conducted in three schools provides information on bullying behavior that can inform such programs.

A Middle School Survey on Bullying

To measure students' experience with physical, verbal, and relational[1] bullying, we administered surveys in spring 2006 to 211 7th and 8th grade students in three K–8 schools in New England. The three schools differ significantly by race, socioeconomic status, and urbanicity. Rural School,[2] located in a small town, serves a student population that is socioeconomically diverse but is 94 percent white; 25 percent of the students are eligible for free or reduced-price lunch. Big City School is located in a low-income urban neighborhood and serves primarily Latino (65 percent) and black (33 percent) students; 93 percent are eligible for free or reduced-price lunch. Small City School has a socioeconomically and ethnically diverse student body composed of 40 percent white, 36 percent black, 11 percent Latino, and 10 percent Asian students; 30 percent of the students are eligible for free or reduced-price lunch.

We surveyed nearly all the students in each grade, with the exception of 8th graders at Rural School, where we were able to survey only half of the class. The surveys included multiple-choice and open-ended questions. Respondents were evenly split between boys and girls. Most of our findings were consistent with what other research has found and what middle grades teachers know about bullying in the adolescent years. Some of our most significant findings follow.

Extent of Bullying

Most students (76.5 percent) felt safe most of the time. However, students at Big City School reported feeling safe much less often than did their peers at the other two schools (65 percent, compared with 83 percent at Small City School and 81 percent at Rural School). They also feared bullying more, even though students at Rural School reported seeing it occur more often. We believe this reflects the greater incidence of community violence to which Big City School students are exposed.

Rural School was the only school in which a majority of students (about 2 in 3) said that bullying was a serious problem. Many of the respondents from Rural School spoke about the difference between physical and emotional safety. As one 7th grade girl said, "I feel safe physically but my emotions take a blow here."

In terms of grade level, bullying was more common for 7th graders than for 8th graders at the three schools we surveyed, with two notable exceptions:

Verbal bullying affected 8th grade girls more than any other subgroup at Small City School, and physical violence affected 8th grade boys and girls more than 7th graders at Big City School.

Finally, across schools, boys and girls experienced physical and verbal bullying to a similar extent, but girls experienced more relational bullying than boys did. Girls at all three schools worried more often than boys that if they did or said something wrong, their friends would gang up on them and decide not to be their friends.

Choosing a Social-Emotional Learning Curriculum

Look for a curriculum that

- Becomes part of a schoolwide and comniunitywide discussion (with parents) about values, beliefs about how to treat one another and policies that reflect these values.
- Poses developmentally and culturally appropriate social dilemmas for discussion.
- Challenges the idea that aggression and bullying are inevitable and expected behavior.
- Demonstrates how people can resolve tensions and disagreements without losing face by giving detailed examples of people who responded to violence in an actively nonviolent manner.
- Encourages students to express their feelings and experiences concerning bullying and enables students to generate realistic and credible ways to stay safe.
- Supports critical analysis of the issues and rejects explanations of behavior based on stereotypes (such as the idea that boys will use physical violence and girls, will use relational violence).
- Helps children and teens become critical consumers of popular culture.
- Addresses all types of bullying.
- Discusses how bullying reflects broader societal injustice.
- Gives ideas for what the adults in the school can do as part of a whole school effort.

Beware of any curriculum that

- Ignores such issues as injustice, stereotype, and imbalance of power regarding gender, race, social class, and sexual orientation.
- Focuses on the victim's behavior as the reason for being a target of bullying.
- Focuses on student behavior without addressing schoolwide climate.
- Emphasizes having students tell the teacher about the bullying and ignoring bullying assaults.
- Focuses on either bullying only or victimization only.
- Portrays victims or bullies as unpopular misfits.
- Promotes simplistic or trendy solutions (for example, "boys will be boys").
- Promotes good solutions, such as peer mediation, but does not provide clear guidelines for when these strategies should and should not be used.
- Lacks evidence-based, population-specific suggestions for design, implementation, training, and evaluation.

This problem appeared to be most dire for girls at Rural School: A full 72 percent of them reported suffering relational bullying either "every once in a while," "often," or "every day," compared with 58 percent of girls at Big City School and 48 percent at Small City School. This finding raises the question of the effect of socioeconomic status and cultural background on the bullying phenomenon. The almost entirely white population of girls at the school with the widest gap between wealthy and poor students was the group most at risk of relational aggression.

Boys were more likely to admit to bullying other students than girls were (which may have something to do with the way bullying is traditionally defined), but no significant gender difference was expressed overall when we asked students whether boys or girls bullied other students more. We also found that boys bullied both boys and girls, whereas girls typically only bullied other girls. We were troubled by girls' graphic narrative responses that demonstrated that boys often bullied girls with demeaning comments about the girls' appearance and demands for sexual interactions, particularly oral sex.

Location of Bullying

In all three schools, bullying happened most frequently in the hallways. When asked how to mitigate bullying at their school many students suggested putting more adult supervisors in the hallways between classes. The second most common place in which bullying occurred differed across the three schools. At Big City School, bullying tended to happen in the bathrooms, where there was generally no adult supervision. At Small City School and Rural School, bullying happened on the playground and in the cafeteria, both places where adults were on duty.

Reasons Students Are Bullied

Students at all three schools perceived that "being overweight" and "not dressing right" were the most common reasons an individual might be bullied. At Small City School and Rural School, the second most common reason stated was being perceived as gay, which suggests rigid behavior expectations for boys and girls. Many students commented that someone might be a target for bullying if they look or act "different" or "weird."

Students' Reactions to Bullying

The most common strategies students reported using when confronted by bullies were walking away, saying mean things back, hitting back, or telling the bully to stop. The least common strategy was telling an adult at the school. Hitting back was a particularly popular response to bullying at Big City and Small City Schools, particularly among the boys. Given steadily increasing numbers of violent deaths over the last few years in many urban communities, we believe that this finding highlights the importance that urban youth put on maintaining a tough appearance to survive, as well as a perceived lack of options for nonviolent conflict resolution.

Student reactions to bullying also differed according to gender. More boys than girls believed that they had the right to use violence to protect themselves from physical violence or someone hurting their feelings or reputations. Girls reported being more likely to help a victim of bullying than boys did and more often said that bullying is wrong.

Inadequate Adult Response

Most students said they were not confident that adults could protect them from being bullied. Students at Rural School had more faith that their teachers could stop the bullying when they were told about it than did students at the other two schools. However, students in this school agreed with their urban peers that teachers did not seem to notice bullying and did not take it seriously enough. Most students said they wanted teachers to be more aware of all types of bullying and to intervene more often. These findings are consistent with past research in which students reported that most bullying goes undetected by school staff (Skiba & Fontanini, 2000).

When we talk with students in a variety of settings, they have many thoughts about how adults can help to make school safer and stop bullying. They frequently answer with statements like these: "Watch out for us and don't ignore us." "Pay attention." "Just ask us what's wrong." "Talk to the students who have been bullied to see how to stop it." "Start caring more." "Believe us." "Punish the bullies." "Do something instead of nothing." One thing seems certain: Most students want adults to see what is going on in their world and respond to bullying in caring, effective, and firm ways.

What Schools Can Do

The following recommendations for a schoolwide approach to bullying prevention are derived from our review of the literature, our survey findings, and a report generated by Northwest Regional Educational Laboratory (Railsback & Brewster, 2001). All sources agree that schoolwide strategies must complement classroom curriculum. Schools should not frame the issue of how students and educators treat one another as an issue of behavior. Instead, they should opt for a more comprehensive set of goals that address social and moral development, school and classroom climate, teacher training, school policies, and community values, along with student behavior.

Conduct an assessment

The first step toward creating an effective school-wide antibullying program is identifying where, when, and how students experience bullying at a particular school. As our study demonstrated, different types of bullying occur with different frequency and magnitude among different populations in different school settings; therefore, a one-size-fits-all approach is not an appropriate solution. Schoolwide bullying intervention programs are more purposeful and relevant when they are informed by students' views. We strongly recommend using a participatory action research approach that involves students in framing a problem statement; constructing a

survey; summarizing, analyzing, and reporting the results; and generating ideas for how staff and students can respond to the issues uncovered by the survey.

Create a committee to focus on school relationships.

A committee involving students, parents, and community members along with school staff should focus on schoolwide relationships, not only on student bullying. This committee will assist the school in generating developmentally and culturally sound prevention and intervention ideas.

Implement an antibullying policy.

When asked what teachers could do to stop bullying, many of the students we surveyed said that teachers should be stricter with bullies. An effective policy should be developed through collaboration among students, teachers, parents, and administrators.

Pepler and Craig (2000) say that a whole-school policy is the foundation of antibullying interventions, and they recommend that a policy include the following: a schoolwide commitment to address bullying; a statement of rights and responsibilities for all members of the school community; a definition of bullying, including types and dynamics; the process for identifying and reporting bullying; expected ways for students and staff to respond to bullying; strategies that will be implemented; and a way to assess the effectiveness of antibullying efforts.

Train all school employees.

Bullying can be subtle and hard to detect, making it challenging for adults to intervene effectively. To stop bullying, school staff (including custodians, clerical staff, bus drivers, and lunchroom staff) must first have an opportunity to discuss the various ways and locations in which bullying occurs. From there, they can develop structures for communicating across roles within a school district and decide on an appropriate unified response. Considering that the majority of students in our study did not believe they could count on adults to protect them from being bullied, ongoing training and communication in this area is key. For students to develop positive attitudes toward school, they need to know that all staff members are committed to making it a safe and friendly environment.

Help the bullied and the bullies

Another step in implementing a school wide anti-bullying program involves providing resources for those most affected by bullying. Many of the students we surveyed who had experienced bullying said that they wanted adults to listen to their stories. Some schools have had success with facilitating groups in which students address issues directly with their peers. The PALS program at Rocky Mountain Middle School in Idaho trains teachers to facilitate these groups, which increase communication and social skills and give stigmatized students a chance to experience a positive interpersonal connection with others and with the school.

Some students who are highly involved in bullying (either as perpetrators or victims) will need one-to-one support. It is important to involve parents and provide referrals for mentoring or counseling. Journaling with a teacher or counselor who reads and replies to concerns and issues may help particularly reticent students. Connecting students to after-school and summer programs will enable them to socialize with their peers outside of the school and form new friendships.

When children have been treated unfairly or violently in their primary relationships, it can be difficult for them to understand why they

and their peers should be treated with respect. Nakkula and Selman (1991) describe an effective intervention called pair counseling as a way for two children who have difficult peer relationships to come together with the help of a counselor to negotiate differences and learn how to be a friend.

Recognize and name all forms of bullying.

Be aware of the relationships among students and of shifts in cliques and friendships as much as possible. Look for subtle signs of relational aggression that may occur between students, such as whispering, spreading rumors, and exclusion. Let students know that comments and actions against any racial, ethnic, or social group will not be tolerated. Be prepared to explain your ethical position to your students. The students we surveyed suggested that teachers ask students what would benefit them and help students generate realistic and effective ideas. On this topic, one 7th grade girl wrote,

> Teachers do everything, I think, in their power, but if they would just listen to the person who says they're being bullied, instead of just saying "stay away from them" or "ignore it" maybe we would see some change.

Reclaim goodness.

School classrooms and corridors contain a full spectrum of behavior, from countless everyday small acts of kindness to serious acts of aggression. In our effort to mitigate negative student behavior, a commonly overlooked but essential aspect of creating emotionally and socially safe environments is noticing, acknowledging, and actively drawing out acts of kindness. Schools are places of tremendous courage, generosity, and thoughtfulness. Some students risk their own social standing by being kind to an "unpopular" classmate. Some students talk with others who appear lonely and try to offer friendship; they speak up when they see injustice because, in the words of one student, they "don't think it is right to judge people by how they dress." In past research (San Antonio, 2004) and in the survey we describe here, students frequently spoke with admiration about teachers who actively intervened against stereotyping and teasing based on gender, social class, race, and learning needs. Naming and reclaiming goodness in the school community is an important step toward reducing bullying.

Integrate social-emotional education into the curriculum.

An effective curriculum for social, emotional, and ethical learning addresses bullying as a social and moral development issue. Activities in such a program focus on self-understanding, understanding of others, appreciation for diversity, and responsibility to the community. By encouraging empathy, respect, and acceptance and giving students tools for communicating their feelings and confronting conflict positively, an effective social-emotional learning curriculum will likely improve school climate and culture beyond just the mitigation of bullying. (See Choosing a Social-Emotional Learning Curriculum, p. 34, and Social-Emotional Learning Curriculums Online, p. 37.)

Educators Set the Tone

As a primary social environment for young people, classrooms and schools are uniquely good places to learn how to treat others and how to tell others the way we want them to treat us. Dozens of times a day, people in schools negotiate interpersonal exchanges with others from diverse backgrounds, making schools a premier learning environment for social, emotional, and ethical learning. Nel Noddings (2002) has long held that a key purpose of schooling is to educate moral people:

> Naming and reclaiming goodness in the school community is an important step toward reducing bullying.

> An emphasis on social relationships in classrooms, students' interest in the subject matter to be studied and the connections between classroom life and that of the larger world provides the foundation of our attempts to produce moral people. As educators we must make it possible and desirable for students to be good. (p. 85)

Of course, students behave in aggressive or submissive ways for a variety of reasons that are not always easy to discern or manage. Some students may posture aggressively because they face violent behavior at home or in their neighborhoods, some have problems reading social cues or controlling their impulses, and some are simply scared. But in our work with schools, we have found that when educators take students' concerns seriously, teach them alternative ways to communicate their needs assertively but not violently, and provide adult guidance, vigilance, safety, good role models, and support, students are more likely to interact positively with their peers.

The findings from the survey we conducted among middle grade students support the concept that educators can influence the social and emotional climate of schools. Students' written comments on the survey make it clear that they value fairness, respectful communication, and adults who make them feel physically and emotionally safe and cared for. By implementing an effective social-emotional learning curriculum and addressing the systemic factors that determine school climate, we can create schools where bullying is rare and where all students are ready to learn.

Notes

1. *Physical bullying* includes hitting, kicking, or otherwise physically attacking the victim, as well as taking or damaging the victim's possessions. *Verbal bullying* includes name-calling, aggressive teasing, or making insulting comments designed to humiliate the victim. *Relational bullying* includes any behavior that intimidates and hurts the victim by harming or threatening to harm relationships or feelings of friendship and belonging (Crick & Bigbee, 1998). *Cyber-bullying* involves the use of information and communication technologies, such as e-mail, cell phone and pager text messages, instant messaging, and Web sites to deliberately harm others (www.cyberbullying.org).

2. To preserve confidentiality, schools are identified by community type rather than by name.

References

Banks, R. (1997). *Bullying in schools*. Champaign, IL: ERIC Clearinghouse on Elementary and Early Childhood Education. (ERIC No. ED407154)

Crick, N. R., & Bigbee, M. A. (1998). Relational and overt forms of peer victimization: A multi-informant approach. *Journal of Consulting and Clinical Psychology, 66,* 337–347.

Fried, S., & Fried, P (1996). *Bullies and victims: Helping your child survive the schoolyard battlefield.* New York: M. Evans and Company.

Gladstone, G., Parker, G. B., & Malhi, G. S. (2006). Do bullied children become anxious and depressed adults? A cross-sectional investigation of the correlates of bullying and anxious depression. *Journal of Nervous and Mental Disease, 194(3),* 201–208.

Hoover, J. H., & Oliver, R. (1996). *The bullying prevention handbook: A guide for principals, teachers, and counselors.* Bloomington, IN: National Educational Service.

Kaltiala-Heino, R., Rimpelae, M., Rantanen, P, & Rimpelae, A. (2000). Bullying at school: An indicator of adolescents at risk for mental disorders. *Journal of Adolescence, 23(6),* 661–674.

Nakkula, M., & Selman, B. (1991). How people "treat" each other: Pair therapy as a context for the development of interpersonal ethics. In W. M. Kurtines & J. Gewirtz (Eds.), *Handbook of moral behavior and development* (Vol. 3, pp. 179–210). Hillsdale, NJ: Erlbaum.

Noddings, N. (2002). *Educating moral people: A caring alternative to character education.* New York: Teachers College Press.

Olweus, D. (1993). *Bullying at school: What we know and what we can do.* Maiden, MA: Blackwell.

Pepler, D. J., & Craig, W (2000). *Making a difference in bullying (Report #60).* Toronto, Ontario: La Marsh Centre for Research on Violence and Conflict Resolution.

Railsback, J., & Brewster, C. (2001). *School-wide prevention of bullying.* Portland, OR: Northwest Regional Education Laboratory. Available: www.nwrel.org/request/dec01

San Antonio, D. M. (2004). *Adolescent lives in transition: How social class influences adjustment to middle school.* Albany: State University of New York Press.

Skiba, N., & Fontanini, A. (2000). *Fast facts: Bullying prevention.* Bloomington, IN: Phi Delta Kappa International. Available: www.pdkintl.org/newsroom/newsletters/fastfacts/ff12.pdf

U.S. Department of Education. (1998). *Preventing bullying: A manual for schools and communities.* Washington, DC: Author.

Weinhold, B. K., & WemholdJ. B. (1998). Conflict resolution: The partnership way in schools. *Counseling and Human Development, 30(7)*, 1–2.

Discussion Questions

1. How should bullying be defined? What are the three types of bullying?

2. What are some effects of bullying on the school as a whole, and on students?

3. Is bullying likely to be more common in urban, suburban, or rural schools? Why?

4. What are some essential aspects of an anti-bullying program?

5. Which populations of students are more likely to be bullied?

6. Who bullies more: males or females? What types of bullying are most common among females?

7. What do students want teachers to do to prevent bullying?

8. What policies and practices are imperative if schools want to prevent more bullying from occurring?

9. How can teachers and administrators include parents in bullying prevention?

Reasonable Expectations or Impossible Standards?

by Dave F. Brown

Are you going to expect a kid in a wheel-chair to run the 100-yard-dash as fast as a kid who's running on two feet?

Pete, Philadelphia high school teacher

Using only one set of standards for the entire city cheats students from differing neighborhoods because you're lowering standards for one set of students and setting the bar too high for others.

Jackie, New York City elementary teacher

Decisions about whether or not students are learning should not take place in the legislature, the governor's office, or the department of education. They should take place in the classroom, because that is where learning occurs.

Douglas Christensen, cited in Roschewski, Gallagher, and Isernhagen (2001, 611)

What Are Standards?

Standards is such a powerful word because for many it signifies excellence, a quality product, and a promise of "the best." There are two types of educational standards: content standards and performance standards. *Content standards* are explicitly stated learning outcomes designed for a specific grade level, unit of study, or content area. Content standards, or what students should know, are developed by state boards of education, local school districts, professional organizations, and in rare cases, local teachers. Most classrooms in America contain a copy of the document that describes a school district's or state's standards for learning.

Content standards have different names depending on where one teaches. The school district of Philadelphia, for instance, calls its standards *curriculum frameworks;* other districts have their benchmarks; and, the state education department in Virginia has its Standards of Learning (SOLs) for students across the state. Generally, teachers are responsible for teaching both local school district standards and state standards as well. You might be surprised to discover that the standards from the two organizations don't always match, placing teachers in a precarious position of attempting to help students meet both sets of standards.

Performance standards describe expected levels of success, usually on standardized tests. Performance standards may also specify how students will demonstrate their learning and the "[K]nowledge they need to demonstrate" (Lewis 1999, 19). In general, the word *standards* is issued in reference to performance standards. Politicians and legislators foolishly believe they can improve students' test scores merely through enacting legislation linking test scores to teachers' compensation or funding for the schools. In these circumstances, higher scores lead to more funding and lower scores less state monetary support.

The premise of linking test results to funding is that with enough pressure from legislators, educators will work more diligently (assuming that they haven't been doing their jobs already) so that their students will attain higher test scores; and, that those higher scores represent more learning. A number of fallacies exist in this belief:

- Teachers are primarily responsible for student academic success.
- All students are capable of performing at or above grade level.
- Students enter school with similar backgrounds of academic success.
- Standardized tests are valid indicators of student growth.
- Standardized tests reflect local and state content standards.
- Standardized tests measure meaningful learning.
- Effective teaching can erase the significant barriers to learning that many students experience.
- Urban students are less entitled to receive funding due to their academic backgrounds.

Every one of these statements is false. When you hear the words *high standards,* listen carefully to the remarks that follow, because they are likely to be based on these entirely inaccurate statements about teaching, learning, and testing. Anyone who accepts the belief that students' performances on state assessments is an accurate indicator of effective teaching and learning has never really taught children and adolescents—especially in urban environments!

Teachers' Limitations

It is absurd to believe that your efforts as teacher will help all of your students score above the fiftieth percentile on certain standardized tests. You should understand the limitations of standardized tests to accurately assess the growth that your students will experience in a year and comprehend the realistic limitations of effective teaching on your students. Falk (2000) reported that New York City's Board of Education recently passed a policy that no student would be promoted from the third, sixth, or eighth grade unless she or he passed the district's reading and mathematics tests (22). Falk added, "Nearly one-third of the more than one million student population (more than three hundred thousand students) are expected to be retained in their grade this year" (22).

How will this testing policy improve teaching and learning, or help failing students? Students need help *before* the tests are given. Why give students a test to identify weaknesses of which their teachers are already aware, and then tell students and teachers that they have failed?

Students and teachers obviously know about their needs. Members of the New York City Board of Education are responsible for seeing that students' learning needs are met now—not a year from now. Administering a high-stakes test and holding students back a grade to learn the same things will do nothing to advance students' knowledge or improve teaching. Using test scores as punitive measures is not an equitable means of helping urban students. As a matter fact, when students are retained, it increases their risk of dropping out by as much as forty to fifty percent (Carnegie Council on Adolescent Development 1989).

Academic performance standards should never be associated with students' standardized test scores in any school, and especially not in urban schools. Urban students are not at all "standard." Standard American children would all have similar academic backgrounds, motivation for learning, support for learning at home, speak English from birth, possess reasonably high reading and mathematics skills and would all come to school every day ready to learn. The probability of this occurring is impossible in any suburban school district in America, much less in urban schools. Susan Ohanian (1999) clearly explains in her book, *One Size Fits Few: The Folly of Educational Standards,* that educational performance and content standards should never be applied to students as a way of determining which schools receive more funding; which teachers receive raises or are fired; or, which students receive the resources they need to succeed.

Teachers' Perceptions of Standards

Standards Linked to Tests

Jeff, who teaches high school English in Wichita, shares a valid concern among many teachers about the value of standardized tests: "We shouldn't worry about high-stakes tests because we need to help the kids. They don't care about the tests. They don't see how it affects them. I lost four weeks of teaching time giving tests this year." Effective teachers don't need a standardized test to explain

learning gaps or students' strengths. They become familiar with their students' learning needs and design instructional activities and curricula to meet those needs. Standardized state and national test demands create time and instructional barriers to the learning progress teachers could be making with their students if these tests weren't used.

Shanika, a fifth-grade teacher in Philadelphia, agonizes over her students' preparedness for their curriculum and tests: "Sometimes I think the expectations for students are realistic. I think, maybe I haven't expected enough of them. I may be lowering my expectations. When I gave out the state tests and realized what students are supposed to know by fifth grade, I felt so sad. Many students said, 'What's this?' and 'We don't know what this is!' I felt like I had really failed them because there were so many concepts and questions that were beyond them that we hadn't even touched." Taking some responsibility for how much students learn throughout the year in your room is reasonable; but being responsible for how students score on standardized tests is unrealistic considering students' baseline knowledge.

Kathleen teaches third graders in Chicago and indicates that the school has developed quarterly assessment tests for all of the five subject areas. Every third-grade teacher gives the same test in her school. Teachers at this school have developed their own performance standards, hopefully designed to indicate students' growth throughout the year within their curriculum. Local assessment instruments provide a more valid link with the school's curricula than externally administered state or nationally designed tests.

Lisa teaches third grade in Los Angeles and speaks of how her district has restructured standards to address the needs of her students: "We reworded the state standards to create our own here. We now have criterion-referenced tests that are linked to report card grades." Lisa wasn't especially happy about the test scores representing report card grades. However, I do see the advantage of the school district adapting state standards to local students' needs. Standards can be more appropriately matched to specific students' needs when locally rather than state determined.

Shanika is not satisfied with the unrealistic standards external tests impose on her fifth graders: "I think the fourth-grade standards would be more realistic for these fifth graders. There are certain general standards that these students can do, like writing creatively, but certain concepts we can't do! Mathematics and grammar are the greatest challenges I see for my students." Student performances on standardized tests frustrate teachers and parents, and provide no information about how students are growing or enough specifics about how they can be helped to improve reading and mathematics achievement. Shouldn't standardized tests at least help students and teachers, considering all the money and time spent purchasing, administering, and scoring them?

The result of using high standards for high-stakes decisions such as graduation requirements frequently causes:

- an increase in the dropout rate (Kohn 2000; Darling- Hammond 1991)
- a decrease in teachers' use of effective teaching strategies (Kohn 2001; Madaus et al. 1992)
- a decline in students' ability to transfer discreet skills to more complex learning situations (McNeil 2000).

These are a few negative impacts of using high-stakes tests to determine the educational future of students. Wasley (2001) stated, "The standards are a very good thing from kids' perspectives when they feel that their school, their teachers, their principals, and community members are going to make sure that they can meet the standards. It's when the standards feel punishing to kids that they really have problems with them" (7). Many districts and states unfortunately have adopted "punishing" rather, than "helpful" standards within the past few years.

Deeding with Content Standards

Kathleen speaks of the Chicago school district content standards she adheres to for her third-grade students: "We all have a copy of both state and city standards. I think the math and reading standards are fine; but the science and social studies standards are much too difficult to cover in a year. The system is very bureaucratic: the curriculum supervisor comes around to check off which standards we've covered."

Shanika faces similar challenges with the expected content students will learn in fifth grade: "Because these kids are the product of kindergarten through fourth grade as well as this year; the concepts that they've been missing snowball. I don't think these [external standardized] tests are appropriate. At the same time, I do think I've brought down my expectations. I think about math … so few of my students understand division, so after a while I say to myself, 'Let me just move on because I'm wasting time.' When I make a decision to move on, it's based on my frustration and their frustration." Shanika adds, "I don't really follow the school district standards because I don't think they're realistic. The things that the standards suggest really don't apply to my kids."

Teachers are often forced to make decisions concerning how they will use standards primarily due to time constraints. Stoskopf (2000) reported, "[T]hat it would take 6,000 extra hours of classroom time to cover all the information required on most state standards" (38) (cited in Falk 2000). This information provides a valid reason for you as the teacher to use discretion and professional judgment in choosing which standards students will meet and which ones will need to be postponed until students acquire the skills and developmental abilities to successfully learn them.

Susan, from San Francisco, shares her perceptions of California's content standards: "The state standards are bad—they are development tally inappropriate. I refuse to use those state standards to determine my students' levels of ability. They are absurd, and I refuse to adhere to them piece-by-piece. I have my own standards for students. I like to see where they are, and then challenge them." That last statement describes the appropriate level of teacher responsibility for assessment and standards in all schools!

Jackie, from Philadelphia, has similar concerns about standards: "The difficult thing about standards is that it's an outside entity giving you goals—and it never works! If you want to lose weight, you have to decide you want to do it. If you want to quit smoking, you have to decide that that's your goal. Standards have to be more individualised. What's going to work in one area of Philadelphia is very different from what's going to work in areas of North Philly. Or, standards for the upper-East Side of New York are going to be very different from what is expected from students in East Harlem."

Teachers realize how inappropriate standards can be when they are established behind closed doors, thereby preventing the developers from comprehending the lives of the learners they intend to affect. Students' backgrounds *should* be a factor in designing curricula, choosing instructional strategies, and establishing standards for learning. What if every automobile repair shop provided the same repairs for every car even though each one has a different problem? What if the state automobile repair examiner declared that every mechanic spend only forty-five minutes changing all mufflers regardless of the problem or type of car being worked on? That idea sounds absolutely absurd to me; yet, that's what state content standards do to teachers—require educators to teach the same material to every child, at the same pace regardless of students' backgrounds and genuine academic needs and interests.

The Difference Between Expectations and Standards

The Absurdity of Standards

Imagine you're a seventh-grade student standing in the gymnasium watching the physical education teacher adjust the height of a hurdle used for track meets. Your job is to jump over the hurdle to show that you can meet the "standard." The teacher places the hurdle height at a foot and a half. Your twenty-nine classmates and you line up forty feet away and run to jump over it. Everyone makes it over. The teacher announces, "OK, that was great work. Now, I'm going to raise the hurdle to two feet." You all run and jump again, but two students aren't able to jump over it. Those two students failed to meet the two-foot standard. The teacher explains to the students how disappointed she is at their inability to clear the hurdle. They are considered failures despite their limited physical abilities, attitudes about jumping hurdles, and poor background knowledge about hurdle jumping. The two students are asked to sit down and think about how they can improve their jumping ability before the next class session.

The teacher, meanwhile, decides to-raise the hurdle to two-and a half feet and asks the remaining students to jump over that height. Several more are asked to sit out because they can't meet the standard. They are given low grades for the day and discouraged from practicing hurdle jumping in the future. The hurdle is raised three more times within the hour and each time fewer and fewer students are able to jump over it. Finally class ends and grades are distributed to students based on how high they were able to jump. Only three of thirty students were able to clear the height the teacher designated as a "reasonable standard." The worst part was watching how the teacher treated those students who were not able to jump over each height. Students were not provided with any feedback for how to improve their jumping ability, were not encouraged by the teacher to try different strategies, and were only provided with one opportunity to jump over the hurdle at each height.

This physical education class experience describes how raising standards works against many students in American schools—especially urban schools. Performance standards are most frequently designed and mandated by nonschool personnel; ignore students' varying developmental needs; are unrelated to school curricula, textbooks, or instruction; ignore students' baseline academic data; are measured using an invalid assessment instrument; and are completely unrealistic measures of students' growth potential. How can these externally imposed standards improve educators' teaching strategies or improve student learning based on these enormous inconsistencies?

Establishing Realistic Performance Expectations

Teachers who recognize students' differences in growth rates, ability levels, background knowledge, English proficiency, reading levels, and learning profiles clearly comprehend that individual students need distinct, personalized standards for learning. I prefer to use the term, *expectations* to describe the level of improvement expected of students in learning processes, cognitive strategies, and basic knowledge. Expectations are realistic levels of learning based on each student's baseline data gathered from previous

teachers' reports about each child and your own observations and experiences. Expectations are established throughout the first few weeks of the school year and revisited and revised as teachers conference with each student.

Reasonable expectations are

- challenging to students, but not frustrating
- developmentally appropriate based on students' abilities
- temporarily established to allow for flexibility when needed
- aligned partially with district curricula
- supported through effective instructional strategies to help struggling students improve with reasonable effort.

Standards are not characterized by the same statements. Establish reasonable performance expectations for each student in your class based on his or her abilities if you actually believe in the idea of success for all students. Students will refuse to engage in learning if the tasks they are required to do are greatly beyond their cognitive capabilities. Some states' content and performance standards are frequently beyond the abilities of many urban students.

You can make a difference in children's or adolescents', learning despite the barrier unrealistic standards create to your perceived success as a teacher. "Success for all" implies that teachers identify the starting point of each student's abilities and establish realistic expectations built on this baseline knowledge.

Implementing expectations that strike a balance between students' academic needs and a set of benchmarks that students may reasonably achieve within a school year is an urban teacher's responsibility. Asking questions about what your students know and can do is the most effective strategy for establishing the appropriate expectations for student learning. You role is to discover what each student needs to accomplish to reach success in your classroom. Data gathering starts when you ask, "What do my students know at this point?" You want to collect information on issues such as students' basic skills, English proficiency, learning profiles, attitudes toward learning, and other information, as mentioned in Chapter 8. You will be able to establish a set of reasonable outcomes for each student by using the responses to those questions. Realistic performance expectations should vary for each student based on all of the factors in a student's life that affect learning, including issues such as family dynamics and socio-economic levels.

Anita, who has twenty-five years of teaching experience with Philadelphia middle school students, shares her views of how standardized curricula affect urban students. "You must-know that when you complete a year of teaching seventh graders, many of them are still going to be at the second and third grade level in reading ability. Unfortunately, we don't do enough here to help these kids because of money. These students need more individualized help. They get lost in the large group. The way curriculum is set up, kids get hurt academically, and it gets worse! When they get to high school, what we find is that they just drop out because they just can't keep up—they can't do it! Many students are coming in academically well below where they should be. You can't penalize them for what they can't do!"

Jeff, from a Wichita high school, experienced challenges establishing realistic expectations: "I vary my expectations from honors classes to frosh classes. I expect them to get work done. I was failing so many kids that I had to reevaluate. I changed the way I ran the class. Homework isn't as important as it was before to me. These students are at home babysitting their brothers, working too much at home because Mom and Dad are working two or three jobs. I do more in-class projects now to find out what they know."

Jeff has found a strategy for helping students to succeed instead of applying unrealistic expectations with the result of many failures. Striking a balance between appropriate expectations and standards that are much too high is the ideal for students; however, it will take some time each academic year before you are able to determine which of your expectations are appropriate for each student or an entire class of students.

Colette, from a Philadelphia high school, shares her philosophy on student expectations: "I expect students to do their work, and I try to make the projects interesting enough to motivate them. But students make all kinds of excuses. They're so full of excuses; they really are!

So I tell them, 'It's not personal, it's just business. You have to do your work. As much as I like you, I'm still going to fail you if you don't do your work!' Sometimes I'll ask them if this is too much work, and the honest students will say, 'This is reasonable; we just don't feel like doing it.'"

These homework expectations hopefully focus more on student effort than on performance. One of the greatest challenges facing urban teachers is getting students to complete assignments. Performance standards are insignificant for students who refuse to complete assigned school tasks. It may be necessary for teachers to develop rubrics for completing assignments so students have a clear indicator of how their effort and finished products affect their potential for learning.

Kathleen, who teaches in a Chicago elementary school, explains how eight of her third-grade students attended summer school following their unsuccessful completion of third grade. Four of those eight students did not pass summer school and repeated third grade. Kathleen applied a set of standards based on the quarterly tests given to students at the end of each grading period. She believes the standards are appropriate based on her knowledge of third-grade curricula and her students' abilities.

You can see from these stories that each teacher is charged with determining which standards have significance for his or her students, and how they are applied. You will also decide which students will receive acceptable passing grades based on your knowledge of what students should know, be able-to do, their strengths, and their areas of need. These are both personal and professional decisions based on each individual case every year you teach. No one has a special formula for choosing appropriate standards and applying them. Although many legislators, parents and caregivers, and administrators may mandate specific standards, many of those standards are too inflexible, unrealistic, and inappropriate to measure students' growth in a meaningful manner. You are the judge, the jury, the prosecutor, and the defender of every student you encounter as a teacher. No one has as much knowledge as you do about your students; therefore, you must be the one to protect students by providing them with the greatest opportunities for growth when you teach them.

Balancing Content Standards with Reasonable Expectations

Falk (2000) described the role of teachers as one of "[F]inding ways to uncover" the critical concepts, and principles mentioned in content standards that your students will need for further learning and to advance their own understanding of how their world works (104). l suggest you collaborate with your grade level colleagues as you evaluate mandated state and local content standards to determine which ones are essential for your students to learn. You will have to prioritize principles because completing all of the mandated standards will be difficult for some students. I suggest developing this list early in the year keeping in mind that it will need to be altered

based on your specific students' personal learning profiles and needs. Teacher decision making in establishing reasonable levels of learning should always take precedence over any pre-established state or local content standards.

Establishing Reasonable Levels of Performance

Another component of establishing appropriate expectations for students' growth is to determine reasonable and acceptable levels of student performance that indicate understanding of prioritized learning principles. This may be the most challenging piece of assessment due to the distinct variations in students' background knowledge as they enter urban classrooms. Finding one standard of acceptable performance and applying it to all students is not sound educational practice. A critical aspect of effective assessment is providing students with multiple measures and means to determine their level of understanding.

Kohn (2000) suggested that, "Each school should be encouraged to develop its own criteria for self-evaluation, inviting students, teachers, parents, and others in the community to decide what will help them determine how effectively they've been meeting their goals" (48). One particular school district in Wisconsin, for example, requires students to learn content benchmarks. Students' progress is determined as they reach a certain level of mastery on these general concepts and principles (benchmarks) in each subject area (Hughes 2001). Following completion of each unit of study (benchmarks), success is determined by students' scores on locally developed rubrics in four categories: advanced, proficient (where students are expected to perform), basic, and minimal (6). Students who perform well on various assessments receive an advanced rating. Students receiving a proficient score have also mastered a unit's concepts and principles

at a satisfactory level. A basic or minimal rating indicates less than adequate demonstration of knowledge; thereby requiring review of those concepts and principles. The expectation is that students who reach the proficient level require no more instruction or practice in that content skill, or process area. Appropriate assessment does not compare students' performance to other students as most tests do; but instead, is criterion or standards-referenced—indicating the extent that students comprehend the principles they are expected to learn. As a teacher, you need to know how you can help students, not where they rank with their classmates either in your school or across the state or country.

Benchmarks and rubrics are shared with students in this Wisconsin school district so that they clearly understand what's expected. Hughes (2001) reported that these benchmarks also help teachers monitor students' progress and use those results in planning further instruction.

Carr and Harris (2001) suggested aligning acceptable standards for performance and content standards with report cards. Redesigning report cards to reflect acceptable performance and content standards can be a lengthy process. The advantage, however, of doing so is the possibility of clearly communicating to students, teachers, parents and caregivers, and administrators the most important strategies and knowledge students should learn and what levels demonstrate acceptable learning.

I realize, with much disappointment, that externally developed and mandated student performance standards are a fact of life in most urban schools. However, I encourage you to use other measures of students' performance to determine to what extent each is growing. The few urban schools (Central Park East Schools, Urban Academy, and others in New York City) in which teachers develop standards based on their knowledge of students and instructional expertise have much greater success in helping students to grow (Falk 2000). Teachers are the last line of defense for students. You must be an advocate for every student you encounter to insure that each receives what he or she needs.

How Do Teachers Measure Success?

The 2000 Phi Delta Kappa/Gallup educational issues poll indicated that sixty-eight percent of all respondents preferred that teachers measure student achievement rather than standardized test scores (Rose and Gallup 2000). Respondents to this survey added that the primary purpose of tests should be to determine the kind of instruction that students need rather than measuring the amount of information learned. Determining whether you are successful with students or not depends on so many factors. Reaching success with all students will be elusive if you use one level on the measuring stick as your indicator of success—much as standardized assessments are applied. Success needs to be measured one child at a time and with different instruments for many students.

Diane, who teaches fifth graders in San Francisco, states a broad definition of how she often measures success: "Sometimes I measure success by the fact that everyone [students] comes back the next day." For many of the urban teachers I interviewed, succeeding with students means designing learning experiences that are developmentally appropriate and can be successfully completed. Success means gaining the cooperation of students who are gang members, helping a struggling middle school student read a novel for the first time, and helping a high school student complete a science project during your planning period. The gains may not be immense or noticeable on a large scale.

Influential urban teachers address the needs of every student they can and evaluate their influence based on broader victories than those that are merely academic. Pete, who teaches SLL students in Philadelphia, explains, "I provide as much support as possible with the tools they need. My job is to provide them [students] with as many keys as I can. I can't open all the doors for them, and I can't give them all the information they need. I can provide them with the small pieces that help them to open up the larger pieces."

Carr and Harris (2001) suggested that teachers measure success on several levels:

- *Individual success:* How well has this student learned?
- *Instructional success:* How successful was my instruction?
- *Curriculum success:* How successfully is the curriculum addressing our students' learning needs?
- *Program success:* How well is our instructional program working? (65)

I strongly suggest that teachers look at success beyond academic indicators. Carr and Harris (2001) advised school personnel to consider improvements in attendance, fewer dropouts, greater numbers of students promoted or retained as other indicators of success (65). Classroom teachers should also consider these as signs of success:

- more students engaged in class discussions
- higher percentages of students completing assignments
- students taking more risk with their learning.
- greater effort among certain students
- students cooperating with each other and demonstrating respect
- fewer discipline referrals

- more parents and caregivers involved in their child's schooling.

These are positive signs that you are making a difference in the lives of your students. These signs are much more reflective of you and your students' successes than test scores!

References

Carnegie Council on Adolescent Development. 1989. *Turning Points: Preparing Youth for the Twenty-First Century.* New York: Carnegie Corporation of New York.

Carr, J. F., and D. E. Harris. 2001. *Succeeding with Standards: Linking Curriculum, Assessment, and Action Planning.* Alexandria, VA: Association for Supervision and Curriculum Development.

Darling-Hammond, L. 1991. "The Implications of Testing Policy for Educational Quality and Equality." *Phi Delta Kappan 73*, no. 3: 220–25.

Falk, B. 2000. *The Heart of the Matter: Using Standards and Assessment to Learn.* Portsmouth, NH: Heinemann.

Hughes, J. 2001. "The Benefits of Benchmarks." *Education Update 43*, no. 1: 6.

Kohn, A. 2000. *The Case Against Standardized Testing: Raising the Scores, Ruining the Schools.* Portsmouth, NH: Heinemann.

———. 2001. "Fighting the Tests: A Practical Guide to Rescuing Our Schools." *Phi Delta Kappan 82*, no. 5:.348–357.

Lewis, A. C. 1999. *Figuring It Out: Standards-Based Reforms in Urban Middle Grades.* New York: Edna McConnell Clark Foundation.

Madaus, G. F., M. M West, M. C. Harmon, R. G, Lomax, and K. A. Viator. 1992. *The Influence of Testing on Teaching Math and Science in Grades 4-12.* Boston: Center for the Study of Testing, Evaluation, and Educational Policy.

McNeil, L M. 2000. "Creating New Inequalities: Contradictions of Reform." *Phi Delta Kappan 81*, no. 10: 728–734.

Ohanian, S. 1999. *One Size Fits Few: The Folly of Educational Standards.* Portsmouth, NH: Heinemann.

Roschewski, P., C Gallagher, and J. Isernhagen. 2001. "Nebraskans Reach for The STARS." *Phi Delta Kappan 82,* no. 8: 611–615.

Rose, L. C., and A. M. Gallup. 2000. "The 32nd Annual Phi Delta Kappa/Gallup Poll of the Public's Attitudes Toward the Public Schools." *Phi Delta Kappan 82,* no. 1: 41–48, 53–66.

Stoskdpf, A. 2000. "Clio's Lament." *Education Week 20,* (2 Feb): 38, 41.

Wasley, P. 2001. "Standards from the Students' Perspective." *Education Update 43,* no. 1; 7.

Discussion Questions

1. Describe the difference between *content standards* and *performance standards.* Are you in favor of either? Explain why.

2. Why are performance standards often unfairly applied to children/adolescents?

3. What factors prevent teachers from having an impact on performance standards?

4. How do high stakes tests affect students?

5. How do differences in students' backgrounds affect teachers' abilities to help their students perform on grade level each year?

6. What are realistic standards and how can teachers establish those for students?

7. How can teachers explain that their students are growing despite the fact that they have not met performance standards?

8. What does success really look like in a classroom?